THE CANADIAN FEDERAL ELECTION OF 2019

McGill-Queen's/Brian Mulroney Institute of Government Studies in Leadership, Public Policy, and Governance

Series editor: Donald E. Abelson

Titles in this series address critical issues facing Canada at home and abroad and the efforts policymakers at all levels of government have made to address a host of complex and multifaceted policy concerns. Books in this series receive financial support from the Brian Mulroney Institute of Government at St Francis Xavier University; in keeping with the institute's mandate, these studies explore how leaders involved in key policy initiatives arrived at their decisions and what lessons can be learned. Combining rigorous academic analysis with thoughtful recommendations, this series compels readers to think more critically about how and why elected officials make certain policy choices, and how, in concert with other stakeholders, they can better navigate an increasingly complicated and crowded marketplace of ideas.

1 Braver Canada
  Shaping Our Destiny in a Precarious World
  Derek H. Burney and Fen Osler Hampson

2 The Canadian Federal Election of 2019
  Edited by Jon H. Pammett and Christopher Dornan

The Canadian Federal Election of 2019

Edited by

JON H. PAMMETT
and
CHRISTOPHER DORNAN

McGill-Queen's University Press
Montreal & Kingston · London · Chicago

© McGill-Queen's University Press 2020

ISBN 978-0-2280-0400-4 (cloth)
ISBN 978-0-2280-0401-1 (paper)
ISBN 978-0-2280-0495-0 (ePDF)
ISBN 978-0-2280-0496-7 (ePUB)

Legal deposit fourth quarter 2020
Bibliothèque nationale du Québec

Printed in Canada on acid-free paper that is 100% ancient forest free (100% post-consumer recycled), processed chlorine free

Funded by the Government of Canada | Financé par le gouvernement du Canada | Canadä Canada Council for the Arts | Conseil des arts du Canada

We acknowledge the support of the Canada Council for the Arts.

Nous remercions le Conseil des arts du Canada de son soutien.

Library and Archives Canada Cataloguing in Publication

Title: The Canadian federal election of 2019 / edited by Jon H. Pammett and Christopher Dornan.

Names: Pammett, Jon H., 1944- editor. | Dornan, Chris, editor.

Description: Series statement: McGill-Queen's/Brian Mulroney Institute of Government Studies in Leadership, Public Policy, and Governance; #2 | Includes bibliographical references.

Identifiers: Canadiana (print) 20200312243 | Canadiana (ebook) 20200312278 | ISBN 9780228004011 (softcover) | ISBN 9780228004004 (hardcover) | ISBN 9780228004950 (PDF) | ISBN 9780228004967 (ePUB)

Subjects: LCSH: Canada. Parliament—Elections, 2019. | LCSH: Elections—Canada—History—21st century. | LCSH: Voting—Canada. | LCSH: Canada—Politics and government—21st century. | LCSH: Canada—Politics and government—2015-

Classification: LCC JL193 .C36 2020 | DDC 324.971/074—dc23

This book was typeset by Marquis Interscript in 10.5/13 Sabon.

Contents

Figures and Tables   vii

Preface   ix

1 The Unspoken Election: The Context of the Campaign   3
  Christopher Dornan

2 Second Chance: The Chastened Liberals   15
  Brooke Jeffrey

3 The Conservative Campaign: An Opportunity Squandered   43
  Faron Ellis

4 Making the Best of It: Political Marketing and the Federal NDP's Fight for Relevance   73
  David McGrane

5 The Battle for Quebec   101
  Eric Montigny

6 The Climate Referendum? The Greens, the Others, and the Politics of Climate Change   128
  Sarah Everts and Susan Harada

7 A Close Race from Start to Finish: Polling in the 2019 Federal Election   155
  Éric Grenier

8 The Media: Challenges of Covering the Campaign   174
  Paul Adams

9 Digital Campaigning in the Era of Misinformation 198
   Tamara A. Small

10 From Sunny Ways to Cloudy Days: Voting in the 2019 Federal Election 221
   Harold D. Clarke and Marianne C. Stewart

11 Voting Turnout in 2019: The Long and the Short of It 246
   Jon H. Pammett and Lawrence LeDuc

12 The Testing Election 265
   Jon H. Pammett

   Appendix: The Results 271

   Contributors 273

Figures and Tables

FIGURES

4.1 Percentage coverage of themes in NDP English TV ads (2019 election) 88
4.2 Percentage coverage of themes in NDP French TV ads (2019 election) 88
5.1 Number of seats by party in Quebec, 2008–19 104
5.2 Léger polls in Quebec from June to 20 October 2019 109
9.1 Example of political ad in the Facebook Ad Library 210
10.1 Evaluations of the Canadian economy, 2011, 2015, 2019 224
10.2 Three most important issues facing the country 224
10.3 Party best on most important issue 225
10.4 Party best on specific important issues 227
10.5 Reactions to Trudeau scandals 229
10.6 Evaluations of party leaders, 2015 and 2019 229
10.7 Federal party identification, 2011, 2015, 2019 232
10.8 Trade-off between climate change and the economy by age group 233
10.9 Statistically significant interactions between evaluations of the economy and climate change versus economy trade-off 236
10.10 Parties' voting percentages in the 2015 and 2019 federal elections 240
11.1 Turnout in Canadian federal elections, 1965–2019, Elections Canada 248

11.2 Turnout in six countries (last five elections), International IDEA 251
11.3 Estimated voting by age groups, 2019 federal election, Abacus post-election survey. 260

TABLES

3.1 2017 Conservative Party of Canada leadership selection (percentage of points won) 46
3.2 Conservative Party revenue: National party annual averages, 2003–19 (thousands) 54
3.3 Conservative Party of Canada election results, 2004–19 65
4.1 Percentage coverage of themes in federal NDP press releases by week 90
4.2 NDP electoral results in 1962–2008, 2011, 2015, and 2019 94
5.1 Number of electoral promises by issue area 108
7.1 Final polls of the campaign and the total error compared to results 165
7.2 Average overestimation (+) and underestimation (–) of each party's support in the final polls of the campaign 167
8.1 How much have you been relying on these media to form your views about this election? 176
8.2 Reliance on these media to form your views about this election 177
10.1 Economic voting model of Liberal support 235
10.2 Change in probability of voting for various political parties produced by changes in statistically significant predictor variables 237
10.3 The flow of the vote, 2015–19 241
11.1 Voting turnout in recent provincial and federal elections, by province 252
11.2 Turnout rises of 4% or more since 1985 in the Canadian provinces 255

Preface

Christopher Dornan

The 2019 Canadian federal election was the forty-third since Confederation and the forty-third to be conducted under an electoral system the governing Liberal Party had promised, during and after the forty-second election, would no longer exist.

In 2015, the Trudeau Liberals were not a government-in-waiting. They were a diminished party with a young, famous, untested leader. They were in a position to promise all sorts of bold initiatives. They vowed to legalize cannabis. If elected, they would transform the rules of how votes count so as to end the dictatorship of majority government.

Proportional representation, however implemented, would yield a more patchwork Parliament than our current system. It would also require a complete overhaul of the existing party campaign machinery. In their first throne speech the Trudeau Liberals promised to "take action to ensure that 2015 will be the last federal election conducted under the first-past-the-post voting system." By 2017 that was over. Minister of Democratic Institutions Karina Gould was told: "changing the electoral system will not be in your mandate."

And yet the outcome of the 2019 election was everything one might have expected if the election had been conducted according to some version of proportional representation. The 43rd Parliament is a political assembly that must be brokered because no party outright commands the confidence of the chamber. The Liberals got exactly what they thought they wanted.

In the end, it was an election in which almost all the parties lost but almost all the parties won. The Liberals lost their majority. The Conservatives lost by failing to unseat the Liberals. The NDP lost 15 of their 39 seats, ending with a caucus of only 24 MPs. The Greens lost because they gained only one seat, for a total of three, and fell short of official party status. Maxime Bernier's People's Party lost because it failed to win a single seat. The Bloc Québécois lost only in the sense that it is not the sole party on which the Liberal minority government must depend in order to remain in power.

At the same time, the Liberals won because they remain in power. The NDP won because it retained official party status, was not eclipsed by the Greens, its leader distinguished himself during the campaign, and with its support the Liberals can remain in power, which gives the NDP a voice in the government. The Bloc won because it can claim to speak for Quebec and because with its support the Liberals can remain in power, which gives it, too, a voice in the government. The Greens won because their core issue – climate change and the environment – is now prominently on the agenda of concern. The People's Party won nothing, but the Conservatives won in that they secured more total votes across the country than the Liberals, making them the stewards of a political viewpoint that cannot be dismissed. Although the progressive, centre-left parties together won far more seats (216) than the Conservatives (121), the distribution of those seats has a geography that makes the Conservative Party indisputably the voice of western Canada. Although it may be the ideological antithesis of the centre-left parties it will nonetheless have to be heard in government.

The chapters to follow document and analyze how a country came to decide to govern itself. They reveal how the collective interaction of the political parties and their competing machines, the news media, unanticipated events, the public, and their use of social media all added up to a campaign dynamic, and how that dynamic led to the election of a minority government of a G7 nation in a time of heightened international uncertainty and domestic tension.

The editors would like to thank our contributing authors for the speed with which they delivered their analyses following the election; the anonymous reviewers of the volume for their helpful insights; and Jaqueline Mason of McGill-Queen's University Press, for her assistance. David Coletto, of Abacus Data, provided us access to the election surveys, which appear in several chapters. And we would also like to thank the office of the Dean of the Faculty of Public Affairs at Carleton University for financial support in bringing this volume to press.

THE CANADIAN FEDERAL ELECTION OF 2019

I

The Unspoken Election: The Context of the Campaign

Christopher Dornan

In Canada, as a parliamentary democracy, general election campaigns are above all exercises in intense competitive political persuasion. They are interludes in which the normal affairs of the partisan arena are suspended and the parties devote themselves to massive, elaborately planned efforts to influence the decisions and actions of tens of millions of voters over a twelve-hour period on a single day. In 2019, there were 27.1 million Canadians eligible to vote, and in the end 65.95 percent of them, 17.9 million, opted to cast a ballot.

The will of the electorate – tallied by a trustworthy, neutral agency – determines how the country is to be governed until the next interlude, and so how the nation's priorities will be set. The campaign period is therefore an occasion for the public to make known to the parties, and to one another, what most concerns them as political citizens as much as it is a contest between the parties over whose priorities should prevail. It is an opportunity to take stock of the factors that might threaten or strengthen prosperity, stability, security, civic institutions, and collective and individual well-being.

And yet an election campaign is rarely an exhaustive audit of the circumstances that may favour or jeopardize the national condition. The parties invariably conduct themselves in the service of a singular ambition – to win; or, in the case of those with faint hope of forming a government, to achieve an electoral goal. Some otherwise important issues may not be politically advantageous for anyone to mention. For example, from January 2016 to June 2019 – almost the span of the Trudeau government's first term – nearly fourteen thousand Canadians died from opioid use,[1] more than six times the homicide rate. The opioid crisis is a blight and a tragedy that has affected communities across the country, and yet it barely registered as an election issue. Similarly, for the past few years the Bank of Canada has been warning with increasing urgency that the greatest vulnerability to the country's economy is the level of individual household debt, but consumer debt was hardly mentioned over the course of the campaign. Election platforms are built on promises, not on hectoring voters to tighten their belts.

Sometimes, in the interests of one's electoral prospects, it is best to leave certain things unsaid and not to draw attention to the silence. As Progressive Conservative leader Kim Campbell famously remarked to her detriment during the 1993 campaign, elections "are the worst possible time" to debate key issues "because it takes more than 47 days to settle anything ... that serious."[2]

In the 2019 campaign, almost everyone instinctively shied away from mentioning certain things. International politics almost never loom large in Canadian elections, but this election was especially insular given global realities; and even matters of manifest domestic concern received muted attention.

A WORLD UPENDED

Canada has its faults and injustices, certainly, but by any measure it is a fortunate country. It is materially wealthy, culturally rich, and politically stable. Its citizens in the main enjoy an enviable standard of living and are concerned for those of their fellow citizens who may not. The nation's federalism, ungainly though it may be, manages to accommodate regions and peoples of very different character. Crucially, Canada has been able to broker fundamental and rancorous political differences through resilient civic institutions.

However, in the four years between the 2015 Canadian election and the 2019 election, the world beyond Canada's borders was convulsed more radically than at any time since the abrupt end of the Soviet Union thirty years ago. Simply put – although it is not that simple – the 2015 election took place in a world before Donald Trump occupied the US presidency. Trump is both an architect and a symptom of the world in which the 2019 election took place, and yet Trump and all that he has brought about was barely mentioned by any of the major political actors over the course of the campaign.

Elsewhere, the politics of authoritarianism, nativism, and an unforgiving populism were threatening the institutions of political compromise that are so essential to liberal democracy. Authoritarian politics cares little for political compromise or managing difference. Authoritarianism seeks to eradicate difference and subjugate dissent. But while academics and intellectuals throughout the West were sounding an alarm about "the crisis of liberalism," the Canadian election unfolded as though untouched and unconcerned by such developments beyond our borders.

Political authority, meanwhile, was being challenged around the world in massive street protests, and not simply in places of traditional unrest. In Chile, the wealthiest country in Latin America, a 4 percent hike in mass transit fares was the pretext for demonstrations that claimed twenty-three lives and led to a constitutional crisis.[3] In Spain, a week before the Canadian vote – in a development surely painfully pertinent to a country that has had to handle the sovereigntist aspirations of one of its own provinces – nine Catalan independence leaders were sentenced to prison terms of between nine and thirteen years, triggering days of demonstrations that brought half a million people into the streets of Barcelona. In Britain, throughout the Canadian election period, there were ongoing massive demonstrations protesting the Conservative government's intention to ram through the United Kingdom's withdrawal from the European Union. And on the day the Canadian election began, in Hong Kong – home to some 300,000 Canadian citizens – pro-autonomy and pro-democracy protests were entering their sixth month. All this and more was the background noise to the Canadian election. Nightly newscasts would show unhappy chanting crowds marching in the streets somewhere in the world, often in confrontations with riot police, and then in the same broadcast show happy chanting crowds of party loyalists here at home cheering their candidates in rented halls.

DONALD TRUMP

As a middle power, Canada's security and prosperity depends on a network of alliances, international law, and trade agreements, but especially on a close and friendly relationship with the United States. Trump came into office determined to tear down the architecture of international conventions and treaties that ordered political and economic relations between nations – that indeed constituted the global order – because these were the product of a negotiated world, a world answerable to shared understandings. Trump had his own global order in mind. He repudiated the Trans-Pacific Partnership, the Paris Climate Accord, and the Iran nuclear agreement; he disparaged NATO, the WTO, the G7, and the European Union as schemes to take advantage of the United States; he erected trade barriers against adversaries and allies alike, including imposing tariffs on Canadian steel and aluminum. He insisted at his rallies and via Twitter that "our allies treat us worse than our enemies" – the corollary being that he intended to do the same in return. His slogan "Make America Great Again" amounts to a promise to reaffirm America's dominance over other nations. Since he cannot assert dominance over the rival power blocs of China and Russia, and since there is no political advantage on the US home front to asserting dominance over what Trump denigrates as the "shithole" countries of the developing world, it is his Western democratic allies who must be seen to be subordinate to American superiority.

Hence the initial bewilderment and exasperation of Europe, Australia, and Canada at the treatment to which they were subjected. They had assumed they were friends and allies of the United States, partners with America in the project of the West, joined by a common commitment to democratic aspirations, humanitarian ideals, and mutually beneficial economic relations, only to discover that Trump views them as little more than impertinent ward heels in an American syndicate to which they owe their fealty and from which they will take their orders. When the Trudeau Liberals were elected in 2015, they never imagined they would shortly have to renegotiate the continental agreement that had governed trade in North America for twenty-five years, much less bargain against an adversary with the moral compass of a mob boss and an ego so infantile he must always be hailed as triumphant over those with whom he negotiates.

The foremost single factor on which the well-being of Canada turns is the country's relations with the United States and, in specific, the terms of its trade relations. And yet the deal struck with the United States and Mexico in the renegotiated North American Free Trade Agreement (NAFTA) hardly figured in the election, even though the Liberals were not just relieved at what they had accomplished but satisfied, and quite possibly proud.

Although the thirteen months of negotiations had concluded in September 2018, by the time of the election the agreement had yet to be ratified by either Canada or the United States. The government and opposition had sparred over the NAFTA renegotiations before the election, Conservative leader Andrew Scheer insisting on the floor of the Commons in May that the deal amounted to a "historic humiliation" for Canada.[4] Conservative partisans viscerally detest Justin Trudeau. They see him as a preening, vacuous lightweight. They cringe whenever he opens his mouth, and no more so than when he speaks on the international stage. They are embarrassed by him, convinced he is out of his depth among the grown-ups of global politics. They are adamant that Trudeau not only accepted a bad deal for Canada but did so in a way that humiliated the country. As deeply felt as this may be among convinced Conservatives, in May 2019 few outside the party's base were buying the argument that the negotiations had been a disaster.

Three months later, with only two weeks to go until the election, Scheer tried this line of attack again. Attempting to goad Trudeau into participating in an election debate on foreign policy to be staged by the Aurea Foundation, which runs the Munk Debates, Scheer accused Trudeau of allowing Trump to take Canada to the cleaners. This prompted a mild rebuke from Rona Ambrose,[5] the former interim Conservative leader who had assisted the government of Canada in the negotiations, who politely insisted this was not true. Four days into the election period, in a late-night scrum with reporters aboard his campaign plane, Scheer reiterated the accusation, charging that Trudeau, weak on the international stage, had capitulated to Trump.[6] Nonetheless, Scheer allowed that if elected he would ratify the agreement since to renege would throw the country into economic chaos. And that, for all intents and purposes, was the last opposition attack on the government's handling of the NAFTA file. It is likely that Scheer and his team realized the charge lacked political resonance. It needed to be stated, to be put on the record for the benefit of the party faithful who wanted to be told how craven Trudeau had been, but it was not a line of attack that was going to unseat the Liberals. There was no groundswell of popular outrage at what the agreement contained.

For their part, the Liberals released a radio ad featuring Chrystia Freeland, the foreign minister and Canada's chief negotiator in the trade talks, describing how Canada "fought tooth and nail" and "stood up to Donald Trump."[7] The deal was pitched to the electorate not on its specifics but on the basis that the country had not allowed itself to be bullied or outmanoeuvred. At no point in the campaign did either the Liberals or the opposition parties methodically unpack the agreement to show what had been won or lost, or to describe how it would reshape the flow of continental commerce, if at all. Pivotal though it might be to the Canadian economy, the deal was merely background in the election.

CHINA

When the campaign began on 11 September, two Canadians had languished in appalling conditions in Chinese prisons for 275 days. Michael Kovrig is a former diplomat and Michael Spavor a sports entrepreneur. Charged with espionage, they were in fact hostages, denied access to lawyers or visits from family members and permitted only one highly supervised thirty-minute meeting a month with Canadian diplomatic officers. They had been seized by Chinese authorities ten days after Canada detained Meng Wanzhou, chief financial officer of the Chinese telecommunications giant Huawei and daughter of the company's founder. Meng had been arrested on 1 December 2018 while in transit at Vancouver International Airport, at the request of the US government, which accuses her of defrauding banks by siphoning money to a Huawei subsidiary that does business with Iran, in violation of US sanctions. Under house arrest at one of her two Vancouver mansions while fighting extradition to the United Sates, she was able to read, paint, and move about Vancouver in the company of a security detail.

China, meanwhile, sought to punish Canada for its part in Meng's detention, and not only by the cruel and arbitrary arrest of two Canadian citizens. In March 2019, China halted imports of Canadian canola seed; China was at that point Canada's largest market for canola exports, accounting for some $4.4 billion of annual sales.[8] In June, China blocked Canadian pork and beef exports (although this ban was lifted in November, after the Canadian election, likely as a result of an outbreak of swine flu in China, which forced China to resume importing meat).[9]

The dispute placed Canada at the nexus of a much larger conflict between China and the United States, which, by the time of the Canadian election, had been locked in an escalating trade war for fifteen months. Central to US complaints are allegations that China illicitly acquires Western intellectual property, particularly in the area of communication and computer technology. The Trump administration has all but insisted that Canada exclude Huawei from participating in building the country's 5G mobile communication infrastructure.

Canada prevailed upon its allies to exert diplomatic pressure on the Chinese government to release the two Canadians, but on this matter its most powerful ally, the United States, is itself implicated in the dispute. The Canadians were in Chinese prisons because Canada acted as it was required to do in accordance with the terms of an extradition treaty between Canada and the United States. As the recipient of Chinese retaliatory action, Canada is merely the proxy for China's animosity towards the United States. In order to be effective, diplomacy most often has to be conducted calmly and quietly, out of the public spotlight. It is difficult to imagine what might be gained in this instance by Canadian politicians fulminating at China, or at one another. Nevertheless, the question of how Canada should conduct itself with China – and, even more thorny, how it should conduct itself in light of the China-US dynamic – is crucial to the well-being of the country, and it might well have been a matter for debate as the electorate considered how it wished to be governed. But, as with the NAFTA renegotiation, in as much as the issue was addressed at all it was framed in terms of whether the government had been sufficiently "tough."

In the months leading up to the election, Scheer had repeatedly called for Canada to institute its own retaliatory measures against China, including imposing tariffs on Chinese imports, subjecting Chinese products to ever greater inspection before being allowed into the Canadian market, and revoking Canadian membership in the Asia Infrastructure Investment Bank. The Liberal government, unwilling to further escalate the dispute, considered such measures imprudent if not counter-productive. During the official French-language leaders debate on 10 October, the opposition leaders took turns insisting that they would have shown more backbone against China, with Bloc Québécois leader Yves-François Blanchet arguing that the dispute would never have come about had Canada not acceded to the US request to arrest Meng in the first place – leaving open the question of the consequences to Canada of ignoring the terms of an extant treaty with its closest ally and largest trading partner.[10]

The full and public debate on Canada's China policy and the imprisonment of the two Canadians would have to wait until after the election. On 10 December, all the opposition parties handed the Liberal minority government its first defeat when they voted to establish a special parliamentary committee to review all aspects of Canada's relations with China.

RACISM

Intent on portraying the Conservatives as intolerant of sexual or racial difference, home to anti-abortion activists, and therefore out of step with mainstream Canadian values, the Liberal electoral machine had been assiduous in its research on individual Conservative candidates, and, in the opening days of the campaign, it released one embarrassing example after another of Conservative candidates making anti-Québécois, Islamophobic, homophobic, or anti-abortion remarks. This had the twin effects of knocking the CPC off-message and – unfairly or not – insinuating that Conservatives were all too commonly insensitive on questions of race, ethnicity, sexuality, and gender rights.

The Liberals would have done well to conduct the same type of "oppo research" on their own leader. A week into the campaign, *Time* magazine published a photograph taken in 2001 of a twenty-nine-year-old Trudeau at an "Arabian Nights" party at the Vancouver private school where he then taught. Dressed in an elaborate costume topped by a turban, he is wearing dark skin makeup on his face, neck, and hands. In short order other images emerged of him in dark skin colouring: a grainy video of him in blackface from the early 1990s and a photograph of him in blackface and an Afro wig performing the traditional Jamaican folk song "Day-O" at a high school talent show.

The images were an international sensation and sent an immediate shudder through the campaign. If these had been photographs of an unknown Conservative candidate unearthed by the Liberal war room they would have been incendiary enough, but Trudeau had constructed a political persona as a progressive, a feminist, a friend and champion of refugees and immigrants and people of colour – a man sensitive to the lived experience of others. The disjuncture between that persona and the evidence of these photographs – not to say the hubris of a man who authorized a systematic hunt for political opponents' past indiscretions knowing full well that these disgraceful images of himself were known to scores of people – momentarily staggered the imagination.

Trudeau of course apologized immediately, acknowledging that his behaviour was racist but claiming he was not aware of that at the time. What he did not address, however, was the perplexing question of *why* he engaged in this behaviour at all. If it was not intended to be contemptuous, if it was all supposedly done in a spirit of good fun, what was fun about it? Who was supposed to be amused, and in what did the amusement lie? What was remotely funny about passing oneself off as a cartoonish – at best – version of another ethnicity? In short, Trudeau never volunteered an answer to the question famously posed by Jay Leno to Hugh Grant, following the actor's arrest for solicitation: "What were you thinking?"

It is possible Trudeau meant no harm by engaging in this manifestly harmful behaviour; after all, he had been a drama teacher, accustomed to dressing up and pretending to be someone he was not. But this is to elide the political and moral charge that attaches to racial identity. If photographs had come to light of a youthful Trudeau dressed as a woman on more than one occasion, it might have been embarrassing – there would have been an uncomfortable national moment, international media attention, the late night comedy shows would have had their fun – but it would not have been so scandalous as to be near-disqualifying because it would not have called into question his moral judgment. For a man to pretend to be a woman as a form of entertainment and enjoyment is one thing. Not so long ago it was seen as a perversion, but today, in an era of gender fluidity, RuPaul is a style maven. However, appropriating the markers of another ethnicity is of a vastly different order. To appreciate why, one only had to compare the Arabian Nights photograph of Trudeau with the leader of the New Democratic Party. If someone were deliberately trying to mock and belittle Jagmeet Singh, this is exactly how he might dress. Small wonder that one of Trudeau's first acts after his public apology was to seek a meeting with Singh in order to apologize in person. Singh graciously accepted, though the meeting was conducted in private since, as Singh said, he "didn't want to be used as a checklist of steps taken to exonerate [Trudeau]."

As dismaying as it was to see the prime minister of Canada in brownface and blackface – in this, at least, the Conservatives were correct: Trudeau had embarrassed Canada at home and on the world stage – many thought that the images would provoke a long-overdue national conversation about racism, bringing the issue to the fore, and that the election was the ideal time to have such a conversation, given how the country was focused on its political future and debating where its values and priorities should lie. "Canada, we need to have a serious talk about racism," wrote Anita Singh and Anjum Sultana in the

National Observer.[11] "Trudeau photos force conversation about racism, history of blackface, experts say," declared a CBC headline.[12]

However, while there were many thoughtful, powerful, and moving pieces written by journalists, academics, and social commentators, by people of colour and by whites, the issue of racism – overt and latent, deliberate and unwitting, systemic and extrinsic – simply did not take hold in the election discourse. For the Conservatives, the blackface images were a stark validation of their long-standing insistence that Trudeau was "not as advertised" – that he is and always has been a fraud. This was the line Scheer used at the start of the English-language leaders debate when he accused Trudeau of being a "phony," of always "wearing a mask." From a tactical point of view, this is altogether understandable. One does not win elections by stoking a soul-searing national debate on an issue as barbed as racism. ("It takes more than [forty-one] days to settle anything ... that serious.")[13] But the drift of the complaint into the falsity of Trudeau's character blunted the focus on racism. It also, inadvertently, caused difficulties for the Conservatives. By making authenticity the measure of character, Scheer entrapped himself when it was revealed that he had not been, as he claimed, a licensed insurance broker in Saskatchewan. More than that, if Scheer had been truly authentic he would have spoken candidly about why he chose not to march in Pride parades or in protests demanding action on climate change. Instead, he equivocated.

There was, however, a more pressing reason that the issue of race and ethnic identity was left largely unspoken by the parties and their leaders. Quebec, with its seventy-eight seats, was a key element of the campaign strategies of the Liberals, the Conservatives, and the NDP. The Liberals knew they would lose seats in Atlantic Canada and the west. They counted on gaining seats in Quebec to offset those losses. The Conservatives calculated they would need to gain seats in Quebec to unseat the Liberals. The NDP hoped to retain, even perhaps gain, seats in Quebec for the chance of holding the balance of power in what might be a minority Parliament.

But just as the federal election began, Quebec's Act Respecting the Laicity of the State had come into effect, in the name of preserving and protecting the character of the province's own proud ethnic identity. The act prohibits the display of religious symbols, artefacts, and dress on the part of newly hired public servants in positions of "authority," and it requires that one's face be uncovered to provide or receive public services that require identification, such as boarding a bus with a reduced-fare photo ID. Thus, teachers, police officers, judges, and other government employees joining the public service workforce will not be allowed to wear turbans, hijabs, yarmulkes, or crucifixes. The law is overwhelmingly popular in Quebec.

If to appropriate the markers of ethnic or religious identity is a racist act, surely to strip a person of the markers of their ethnic or religious identity is even more so? The act has come under fire as a form of institutionalized racism from those who see it as directed at populations for whom religious symbols and ethnic attire are part of their identity, primarily Muslims and Sikhs. So, the will to build a society *chez nous* founded on "Quebec values" collides with the cultural need of minorities to dress in accordance with their customs and beliefs.

For the parties wooing the voters of the province, to forcefully defend the rights of those minorities in the face of the law of Quebec would have meant forfeiting their electoral prospects in the province and therefore jeopardizing their electoral prospects nationally. Outright confrontation with Quebec on the question would most likely provoke a national crisis. And so the three major parties decided that discretion was the better part of valour. Both the Conservatives and NDP vowed not to intervene. Only the Liberals left the door open to a possible court challenge, and even then they did so coyly. None made the law an election issue.

And so, for reasons of brute pragmatism an issue of fundamental import about ethnic identity and the rights of Canadian citizens was passed over in near silence. Curiously, only two weeks after the election, anglophone Canada got the pent-up conversation about race, insult, and identity that had been simmering during the campaign when an octogenarian hockey commentator blathered on television about immigrants ("you people") not wearing poppies to honour military veterans on Remembrance Day and lost his job as a result. Francophone Canada would hardly have noticed except that the hockey commentator had said much worse for years about French Canadians and had kept his job.

NOTES

1 Special Advisory Committee on the Epidemic of Opioid Overdoses, *National Report: Opioid-Related Harms in Canada* (Ottawa: Public Health Agency of Canada, December 2019), https://health-infobase.canada.ca/substance-related-harms/opioids.

2 Christopher Dornan, "The Media and the Unmaking of a Prime Minister: The Spectacular Rise and Fall of Canada's Kim Campbell," *Media Information Australia* 73 (August 1994): 84.

3 Martin Gurri, "2019: The Year Revolt Went Global," *The Fifth Wave*, 10 December 2019, https://thefifthwave.wordpress.com/2019/12/10/2019-the-year-revolt-went-global/.

4 CTV News, 29 May 2019, https://www.youtube.com/watch?v=Rbo5GZOfhGs&list=PLLzHOgGvydCmQ6eDjl-drq4aSM3swdCUB&index=48.

5 Joan Bryden, "Rona Ambrose Disagrees with Scheer's Assertion That Trudeau Caved to Trump on NAFTA," *National Post*, 27 August 2019, https://nationalpost.com/news/canada/ambrose-disagrees-with-scheers-assertion-that-trudeau-caved-to-trump-on-nafta.

6 Mia Rabson, "Scheer Says He Will Ratify CUSMA Despite Saying Trudeau Gave Everything to Trump," *Canadian Press/Global News*, 15 September 2019, https://globalnews.ca/news/5904932/andrew-scheer-ratify-nafta/.

7 Janice Dickson and Michelle Carbert, "Scheer Accuses Trudeau of Negotiating a Weak NAFTA Replacement after Pressure," *Globe and Mail*, 15 September 2019, https://www.theglobeandmail.com/politics/article-scheer-accuses-trudeau-of-negotiating-weak-nafta-replacement-after/.

8 Jaquie McNish, "Chinese Dispute Strikes Canada's Canola Farmers," *Wall Street Journal*, 16 April 2019, https://www.wsj.com/articles/chinese-dispute-strikes-canadas-canola-farmers-11555412400.

9 Catherine Tunney, "Canadian Pork and Beef Exports to China Resuming, Trudeau Says," *CBC News*, 5 November 2019, https://www.cbc.ca/news/politics/canada-pork-beef-trudeau-1.5348532.

10 Brian Hill and Rachel Browne, "Federal Leaders Spar over the Detention of Canadians in China," *Global News*, 10 October 2019, https://globalnews.ca/news/6019475/federal-leaders-debate-china/.

11 Anita Singh and Anjum Sultana, "Canada, We Need to Have a Serious Talk about Racism," *National Observer*, 24 September 2019, https://www.nationalobserver.com/2019/09/24/opinion/canada-we-need-have-serious-talk-about-racism.

12 Ahmar Khan, "Trudeau Photos Force Conversation about Racism, History of Blackface, Experts Say," *CBC News*, 19 September 2019, https://www.cbc.ca/news/canada/manitoba/trudeau-blackface-historical-significance-1.5290761.

13 When Kim Campbell made this remark in 1993, the election campaign was forty-seven days long. The 2019 campaign was fought over forty-one days.

2

Second Chance: The Chastened Liberals

Brooke Jeffrey

On 21 October 2019, the Trudeau Liberals were returned to office for a second term, but this time with a minority rather than the sizable majority they received in 2015. This was probably the best they could have hoped for, given the precarious situation in which they found themselves only a few months earlier. Although some optimistic Liberal insiders had believed a majority was still in the cards, a loss of seats was definitely expected. Nevertheless the extent of their loss was greater than anticipated, and the extent of the regional divides the election revealed was equally surprising. The election results were widely seen as a lukewarm acceptance of the Liberals as the best option. But the enthusiasm and high hopes of 2015 were absent during the divisive and frequently negative campaign. In the end it was a chastened Prime Minister Justin Trudeau who acknowledged that Canadians had given his government a second chance, on the understanding that he and his team must do better.

Certainly the results were a dramatic contrast with the party's stunning 2015 election victory. Not only had the Liberals come from behind in that campaign, surging from third place at the start to win a solid majority of 184 seats, but their 148-seat gain represented the largest single seat increase in Canadian electoral history. This time the Liberals lost seats in every region of the country, and their 157 seats fell thirteen short of a majority. With only 33 percent of the popular vote (down from 39 percent in 2015), they formed a government with the lowest percent of the vote ever. And, having won no seats in Alberta or Saskatchewan, the regional divide between the two western oil-producing provinces and the rest of Canada was starkly evident. At the same time, the heightened importance of environmental issues throughout the campaign, especially in Ontario and Quebec, seemed to ensure the Liberals would face a significant challenge in navigating difficult policy choices in a minority Parliament.

Looking back, the Trudeau Liberals' 2015 victory was extraordinary for many reasons. When that campaign began the Liberals had been in opposition for nearly a decade, enduring four leaders and three disastrous election losses during their sojourn in the wilderness. Their once-famous Big Red Machine was on life support and the party was nearly bankrupt. The slow process of rebuilding had barely begun when supporters chose Justin Trudeau as the next leader in 2013. But hard work – including a massive restructuring of the party organization, improved fundraising efforts, and the adoption of advanced campaign technology – paid off. The Liberals' victory in 2015 was due in large measure to their impressive technical campaign as well as a progressive but credible platform. But it was also due to their charismatic leader and his refreshingly positive campaign, promising a return to "sunny ways," hope for the future, and a less partisan, confrontational way of doing politics. Not surprisingly, the expectations of Canadians were high, if not unrealistically high, as the Liberal victory brought an end to the Harper Conservatives' decade in power.

From his early symbolic gestures of ensuring gender parity in cabinet and marching in Pride parades, to promoting reconciliation with Indigenous communities and accepting Syrian refugees, Justin Trudeau initially was seen to follow through on his commitment to do politics differently. Aided by his extensive use of social media, the image of the so-called "first prime minister of the Instagram age" was carefully crafted to demonstrate sensitive but forceful leadership. His popularity and that of the Liberal Party actually increased after the election.[1] As a result the party's honeymoon with voters lasted far longer than usual. Having won the 2015 election with 39.5 percent of the vote, the Liberals polled a stratospheric 40 to 50 percent throughout 2016 and 2017, only coming down to earth in early 2018 after an unprecedented 125 weeks in first place.[2]

Canadians' love affair with Trudeau finally came to an end largely as a result of a series of self-inflicted wounds. The first involved a family vacation at the Aga Khan's private island in the Caribbean in December 2016. The opposition Conservatives vigorously attacked the trip as a conflict of interest. Trudeau, taken aback by the charge, said he had not consulted the ethics commissioner about the trip because the Aga Khan was a family friend, a category specifically exempted from the newly introduced conflict of interest legislation. The commissioner eventually issued a report that disagreed with the prime minister's interpretation of the guidelines, but polls indicated the affair had little impact on public opinion. Still, the incident had raised potential concerns about the prime minister's judgment.

An ill-fated trip to India in February 2018 finally broke the spell. The perceived diplomatic failure was compounded by Trudeau's decision to dress in formal Indian attire throughout most of the trip, leading to widespread ridicule in Canada and internationally. As one media headline declared, "Trudeau's India Trip Is a Total Disaster, and He Has Only Himself to Blame."[3] Barely a month after the gaffe-filled trip an Ipsos poll on 2 March found the Liberals' support was down to 33 percent, more than five points behind the Conservatives. Ipsos CEO Darrell Bricker concluded "there was something about this trip to India that was just a bit of a tipping point for them."[4] His counterpart David Coletto of Abacus Data agreed: "His trip to India struck a nerve with the public and raised quite a few doubts."[5]

Shortly after his return to Canada the prime minister launched a cross-country town hall tour. The format had proven effective for Trudeau in the past, and it appeared to work again as the polls slowly improved. Trudeau also benefitted from comparison with his opponents. Although his approval rating had fallen to roughly 41 percent by late 2018, Conservative leader Andrew Scheer's was only 22 percent, barely ahead of the NDP's Jagmeet Singh at 19 percent. By late 2018, it appeared Trudeau had put his personal image problems behind him. Polls suggested the Liberals were likely to be returned with another comfortable majority.[6] Meanwhile, the party's organization had begun to gear up for the 2019 election.

THE ONGOING FUNDRAISING CHALLENGE

After the 2015 election Christina Topp continued to act as senior director, fundraising, at party headquarters. Her frequent messages to donors urged them to support the party's efforts to counter the Conservatives' well-funded propaganda machine, now a permanent feature of political life in Canada. Her concern was well-founded. The Liberal Party ended 2018 with an impressive $15.9 million raised from 66,192 contributors. But the Conservatives reported a total income of $24.2 million for 2018 from 104,183 contributors. The fundraising gap between the two parties continued in the first two quarters of 2019 (the only ones for which reports would be available before the 21 October election), despite increased pressure from the Liberals on their base. Liberal Party spokesperson Braeden Caley proudly announced the party had raised a total of $8.9 million in the first half of 2019. The Conservatives raised twice as much.[7]

The significance of this imbalance became clear when more details of the parties' financial situation were made public. The Conservatives had an operating surplus of $3.6 million, net assets of $5.1 million, and an astonishing $9.9 million cash on hand. The Liberals reported an operating surplus of only $4,000 (still an improvement over the previous year's $400,000 deficit), net assets of $1.7 million, and roughly $2.3 million in cash on hand.

This somewhat gloomy report was tempered by the fact the Liberals raised by far the most amount of money at the riding level, a direct consequence of their candidate nomination criteria (discussed below). While 201 local Liberal associations reported raising some $4.6 million by the end of 2018, more than 262 Conservative associations only managed $4 million. Another piece of good news for the Liberals was that their new fundraising practices were more efficient than those of the Conservatives. They spent only 19 percent of their revenue on fundraising activities, while the Conservatives devoted fully 38 percent of their revenue to such activities. Put another way, the Liberals earned $5.14 for every dollar spent compared with only $2.62 for the Conservatives.

By 2018, the upcoming election was on every Liberal's mind. As an incentive to donors, late in the year the party instituted a "$400K-for-400-days" fundraising campaign to highlight the time remaining until the writs were dropped. The party's communications emphasized that funds would be used to prepare for the upcoming election, citing "building and training our campaign teams, ensuring our volunteers have the most innovative campaign tools, and equipping our regional offices and organizers with every resource they need on the road to 2019."[8]

Meanwhile, in Parliament the Liberals had introduced Bill C-76, an act to amend a number of features of the Canada Elections Act in keeping with their 2015 election platform commitments. The bill came into effect in late 2018, in time for the 2019 election. Among the changes was the introduction of a new "pre-writ period" (beginning on 30 June) when parties would be strictly limited in their expenditures on such items as advertising, over and above the existing limitations on spending during the campaign period itself. This move was recommended by the chief electoral officer and was widely supported. Its effect was to restrict but not entirely prevent the permanent campaign model perfected by the Conservatives.[9] As a result, many Liberal organizers were far more sanguine about the Conservatives' fundraising edge this time around. "You can only spend so much. We have more than enough to finance the campaign and some pre-election ads," one insider noted, "and their ads will have limited impact if they are shown too far ahead of the real game."

ELECTION READINESS

In December 2017, the Liberal Party announced the appointment of its new national director, Azam Ishmael. Having served as the party's get-out-the-vote director during the 2015 election campaign, he was selected to run the party headquarters and lead preparations for the 2019 election. Described as a leading campaign mobilization expert, Ishmael's appointment reflected the party's shift in focus from fundraising (job well done) to election readiness (still work to do). His first task was to organize the next biennial convention of the party, in Halifax in April 2018, where the agenda was unapologetically focused on election readiness. Roughly half of the forty workshops and panels over the three-day event were devoted to aspects of party organization and election planning, most of which were presented by a group of Trudeau advisers referred to as the "Team Trudeau Hub." These sessions covered such topics as "Organizing a Day of Action," "Invite Her to Run and Help Her Win," "Volunteers and Growing Our Movement," "Youth Engagement," and "Hope and Hard Work on the Campaign Trail."

A few weeks later the party launched the Team Trudeau Field Program. The innovative Days of Action the party organized in 2014–15 allowed the Liberals to engage in direct "conversations" with over 4 million voters in advance of the 2015 election. These activities were viewed as a major success, and now the Liberals planned to expand their reach by starting earlier and conducting more of them. Special Days of Action would take place on seven weekends in the spring and fall in addition to the regularly scheduled Days of Action held every weekend in July and August. The rationale for such days was equally clear: a combination of information exchange, voter identification, and pre-campaign training for volunteers. As party communications stressed, "Days of Action are mass mobilizations of our supporters, on the doorstep, on the phone or at community events." By identifying specific dates far in advance, they noted, "We want to give ridings time to plan and organize their teams with specific goals in mind – to engage our movement of supporters, increase the number of active volunteers, and identify more Liberals for 2019."[10] In late 2018, party spokesman Parker Lund reported the plan had exceeded expectations: "Throughout 2018 the party had more field organizers on the ground than had ever been seen in a non-election year, and campaign readiness has been a major focus at special regional conventions the party continues to host across Canada."[11]

In addition, organizers noted the party had defied the traditional pattern of governments losing seats in by-elections. The Liberals held five of their existing six seats in contests between 2015 and 2018 and even took two from the Conservatives as well as regaining the Quebec riding of Outremont, which had been held by the NDP's Tom Mulcair. For many commentators these results were evidence of the party's organizational competence, and they also reinforced the Liberals' lead over the Conservatives, while confirming the near total collapse of the NDP in Quebec.[12] Expectations of Liberal gains in that province were therefore high as the party began to nominate candidates for the next election.

ASSEMBLING "TEAM TRUDEAU": NOMINATING CANDIDATES

In June 2018, the party announced its sitting MPs would be acclaimed, providing they met certain basic conditions on fundraising and voter engagement. These included participating in at least two Day of Action engagements (where, together with volunteers, they would achieve thirty-five hundred doors knocked or five thousand telephone calls made), obtaining the signatures of 150 registered Liberals in their riding who supported their candidacy, and raising at least 50 percent of the funds required for the 2019 local campaign. For those MPs who had fulfilled these requirements the nomination meetings were expected to take place over the summer.

On 27 June 2018, Innovation and Economic Development Minister Navdeep Bains became the first MP to be acclaimed. In short order more than half of the caucus was acclaimed, including Trudeau himself. Then on 31 August the remaining 155 "non-held" ridings were opened up. Here, too, a significant number of conditions needed to be met before the meeting date would be scheduled. These included a requirement that the local riding association have banked at least 15 percent of the allowable expense limit for the election campaign, that the riding have a minimum of 150 registered Liberals, and that the local executive had conducted and documented a serious search for female candidates. Nomination meetings in those non-held ridings were expected to be scheduled throughout the late fall of 2018 and early winter of 2019. The drive to achieve gender parity was reinforced by the National Women's Liberal Commission, which held special campaign colleges across the country to encourage greater female participation as candidates and party officials. (In the end some 40 percent of the Liberals' candidates were women.)

At a special caucus meeting in Saskatoon in September of 2018, President Suzanne Cowan commented: "We're feeling in good shape, both on the ground and here, with our caucus team." "I'm feeling very optimistic about where we're at," she concluded.[13] But not everyone shared that view. As 2018 drew to a close there were murmurs of concern from some Liberal activists about what they saw as the party's slow start to election readiness. "It's critical to have the full campaign structure in place well in advance ... especially when the government is expecting a tough and nasty fight in the upcoming election."[14] By June 2019 it was obvious the fast-tracking of candidate nominations had stalled. The party needed 338 candidates for a full slate but had only nominated 197, almost all of whom were sitting MPs. Even so, it was 26 August before the last of the Liberals' incumbent MPs who planned to run again – former cabinet minister Bob Nault – was formally nominated. (Quebec Liberal MP Eva Nassif [Vimy] had indicated only days earlier that she would not seek re-election.)[15]

According to the party's senior director of communications, Braeden Caley, one reason for the slow progress in ridings the Liberals did not hold was the high number of aspiring candidates. "We have seen more potential candidates expressing interest than we've ever seen before," Caley said,[16] noting that over five hundred individuals had requested nomination forms for the 141 unfilled ridings. A consequence of this high number of Liberal hopefuls was the need to vet far more individuals than in 2015. On 17 July 2019, the party announced that Toronto lawyer Suh Kim, former chief of staff to retired MP Bill Graham, would serve as national chair of the Green Light Committee in charge of vetting, having been co-chair of the Ontario committee in 2015. (In the end the Liberals withdrew only one controversial candidate, Hassan Guillet [St Leonard-St Michel] whom they themselves had recruited.)[17]

By the end of July the Liberals still had no candidate in eighty ridings. On 10 August, the party invoked its "national electoral urgency clause," allowing the party to bypass nomination rules and appoint candidates if necessary. According to Braeden Caley this was a "long-standing" administrative measure that "always" comes into effect this close to an election "to help finalize the last few steps of the Liberal nominations process."[18] He noted that it was triggered ahead of the 2015 election as well. Several hopeful candidates expressed alarm, fearing the measure had been enacted in order to allow the party to simply appoint its preferred choice, but this did not happen. Nomination meetings continued beyond the start of the election campaign on 11 September, and the party finally fielded a full slate by the cut-off date of 30 September. Few of the party's nomination meetings were controversial and only a handful of new "star" candidates – including former Olympic kayaker Adam van Koeverden and former provincial Liberal minister Marie-France Lalonde in Ontario and well-known environmental activist Steven Guilbault in Quebec – were nominated.

THE CAMPAIGN ORGANIZATION

Many of the same Liberals who were concerned with the slow pace of nominations were also anxious about what they considered tardy decisions on campaign organization and strategy. It was not until fall 2018 that the composition of the national platform committee was announced, including co-chairs Ralph Goodale (minister of public safety) and Mona Fortier (first-time Liberal MP). But the national campaign chairs and their provincial counterparts had not been appointed, making it difficult to proceed with nomination meetings since they had to sign off on potential candidates. Even more important for many nervous staffers was the uncertainty over who would fill the staff positions of national campaign director and the team that would serve on the ground and on the plane. As one former Liberal organizer stated: "There's been a lot of complaints and concerns right across the country ... The formalization has not occurred. The PMO needs to sign off on who will be members of the national campaign committee ... so we can move forward quickly."[19]

Some of these concerns were addressed in January 2019, when Trudeau announced the appointment of no fewer than five national campaign co-chairs, an evident attempt to ensure both regional and gender balance: Intergovernmental Affairs Minister Dominic LeBlanc, Innovation Minister Navdeep Bains, former Prime Minister's Office (PMO) adviser Brittney Kerr, and former party organizers Nikki Hipkin and Sylvie Paradis. However, these posts were expected to focus on the overall conduct of the campaign rather than on day-to-day operations. Many insiders anxiously awaited the appointment of the national campaign staff who would handle the nuts and bolts of campaign planning. This had been the responsibility of Katie Telford and Gerald Butts in 2015. But with the advent of the SNC Lavalin issue in February 2019 (discussed below) and the subsequent resignation of Butts, Trudeau's top aide, the situation deteriorated and announcements came to a halt. Butts had been expected to lead the campaign team once again along with Telford. With Butts out of the picture the remaining key players in the PMO, and notably Telford, were forced to put aside or significantly delay their plans to leave and, instead, take over various roles with the party.

On 1 May, at a meeting of the national caucus in Ottawa, the prime minister announced that Jeremy Broadhurst – chief of staff to Foreign Affairs Minister Chrystia Freeland – would leave that post to serve as the national campaign director. Broadhurst had already served as the party's national director from 2013 to 1015 and was seen to be both knowledgeable and competent. Similarly, Tom Pitfield would return to manage the party's digital operations, including the Liberalist voter contact database that had been so successful in 2015. Kate Purchase, a director of communications in the early days of the Trudeau PMO, was named chief content strategist, responsible for the supervision and coordination of advertising, leaders' debates, and platform announcements.

At a special retreat in Ottawa on 11 July, some sixty Liberal advisers and party workers met to finalize the party's election strategy and organize the campaign team. Veteran adviser Cyrus Reporter, who accompanied Trudeau on the plane during the 2015 election, took leave from his law firm to do so again. Also on the Leader's Tour would be Finance Minister Bill Morneau's former chief of staff, Ben Chin, who had moved into the PMO after the departure of Butts. A former adviser to BC premier Christy Clark, Chin was known to Trudeau from his earlier stint in the PMO as an adviser on western issues. And, finally, John Zurucelli would again be the director of the Leader's Tour, overseeing logistics and technical matters.

This announcement was quickly followed by an unexpected one on 20 July confirming that Gerald Butts would be involved in the Liberal campaign after all, serving as an informal adviser to Trudeau and the senior campaign team. The final line-up of Liberal campaign staff soon followed, highlighted by the fact that Butts and Telford would be switching roles. This time Telford would be on the plane with the leader and Butts would be located at party headquarters. In addition to Chin and Reporter, Telford's team on the plane would also include two media relations officers from the PMO, Cameron Ahmad and Chantal Gagnon. Meanwhile, at party headquarters in Ottawa, Olivier Duchesneau, a former ministerial chief of staff, was named deputy campaign director with responsibility for Quebec.

Another important piece of the campaign organization was put in place in early July when party officials announced they had chartered a plane and several buses for the Leader's Tour. Before the actual campaign began, then, it appeared the Liberals were well prepared technically for the upcoming election. The Big Red Machine was back, and if solid campaign organization alone could produce another win, the Liberals were in good shape. But the campaigns of governing parties must also be fought on their record in office and here, despite progress on many files, several unexpected spanners were thrown into the works.

THE GOVERNMENT'S RECORD: PROGRESS IN KEY AREAS

When they announced their campaign slogan, "Choose Forward," in August 2019, Liberal strategists believed they had a solid record of accomplishments on which to build. There can be little doubt that the Trudeau government was seized with the importance of demonstrating its commitment to liberal values, especially the progressive social values with which Trudeau himself had been identified from the beginning. The prime minister's symbolic commitment to gender equity in cabinet "because it's 2015" was followed up with concrete changes, including the introduction of gender-based policy analysis and the overhaul of the patronage system, which by 2018 resulted in women being appointed to 55.5 percent of the postings for federal boards and agencies.

Shortly after the 2015 victory, platform commitments had been kept to reduce taxes for low-income individuals, to introduce a Canada Child Benefit, and to provide funding for housing, student aid, and Indigenous communities. The Liberals also made much of fulfilled election promises to introduce legislation on assisted dying, decriminalization of marijuana, LGBTQ rights, and the reversal of many punitive changes to the Criminal Code introduced by the Harper Conservatives.

There was also concrete evidence of progress. A February 2019 Statistics Canada report concluded that the Liberals' income support policies had been highly effective. The poverty rate had fallen significantly, and some 900,000 individuals, including nearly 300,000 children, had been lifted out of poverty as a direct result of the Liberals' Canada Child Benefit.[20] Similarly a Parliamentary Budget Officer report on the impact of the Liberals' tax increase on the top 1 percent concluded that the government's revenue had increased substantially, although it might not fully cover the amount lost through tax cuts for low-income earners.[21] And, while some Indigenous groups complained of slow progress on specific aspects of Trudeau's signature commitment of reconciliation, Assembly of First Nations national chief Perry Bellegarde described the progress made by Trudeau's government after four years as "unprecedented."[22]

In addition, the Liberals were widely perceived to have competently handled the unexpected threat to the North American Free Trade Agreement posed by the election of US president Donald Trump. Public opinion polls consistently showed the vast majority of Canadians approved not only of the resulting deal but also of Trudeau's handling of the file throughout the negotiations.[23] As a result, this unexpected challenge may actually have worked to the Liberals' advantage. With less than a year to go until the next election, they found themselves impervious to attacks from either the Conservatives or the NDP on the trade file.

Canada's positive economic fundamentals represented another major advantage for the Liberals. By June 2019 the national unemployment rate, at 5.7 percent, was at its lowest level since 1976. Statistics Canada's labour market report showed that 700,000 new jobs had been created in the previous two years and that wages had risen a healthy 2.8 percent over 2018. Even more significant, at 30.9 percent Canada's debt-to-GDP ratio was the lowest in the G7 and had actually fallen since Trudeau had come to power. A *Globe and Mail* editorial concluded: "Ottawa does not have a debt crisis, or even a debt problem."[24] Public opinion polls showed Canadians generally agreed. As a result, the Liberals' plan to continue to run small deficits to finance their platform was endorsed by almost all economists and left the Conservatives with little room to manoeuvre on that front.

Another potentially invaluable election tool was handed to the Liberals in August 2019 when two dozen academics released a book titled *Assessing Justin Trudeau's Liberal Government*. It concluded that nearly 90 percent of the Liberals' 2015 platform commitments had been either completely (50 percent) or partially (40 percent) met, while the remaining 10 percent were either unfulfilled or broken. (By contrast, using the same measurements, the Harper government was found to have kept only 77 percent of its promises and broken 16 percent.)[25]

THE GOVERNMENT'S RECORD: ELECTORAL REFORM AND THE ENVIRONMENT AND ENERGY FILES

Despite these advantages there were two areas in which the Trudeau government's record was vulnerable. Both were repeatedly raised by opponents to great effect during the campaign, ultimately overshadowing the Liberals' record of accomplishments. The first, electoral reform, did not seem too significant at the time. Their plan to eliminate the first-past-the-post system before 2019 had encountered opposition from the start, and an online survey conducted by the government indicated there was no public consensus on the issue. With opposition parties also divided, and several polls demonstrating only a minority of Canadians were concerned about electoral reform in the first place, the Liberals felt they could abandon their efforts at little political cost and instead concentrate on delivering other measures they had promised on democratic reform. But the Liberals' failure to deliver on this prominent campaign pledge ultimately allowed both the Conservatives and third-party groups to convincingly accuse them of broken promises.[26]

The second and far more serious problem involved a pair of files: (1) the Liberals' plans for a national environmental agreement to reduce greenhouse gas emissions and (2) the construction of the Trans Mountain pipeline, intended to carry Alberta oil to the coast of British Columbia for transport by tanker to Asia. These two initiatives were closely linked by Trudeau, who saw the combination as exemplifying the pragmatic balancing that had long been a hallmark of the Liberal approach. Shortly after taking office Trudeau was able to follow through on the environmental component as well as his pledge to maintain cooperative working relationships with the provincial premiers. On 9 December 2016, he announced a "historic national plan on clean energy and the environment" at a first ministers' conference that included representatives of Aboriginal groups. [27]

Both environmental and energy projects began to unravel less than a year later. With the election of a minority NDP government in British Columbia in May 2017 Trudeau lost a strong supporter in former Liberal premier Christy Clark. New premier John Horgan, under pressure from his Green coalition partners, began a series of escalating measures to halt progress on the Trans Mountain pipeline over environmental concerns. With her provincial economy and her own political fortunes in danger, Alberta premier Rachel Notley responded by threatening retaliatory measures. Repeated efforts by Trudeau to negotiate a resolution of the interprovincial dispute failed. With the conflict no closer to resolution after a full year the private-sector sponsor of the pipeline, Kinder Morgan, announced it was planning to mothball the project. This led the Trudeau government to announce that it was purchasing the pipeline outright for roughly $4.5 billion, a decision it justified by expressing concern that the economy would lose far more if the pipeline were not built and reiterating its determination to proceed quickly with its completion. Then the Supreme Court ruled the federal government could not proceed with the pipeline until it conducted proper consultations with affected Indigenous communities. This further delay not only exacerbated interprovincial tensions but also increased dissatisfaction with the Liberals in Alberta and Saskatchewan, whose oil-dependent economies were already slumping. The situation intensified with Notley's defeat in the 2019 Alberta provincial election by Conservative Jason Kenney, an aggressive critic of the Trudeau government.

Problems mounted with the defeat of the Ontario provincial Liberals in June 2018; the new Conservative premier, Doug Ford, promptly reneged on his predecessor's commitment to a cap-and-trade system with Quebec and California, and withdrew Ontario's participation in the national climate change plan that Trudeau had negotiated barely a year earlier. The Ontario withdrawal then encouraged Saskatchewan and Manitoba to follow suit, leaving Trudeau's environmental plan in tatters.

The October 2018 victory of the Coalition Avenir Quebec (CAQ) government of Francois Legault in Quebec increased the pressure, with Legault's controversial statements flatly rejecting the possibility of an eastern pipeline adding fuel to western discontent. But it was his introduction of Bill C-21, an act prohibiting government employees from wearing religious symbols, that would cause the most difficulty for Trudeau (see chapter 5, this volume). The bill was overwhelmingly popular in Quebec but less so elsewhere, and it was vigorously opposed by human rights groups. Trudeau's initial reluctance to take a position on the bill satisfied neither side.

THE GOVERNMENT'S RECORD: JODY WILSON-RAYBOULD AND THE SNC LAVALIN SAGA

Another problem area for the Liberals was of their own making, and it created a negative image for both the government and the prime minister, who saw his judgment once again called into question. It involved a prize recruit to Trudeau's cabinet, Jody Wilson-Raybould, who in 2015 was appointed the first minister of justice of Indigenous background, despite her lack of previous political experience or involvement with the Liberal Party. Perhaps not surprisingly, her performance as minister was questioned on numerous occasions over the next three years by stakeholders and opposition parties.[28] But when Wilson-Raybould was effectively demoted to the Veterans Affairs post in a cabinet shuffle in early 2019, a dramatic series of events unfolded that even the most seasoned political observers agreed was not only unexpected but unprecedented.

Wilson-Raybould was visibly unhappy with her new situation and resigned her new post within days. Shortly after, a lengthy string of revelations emerged about the internal workings of the Trudeau government. Wilson-Raybould charged that Trudeau, senior members of his staff, and the clerk of the Privy Council had attempted to interfere with her decision to proceed with the prosecution of a Quebec business icon, SNC Lavalin, by pressing her to invoke a little-known procedure related to criminal charges of corporate wrongdoing called the deferred prosecution agreement. Although all of those accused vigorously denied that their actions had been improper, in short order the demotion of a cabinet minister was transformed into a full-blown political scandal.

Incredibly, the Liberals appeared to have no coherent communications strategy to deal with the affair. It also appeared that Trudeau, who had based much of his personal appeal on his progressive views and tolerance of diversity, was unwilling to take a hard line with his former minister or criticize her actions. Instead, he attempted to straddle a divide between "doing politics differently" and defending his government's actions as legitimate and appropriate. In the end this ambivalence convinced no one. Veteran Liberals watched in disbelief as the scandal was allowed to continue unimpeded for more than two months. Growing opposition party and media pressure resulted in parliamentary committee hearings, public testimony by many of the principals, and sensational nightly news coverage. In the end Trudeau's closest confidante, Gerald Butts, resigned from his post in the PMO and veteran public servant Michael Wernick resigned as clerk of the Privy Council.

Worse still, despite his record as the prime minister who had made gender parity and gender-based analysis a signature policy, Trudeau was increasingly accused by his detractors of being a phony feminist who fired strong women when a second cabinet minister, Jane Philpott, chose to resign from cabinet in sympathy with Wilson-Raybould. At the same time, further evidence emerged that Wilson-Raybould had long been a thorn in the side of the government and many of her cabinet colleagues, and had actually been at loggerheads with Carolyn Bennett, the minister of Crown-Indigenous relations, for months.[29] Many furious Liberal insiders believed she should have been removed from cabinet much earlier. In the end, her secret taping of a conversation with the clerk doomed Wilson-Raybould, and both she and Philpott were expelled from the Liberal caucus. And, on the eve of the election, a damaging report by the ethics commissioner found Trudeau guilty of ethical impropriety, although it stressed no laws were broken. Adding to Liberal woes, Trudeau's statements defending SNC Lavalin in order to protect thousands of jobs in Quebec added more fuel to the fire of western discontent.

The seemingly never-ending saga took its toll. The Liberals' lead in the polls in late December 2018 had disappeared (see chapter 7, this volume). By March 2019 the party was ten percentage points behind the Conservatives. Moreover, some Liberals and pundits believed that Trudeau, who was a principal reason for the party's resurgence in 2015, was now a dubious asset if not a liability, demonstrating conclusively the perils of being a celebrity leader. Meanwhile the Conservatives took full advantage of the pre-campaign period to release television ads reprising their 2015 job interview format, with the actors this time concluding Trudeau was "never ready."

Yet, despite the Trudeau government's inept handling of this file, the Liberals' polling numbers slowly recovered. By late August they had pulled even with the Conservatives and Trudeau himself again enjoyed a ten-point lead over Andrew Scheer as preferred prime minister. With a minority victory now a real possibility after such bleak prospects a few months earlier, and a majority not entirely out of the question, the Liberals' campaign strategists decided on a plan of action that they felt took all of these developments into account.

CAMPAIGN STRATEGY: SUNNY WAYS MEET GOING NEGATIVE

The Liberals' internal polling results at the outset of the campaign showed the party running neck and neck with the Conservatives. How to break away? It was increasingly evident the government's efforts to help the oil patch had failed to make any positive impact, while the decision to buy the pipeline had alienated many voters in British Columbia. Since the Liberals already held all of the seats in Atlantic Canada and could not expect to duplicate that feat, they believed a win could only be achieved by capturing Conservative seats in suburban Ontario, as well as the sixteen seats held by the NDP in Quebec, to make up for seats lost elsewhere.

Over the previous year Justin Trudeau had insisted the Liberals would continue to remain positive despite what many observers predicted would be a highly negative campaign. Reflecting that positive message, on 27 August the party announced its campaign slogan, "Choose Forward." Party spokesman Braeden Caley told reporters "this theme ... speaks to Justin Trudeau's commitment to move forward with progress that helps people every day, and it highlights the choice that Canadians will make in this fall's election."[30] An accompanying video showed Trudeau riding a bus in his riding and speaking with fellow passengers. While much of the conversation revolved around the concerns of the riders and the accomplishments of the government, it also pointedly included Trudeau "warning them that conservative politicians claim to be for the people but cut services."[31] The tone of the video was partly a response to the months of pre-election ads run by the Conservatives attacking Trudeau. Titled "Not as Advertised," they accused the Liberal leader of broken promises (electoral reform), corruption (Aga Khan and SNC Lavalin), and hypocrisy (India trip). Liberal strategists believed the sunny ways of 2015 would have to give way, at least to some extent, to rebut this criticism and take seats in Ontario. Still, the Liberals argued that their criticism was focused on opposition policies, not personal attacks.

The Liberals' decision to take a more aggressive stance was soon evident. Whenever possible the Conservatives were described as intolerant, and Andrew Scheer's social conservative values (including his opposition to gay marriage and abortion) were highlighted. (To bolster this approach the Liberal war room had compiled a lengthy list of problematic statements by Conservative candidates reflecting racist or homophobic views.) Meanwhile, in order to unite the progressive vote behind the Liberals and to prevent vote splits that allowed the Conservatives to win ridings, the NDP and Greens were described as marginal and ineffective.

With Ontario premier Doug Ford's Conservative government deeply unpopular, another element of the Liberal strategy was to link him, as well as former prime minister Stephen Harper, with Andrew Scheer and the federal Conservatives. Liberal cabinet ministers from Ontario led the charge. Employment minister and Thunder Bay MP Patty Hajdu, for example, called the deep cuts in the Ford government's spring 2019 budget "cruel" and "reckless," concluding: "From my perspective Doug Ford and his cronies are trying to pull a fast one on Ontarians. It's quite clear that Andrew Scheer would take exactly the same tactic."[32]

THE LIBERALS' EFFECTIVE ADVERTISING CAMPAIGN

The Liberals' first set of election ads, with Trudeau riding a bus, was released in late August along with the campaign slogan. Political advertising experts described them as "head and shoulders" above those of their opponents, technically superior and effective in terms of messaging.[33] They were also the most positive aspect of the Liberals' campaign, outlining the government's accomplishments and their positive impact on the lives of ordinary Canadians. Here too, though, Trudeau's comments straddled the divide between optimism and cautionary tale. "We've done a lot together these past four years," he said, "but the truth is, we're just getting started. So Canadians have an important choice to make. Will we go back to the failed policies of the past, or will we continue to move forward? That's the choice. It's that clear. And it's that important. I'm for moving forward for everyone."

In keeping with their ongoing efforts to attract the youth vote, the party led the way in its use of social media to communicate its message. The Liberals spent more money and ran more ads on Facebook than all the other parties combined.[34] While the Conservatives' social media ads had a conventional format and national content, the Liberals focused on individual candidates' pages, a far more effective approach according to experts. The content again was primarily positive, highlighting government accomplishments and platform commitments, albeit tailored to local priorities and targeting whichever party posed the greatest threat to the Liberal candidate. The Liberals' emphasis on social media was validated by communications experts who noted that television remains the most expensive medium but is less effective in reaching young, undecided, or leaning voters.[35]

The party's ads in all formats evolved over the course of the campaign. One major addition responded to controversial third-party advertising by Conservative-friendly groups such as the Canada Growth Council, Canada Strong and Proud, and Shaping Canada's Future, all of which contained negative personal comments about Trudeau. One full-page ad in major newspapers declared "It's Time for a New Prime Minister," describing Trudeau as a liar and "the ultimate hypocrite."[36] The Liberals responded with a series of ads featuring Trudeau alone, stating: "The Conservatives want you to think this election is about me. We think it's about you." Others featured ordinary Canadians echoing this thought. Again, the messaging was effective since committed voters had already made up their minds on the issues outlined, but undecided voters might be receptive to Liberal arguments.

Another series of Liberal ads aired late in the campaign, responding to Conservative ads in Chinese that falsely accused the Trudeau government, among other things, of planning to legalize all hard drugs.[37] The Liberals denied all of the false claims and accused the Conservatives of using "the playbook of the American far right" to "spread false information to scare and mislead voters."[38] However, their response (in Chinese) was itself a classic example of negative advertising: they accused the Conservatives of opposing gun control and warned voters of potential threats to public safety.

EARLY CAMPAIGN SURPRISES

As in 2015, Justin Trudeau began the campaign in earnest in British Columbia. This time his launch was more problematic, when a minor collision occurred on the tarmac in Victoria damaging the Liberals' plane. However, the party organization regrouped and promptly secured a second plane to carry on. The first week of the campaign then saw the party and the leader on the attack, aggressively campaigning in non-held ridings in the province where they believed they could pick up seats and holding several well-attended rallies of the party faithful.

But the campaign's momentum came to a halt on 18 September when *Time* magazine published a photo of a young Trudeau, in "brownface" and wearing an Aladdin costume, at an Arabian Nights fundraiser for the Vancouver school at which he was a drama teacher. In short order another photo emerged, this time of an adolescent Trudeau wearing "blackface" while performing a Harry Belafonte song at a high school talent contest. Media coverage of the revelations, in Canada and abroad, was universally negative. This time the Liberal campaign was thrown into turmoil and only the leader could resolve the problem. Trudeau issued an apology immediately after the first photo appeared, stating: "I take responsibility for my decision to do that ... I should've known better. It was something that I didn't think was racist at the time, but now I recognize it was something racist to do, and I am deeply sorry." A second apology followed the next day as he told reporters he would be speaking with his candidates, opposition leaders, and his children about the incidents.

One analyst predicted the event would make the campaign "the fight of Trudeau's political life,"[39] but this did not prove to be the case. The following week revealed only a 1 percent deviance from the virtual tie in which the Liberals and Conservatives had been locked on the eve of the bombshell incident. Pollsters concluded the majority of Canadians "either were not bothered by the scandal or had accepted Trudeau's apology."[40] This acceptance was no doubt helped by the flurry of supportive comments from Liberal candidates of colour, epitomized by the statement of Liberal MP Greg Fergus (Hull-Aylmer):

"This is something that happened 20 years ago ... people are willing to cut him some slack and willing to forgive him because he has such a [positive] track record. I have confidence in the man."[41]

The same polls did find that Trudeau's personal ratings were down four points, but his opponents had fared worse. Elizabeth May's numbers were "lower than at any point since March," while "Andrew Scheer's negatives ha[d] hit a new high at 39%."[42] However, the damage to Trudeau's image was potentially more significant for the Liberal campaign since defending tolerance and diversity had been fundamental to his appeal four years earlier. Building on his earlier image problems, the revelations lent some credence to third-party advertising claims of Trudeau's poor judgment and Liberal hypocrisy. In short, both sunny ways and moral superiority – two key elements of Trudeau's original appeal – had now been abandoned or tarnished. The incident also caused problems for the broader campaign strategy of warning voters of the perils of a social conservative victory, and the Liberal war room prudently stopped releasing damaging material on opponents.

Meanwhile, the importance of the climate change issue continued to grow. Both the NDP and Greens had repeatedly criticized Trudeau's decision to buy a pipeline, rejecting his argument of a balanced approach. The Conservatives, by contrast, had cemented support in western Canada with their accusations that Trudeau was intent on shutting down the oil industry. With teenage climate activist Greta Thunberg's arrival in North America the publicity surrounding the issue – and the pressure on the Liberals – grew. Thunberg, too, had criticized the pipeline purchase, accusing Trudeau, "like all politicians," of "not doing enough."[43] When it was announced she would attend a rally in Montreal on 27 September, Trudeau took the initiative. He met her in advance, declared he "was listening" to her concerns, and then participated in the rally with his family. In addition, the party released another environmental platform plank promising to plant 2 billion trees as part of a broader ten-year, $3 billion plan to "use the power of nature to flight climate change."[44] But Trudeau also unapologetically defended his balanced approach and government's pipeline policy. "We have a national climate plan that will reduce our emissions and hit our 2030 targets in a way that also includes getting a better price for our oil resources that allows us to put the profits directly into climate change."[45]

Then on 30 September the entire Liberal platform was released to generally positive reviews. Titled *Forward: A Real Plan for the Middle*

Class, it was comprehensive, credible, and clearly positioned to continue the direction begun in 2015. It was also in stark contrast to Conservative proposals. Platform planks promoted social justice, environmental protection, Indigenous reconciliation, and economic innovation, and included measures to aid students, seniors, and first-time homebuyers; a plan for net-zero emissions by 2050; and signature policies on gun control, a national pharmacare plan, and data privacy. However, virtually no one, including Liberal candidates, paid much attention to the package after its release. In a campaign characterized by mudslinging and personal attacks, and in which the Liberals were obliged to spend much of their time countering attacks on their government's record, serious policy debate took a back seat.

THE LEADERS' DEBATES CHANGE THE NARRATIVE

The newly created Debates Commission organized two formal debates on 7 October (English) and 10 October (French). Trudeau declined to participate in additional debates proposed by *Maclean's* and the Munk School but did agree to a second French debate on 2 October organized by TVA.

The English debate was undoubtedly the least successful, with a complicated format, many moderators, and frequent exchanges in which all the leaders spoke at once. The tone was aggressive from the beginning, set by Andrew Scheer's unexpectedly personal attack on Trudeau. The Liberal leader's plan, by contrast, was to appear prime ministerial and to avoid gaffes. His restrained performance did achieve that objective, but it did little to advance the Liberals' cause. Trudeau responded calmly to questions, highlighting his government's record or platform planks, but failed to make an impression. Only Jagmeet Singh appeared to have struck a chord with viewers, notably when he attacked both Liberals and Conservatives on the environment.

The two French debates, in contrast, were models of organizational competence. Here it was the Bloc's Yves-François Blanchet who made an impact. With support for separatism near record lows, Blanchet carefully avoided the term and convinced many viewers the Bloc would be a lobby group representing Quebec's interests in Ottawa. Trudeau was forced on the defensive, claiming the Liberals were the best choice to represent Quebec interests because they were in power, not opposition. A particular advantage for the Bloc was its unequivocal support of the CAQ's Bill C-21, which Trudeau could not offer. After the debates Bloc fortunes soared and the NDP felt new hope, while the Liberal strategy was in shambles (see chapter 5, this volume). The party now feared it would lose more seats outside Quebec due to a split progressive vote, while the Bloc's remarkable comeback meant it might not capture the NDP's sixteen Quebec seats to compensate. The Liberal Party's response was twofold: first, to double down on its narrative that a Conservative government would mean regression on climate change and cuts to programs and services, and, second, to insist that it was the only party who could stop them.

The post-debate polls showed little change, with the Liberals still tied or trailing the Conservatives. Speaking at a rally in Montreal on 16 October, Trudeau acknowledged his opponents might win. Liberal insiders and volunteers were discouraged. Reports the Manning Centre had funded third-party groups who attacked the Liberals but refused to disclose its sources led Trudeau to describe the Conservative campaign as "reprehensible" and "one of the dirtiest, nastiest" in Canadian history, "based on disinformation," adding: "it's no surprise they don't want to share whose deep pockets are funding their attacks."[46]

However, the final days of the campaign saw support shift to the Liberals. In addition to their own actions, the Liberals were helped by the Conservatives when, hoping to avoid scrutiny, they released their entire platform on the Friday of the long Thanksgiving weekend. The Liberal team quickly found numerous weaknesses. Scheer's vulnerability on climate change had already been heightened by his promise, if elected, to eliminate the Liberals' carbon tax measure as one of his first acts. Now the platform also confirmed Liberal accusations the Conservatives would cut federal programs and services.[47] Liberal ads streamed out on Facebook and Twitter under the hashtag #scheercuts. Then Trudeau gave a rousing performance at the rally in Montreal, focusing on the Liberals' positive message. In addition the Liberals released the ad showing Trudeau declaring "the election is about you," which had been filmed during a major rally in Mississauga days earlier. The late ad proved extremely timely since a post-election study found more than two-thirds of voters did not make up their minds until the final week of the campaign.[48]

Finally, on 16 October, Trudeau received a major boost from former American president Barack Obama. Although Martin Luther King III and Raptors' president Masai Ujiri also endorsed Trudeau, Liberal insiders believed Obama's ringing endorsement was a game-changer.

According to one, "it recharged the base," especially those for whom the blackface incident had been a significant embarrassment.[49] The campaign distributed the endorsement widely.

By election day the Liberals turned potential defeat into a sizeable minority. An underlying factor in the Liberal win was undoubtedly the solid campaign fundamentals established in 2015 and diligently maintained over their first term in office. Moreover, Trudeau himself, while wounded, was still an important factor in their eventual recovery. In addition, the late campaign strategy reinforcing the "us-or-them" scenario had clearly worked. Post-election polls indicated that slightly more than one-third of Canadian voters considered voting strategically, especially if they were considering voting Liberal.[50] Nevertheless, with the numerous advantages the Liberals enjoyed going into the campaign, their difficulty in securing that minority is a cautionary tale.

THE FUTURE OF THE TRUDEAU LIBERALS: DYNASTY OR INTERLUDE?

The Trudeau Liberals had received a substantial majority in 2015 and used their mandate to deliver on many important platform commitments. They had also presided over a period of robust economic growth. In this context the fact they began the 2019 election in a dead heat with the Conservatives is revealing. From early speculation of a new Liberal dynasty emerging,[51] the question they faced in 2019 was how to salvage a minority. What went wrong?

The 2015 victory owed much to Trudeau's personal image and commitment to a positive approach. But with the leader's image tarnished by various scandals (exacerbated by an abject failure of Liberal communications efforts), and the party strategists' subsequent decision to "go negative," these advantages over their opponents were effectively lost. Further unexpected developments over the course of the campaign, as well as the surge in support for the Bloc and the better-than-anticipated showing of Jagmeet Singh, all contributed to the minority result.

Still, the Liberals remain in a relatively strong position. With their 157-seat minority only thirteen seats shy of a majority, they should not have much difficulty obtaining sufficient support to implement the bulk of their agenda. The NDP, Bloc, and Greens are likely to approve the progressive elements of the Liberal platform, and the

Conservatives will have little choice but to support the controversial Trans Mountain pipeline, which the other opposition parties reject.

Moreover, the results of this election resolve the question of whether the Liberals' 2015 victory was merely the result of voters' overwhelming desire to replace the Harper Conservatives. And, with 63 percent of the popular vote going to progressive parties, Trudeau was on solid ground when he declared the election results confirmed Canadians' rejection of Andrew Scheer and Conservative policies. In addition, despite their modest recovery, the NDP's fourth-place finish at the hands of the Bloc, and loss of its Quebec foothold, suggest it is unlikely to be a credible alternative for some time.

The regional implications of the Liberal victory should also be placed in context. Much has been made of the Liberals' failure to win any seats in Alberta and Saskatchewan, but they entered the election with only five – one in Saskatchewan and four in Alberta. In the other two western provinces they retained fifteen seats. They also finished second in three of those four provinces, well ahead of the NDP. Moreover, the electoral system played a part: in Alberta, where they received 14 percent of the vote, the Liberals won no seats; whereas in Quebec the Conservatives received only 16 percent but held ten seats. In Atlantic Canada the Liberals took twenty-six of thirty-two seats; the Conservatives took no seats in Prince Edward Island or Newfoundland and Labrador, only one in Nova Scotia, and four in New Brunswick.

While regional divisions have been underlined by the election results, a Nanos poll conducted at the end of October found that some 60 percent of Canadians (including a majority of Quebecers) were "pleased or somewhat pleased" with the election results. Perhaps more significantly the same poll indicated nearly 50 percent of Canadians wanted Trudeau's government to proceed with *both* the Trans Mountain pipeline and their carbon-pricing plan, validating the Liberals' approach.[52]

For most voters, then, the continued pursuit of balance and positive progress, along with greater humility on Trudeau's part, would appear to be the recipe for redemption for the Liberals. Trudeau's biggest challenge will be in calming the surging discontent in Alberta and Saskatchewan, aggressively stoked by provincial premiers based on real and perceived policy slights. At the same time, it is likely that some Liberal initiatives already in train will moderate oil patch discontent when they come to fruition. The announcement barely a week after the election that the Trans Mountain project would be hiring more than two thousand new workers is one example. Nevertheless, it would appear that greater federal consultation with provinces, and a far better communication strategy, will be necessary. In Quebec, with a rejuvenated Bloc Québécois ready to defend the interests of the province, the Liberals need to re-establish their credentials as the more effective party.

The real unresolved questions are, first, whether the Liberals have learned the correct lessons from their mistakes and, second, whether they will have time to implement the necessary changes in policy and attitude. As many commentators have noted, the situation of Justin Trudeau's Liberals in 2019 is eerily similar to the situation his father faced in 1972. It is too soon to tell whether the next election will confirm the existence of a new Liberal dynasty or relegate the Trudeau Liberals to the margins of history as a mere interlude.

NOTES

1 M. Lalancette and V. Raynauld, "Instagram, Justin Trudeau and Political Image Making," *Policy Options*, 9 April 2018.
2 By almost any measure the Liberals' love affair with Canadian voters was abnormally long, but particularly in comparison with the Harper Conservatives, who first fell below the level of their 2011 election-day support after a mere three months. Even in their first election in 2006, the Conservatives' honeymoon lasted only seven months. And, unlike Harper, Trudeau's personal popularity continued to soar once in office, with approval ratings rising to a stratospheric 60 percent in late 2015 and remaining in first place even after the selection of two new party leaders – Andrew Scheer for the Conservatives in the spring of 2017 and Jagmeet Singh for the NDP in the fall of that year. This was particularly striking since almost any new federal party leader will enjoy at least a brief rise in popularity, and Trudeau himself enjoyed that bump after his selection in 2013.
3 Barkha Dutt, *Washington Post*, 22 February 2018.
4 Abbas Rana, "Drop in Polls a Wake-up Call for Liberals," *Hill Times*, 19 March 2018.
5 Ibid.
6 At 36.7 percent (with the Conservatives at 33.8 percent and the NDP at only 15.3 percent), pollster Eric Grenier concluded the Liberals were on track to obtain 179 seats, far ahead of the Conservatives (135), NDP (22), and the Greens and Bloc (1 each).

7 Data on party financing in this section available at Elections Canada, http://www.elections.ca/content.aspx?section=fin&document=index&lang=e. See also Eric Grenier, "Conservatives Had a Better Fundraising Year in 2017 Than the Liberals," https://www.cbc.ca/news/politics/federal-parties-annual-filings-1.4733189.
8 Liberal Party of Canada, 3 October 2018 (hard copy).
9 See, for example, Mr Mayrand's testimony before the House of Commons Standing Committee on Procedure and House Affairs, 4 June 2018, https://www.ourcommons.ca/DocumentViewer/en/42-1/PROC/meeting-109/evidence.
10 Liberal Party of Canada, "Day of Action" Briefing Note, https://www.liberal.ca/summer-of-action//.
11 Abbas Rana, "Anxious Liberals Want Grits to Fill All-Important National Campaign Director Position Soon," *Hill Times*, 22 April 2019.
12 Annabelle Olivier, "Liberal Parties Rachael Bendayan Wins Byelection in Outremont," Global News, 25 February 2019, https://globalnews.ca/news/4998250/liberals-rachel-bendayan-wins-federal-byelection-in-outremont/.
13 Canadian Press, "Liberal Brass Says Ruling Party in Good Shape," *iPolitics*, 18 September 2018.
14 A. Rana, "Some Liberals Concerned Party Has Not Yet Named Top Campaign Officers," *Hill Times*, 14 January 2019.
15 Her decision was later described as involuntary. See, for example, Canadian Press, 25 September 2019, https://globalnews.ca/news/5950841/trudeau-denies-quebec-mp-forced-out-for-not-lauding-him-as-feminist/.
16 Samantha Wright Allen, "Conservative Party Leads Nominees, NDP Lags," *Hill Times*, 5 June 2019.
17 In the end the Liberals did have a few problematic candidate issues, but fewer than either the Conservatives or the NDP.
18 Allen, "Conservative Party Leads Nominees."
19 Abbas Rana, *Hill Times*, 14 January 2019.
20 Canadian Press, "Liberals Child Benefit Lifting Children Out of Poverty, StatsCan Says," 26 February 2019.
21 Bill Curry, "Tax Revenue from Canada's Richest Increased in 2017 after Liberal Reforms," *Globe and Mail*, 19 April 2019.
22 Amy Smart, "Reconciliation, Indigenous Engagement in Question Ahead of Election," Canadian Press, 13 October 2019.
23 See, for example, Graham Slaughter, "Majority of Canadians Support Trudeau's Trade Tactics with Trump," CTV News, 8 July 2018; and John

Geddes. "Liberals Enjoy Strong Support for Their Renegotiation of NAFTA," *Maclean's*, 23 November 2018, n.p.
24 Editorial, "The Debt, the Deficit, and Other Things This Election Isn't About," *Globe and Mail*, 18 September 2019.
25 Lisa Birch and Francois Petry, *Assessing Justin Trudeau's Liberal Government* (Quebec City: Laval University Press, 2019).
26 See, for example: https://nationalpost.com/news/politics/election-2019/the-liberals-broke-their-promise-on-electoral-reform-will-it-hurt-them-in-2019; https://www.conservative.ca/justin-trudeau-broke-his-promises-to-you-last-time-and-he-will-do-it-again-if-re-elected/; https://nationalpost.com/pmn/news-pmn/canada-news-pmn/ndp-reminds-trudeau-of-electoral-reform-promise-before-last-debate.
27 "Trudeau Reaches Historic National Climate Deal with Provinces," *Globe and Mail*, 9 December 2016, https://www.theglobeandmail.com/news/politics/national-climate-deal-reached-trudeau-provinces/article33281195/.
28 See, for example, Joan Bryden, "Trudeau Rejected Wilson-Raybould's Conservative Pick for High Court," CBC News, 25 March 2019; and Daniel Brown, "Wilson-Raybould's Regrettable Legacy as Justice Minister," *Toronto Star*, 16 January 2019.
29 Randy Boswell, "The SNC Affair: What Role Did Indigenous Clash Play?," *Ottawa Citizen*, 16 April 2019.
30 Rachel Emmanuel, "Grits, Tories Release Campaign Slogans," *Globe and Mail*, 27 August 2019.
31 Ibid.
32 Canadian Press, "Federal Grits Make Ford-Scheer Connection, *Ottawa Citizen*, 13 April 2019.
33 Peter Mazereeuw, "Liberal Election Ad 'Head and Shoulders' above Tory, NDP Offerings Says US Campaign Guru," *Hill Times*, 6 September 2019.
34 Tom Cardoso, "Liberal Campaign Has Most Ads on Facebook," *Globe and Mail*, 10 October 2019.
35 Adam Radwanski, "How Much Is the Conservatives' Fundraising Edge Really Worth?," *Globe and Mail*, 18 May 2019. For more detail see also Mary Francoli, Josh Greenberg, and Christopher Waddell, "The Campaign in the Digital Media," in *The Canadian Federal Election of 2011*, ed. Jon Pammett and Christopher Dornan (Toronto: Dundurn, 2011), 219–46.
36 Adam Hunter, "Regina-Based Group behind Anti-Trudeau Ad Campaign in National Newspapers," CBC News, 11 October 2019.
37 Xiao Xu, "Conservatives Running Facebook Ads Falsely Accusing Liberals of Planning to Legalize Hard Drugs," *Globe and Mail*, 11 October 2019.

38 David Beers, "As Scheer Falsehoods Pile Up, Postmedia Gives Its Blessing," *Tyee*, 9 October 2019.
39 See especially comments by Greg Lyle, Innovative Research, as cited in *Hill Times*, 23 September 2019.
40 See, for example, Abacus Data, "A Sensational Week Yet a Tight Race Remains," abacusdata.ca; and "The Blackface Photos Jolted Voters, But Maybe Only Temporarily," *Maclean's*, https://www.macleans.ca/politics/ottawa/the-blackface-photos-jolted-voters-but-maybe-only-temporarily/.
41 Greg Fergus, statement to media at press conference, Ottawa, 19 September 2019. See also Joanne Laucius, "Candidates Accept Trudeau's Apology, *Ottawa Citizen*, 20 September 2019.
42 Abacus Data, "A Sensational Week Yet a Tight Race Remains," *abacusdata.ca*.
43 Kathleen Harris, "Greta Thunberg Meets Trudeau, Tells Him He's Not Doing Enough," CBC News, 27 September 2019.
44 Liberal Party of Canada, *Forward: A Real Plan for Change* (Ottawa: Liberal Party of Canada, 2019), 35.
45 Ibid.
46 Kathleen Harris, "Trudeau Acknowledges Tories Could Win, Accuses Them of Running Dirtiest Campaign Ever," CBC News, 16 October 2019.
47 John Ivison, "How Barack Obama Revived the Liberal Campaign," *National Post*, 13 November 2019.
48 Angus Reid Institute, angusreid.org/election-2019-exit-poll.
49 Ivison, "How Barack Obama Revived the Liberal Campaign."
50 Joan Bryden, "Poll Suggests Plenty of Canadians Voted Strategically," CBC News, 29 October 2019.
51 For a detailed discussion of the concepts of party dynasties and interludes, see Lawrence LeDuc and Jon H. Pammett, *Dynasties and Interludes: Past and Present in Canadian Electoral Politics*, 2nd ed. (Toronto: Dundurn, 2016).
52 Daniel Leblanc, "Liberals Have Support to Forge Ahead on Both Pipeline and Carbon Tax: Poll," *Globe and Mail*, 11 November 2019.

3

The Conservative Campaign: An Opportunity Squandered

Faron Ellis

The Conservative Party of Canada (CPC) entered the 2019 federal election campaign with much higher expectations for success than at any time since its 2015 defeat. Many observers and Conservatives themselves assumed it would take at least two elections before they could rebuild enough support to challenge for government. But by the spring of 2019 the Liberal brand had become tarnished. A series of scandals and growing fatigue with Liberal leader Justin Trudeau's style propelled the Conservatives into the lead in most public opinion polls. The party was preparing to complete a feat accomplished only twice before in Canadian federal political history: defeat a majority government after its first term in office. The 2019 election results, however, proved mixed for Conservatives. Leader Andrew Scheer and his campaign team secured more votes than the party had received in any of the six elections since it was formed by a merger of the Progressive Conservative and Reform/Alliance parties.[1] Yet, despite winning more votes than the Liberals, the Conservatives won fewer seats, leaving many with the impression that an opportunity had been squandered by a campaign that never managed to communicate a coherent reason for supporting the CPC, to get on or stay on message, or to effectively deal with the widely anticipated identity politics-driven attacks on its leader and candidates.

The Conservative campaign also failed to adequately inoculate itself against opponents' ability to portray it as a continuation of the least popular aspects of the Harper regime. Indeed, the 2019 Conservative campaign undermined a great deal of the Harper legacy by not adequately defending against, and at times reinforcing, its opponents' branding of the party as a bastion for social conservatism and of harbouring a radical fiscal agenda destined to make deep cuts to services and programs.[2] The record shows that Harper pursued an incrementalist[3] strategy during nearly a decade in government[4] based on his "pragmatic electorally driven" approach to policy.[5] He incorporated social conservatives within the larger electoral coalition but for the most part kept the more radical elements in check. He ran deficits when economic circumstances warranted and returned to conservative budgeting principles once the economy improved. But concerns about a hidden agenda resurfaced in 2015 when Conservatives attempted to leverage their version of Canadian values as a campaign issue.[6] Through a series of mistakes, ineffective strategic decisions, and Scheer's inability to portray himself as authentic, the 2019 Conservative campaign failed to defend against its opponents' negative narrative and failed to build support beyond its base of approximately one-third of Canadian voters. Hence, a campaign that began with the promise of victory ended by improving the Conservative Party's parliamentary position but by disappointing the heightened expectations of its members, candidates, and supporters.

THE CONSERVATIVE LEADERSHIP ELECTION

One reason the 2019 Conservative campaign failed to propel the party to victory originates with its leadership election to replace Harper. At its first caucus meeting after the 2015 election, Conservatives selected Alberta MP Rona Ambrose as interim leader. Tasked with keeping the party unified for over a year prior to electing a permanent leader in a contest the party did not intend to hold until well into 2017, Ambrose shone. She toured regions where the Conservatives had been decimated in the 2015 election, rebuilt the party's finances, and proved an effective parliamentary performer. So impressive was her performance that a number of MPs and Conservative operatives launched a "Draft Rona" campaign to coax her into running for the permanent leader position. However, as a condition of her obtaining the interim leader position, Ambrose had promised not to seek the permanent job: she now reiterated her commitment to step aside and also to retire from thirteen years of electoral politics. Rona Ambrose was not the only prominent Conservative to decline an invitation to seek the permanent leader position. Low expectations about what any new leader could achieve in the short term combined with depleted caucus ranks produced a less than optimal slate of candidates to lead the party into the 2019 election. Most of the recognizable potential leaders also declined, including former Progressive Conservative leader Peter MacKay, former Saskatchewan premier Brad Wall, and Harper cabinet stalwarts John Baird and James Moore. Another, Jason Kenney, embarked on an audacious but successful effort to unite Alberta's still warring provincial conservative parties and went on to defeat the NDP government in that province. Despite the lack of available household-name candidates, the Conservatives embarked upon a modified one-member one-vote leadership selection process in which each party member would cast a single-transferable ballot to rank all of the candidates in order of preference. Votes were tabulated for each of the country's 338 electoral districts, with each riding contributing an equal number of points (one hundred) to the total.[7] Candidates were awarded a share of points based on their percentage of votes in the districts. Fourteen candidates appeared on the ballot. On 27 May 2017, the party announced that 141,362 members cast ballots, the largest number to ever participate in a Canadian party's leadership contest.[8] After thirteen rounds of counting, Saskatchewan MP Andrew Scheer, former speaker of the House of Commons, won 17,221.2 points (50.95 percent) and claimed a narrow victory over former Harper cabinet minister Maxime Bernier, who tallied 16,577.8 points (49.05 percent). Scheer also beat Bernier in total votes received – 62,593 (53 percent) to 55,544 (47 percent) – thereby sparing the party the awkward spectacle of having the points system declare a winner who had not received the most votes.[9]

Andrew Scheer was first elected to the House of Commons for the Saskatchewan riding of Regina-Qu'Appelle in 2004 when he was only twenty-five, narrowly defeating NDP stalwart Lorne Nystrom. After the Conservatives formed a minority government in 2006, Scheer was appointed one of three deputy speakers of the House. When the Conservatives achieved their majority victory in 2011, Scheer was elected speaker, the youngest in Commons history at the age of thirty-two. He held that position until the 2015 election. Having spent most of his political career to date in the non-partisan speaker's office, Scheer was one of the least recognizable candidates to seek the CPC leadership. Often referred to as "Stephen Harper with a smile," he was described by colleagues as affable, a consensus builder, and someone who could present conservative ideas with less of a hard edge than

Table 3.1
2017 Conservative Party of Canada leadership selection (percentage of points won)

ROUND	1	2	3	4	5	6	7	8	9	10	11	12	13
Andrew Scheer	21.82	21.85	21.97	22.06	22.17	22.48	22.97	23.85	26.03	28.28	30.28	38.36	50.95
Maxime Bernier	28.89	29.06	29.16	29.36	29.93	30.20	30.51	31.24	31.69	34.23	36.57	40.38	49.05
Erin O'Toole	10.65	10.68	10.75	10.86	10.97	11.15	11.32	12.37	12.79	14.64	18.15	21.26	
Brad Trost	8.35	8.36	8.37	8.39	8.41	8.44	8.47	8.53	12.84	13.71	14.30		
Michael Chong	7.55	7.61	7.64	7.71	7.75	7.89	7.97	8.60	8.70	9.14			
Kellie Leitch	7.00	7.03	7.05	7.09	7.19	7.26	7.45	7.74	7.95				
Pierre Lemieux	7.38	7.39	7.41	7.43	7.45	7.51	7.58	7.67					
Lisa Raitt	3.34	3.37	3.45	3.52	3.58	3.68	3.74						
Steven Blaney	1.26	1.27	1.28	1.30	1.33	1.39							
Chris Alexander	1.12	1.14	1.16	1.21	1.23								
Kevin O'Leary	1.07	1.08	1.09	1.09									
Rick Peterson	0.65	0.66	0.67										
Andrew Saxton	0.50	0.51											
Deepac Obhrai	0.41												

had Harper. Unlike Kelly Leitch and Chris Alexander,[10] he was unencumbered by baggage from the Harper years, and unlike Maxime Bernier he had not to this point demonstrated any inability to work cooperatively with his caucus colleagues. But he was not a well-known commodity within the CPC and was virtually unknown to the general voting population. Scheer used this lack of notoriety to his advantage in the leadership contest, providing members with a low-key alternative to the much more flamboyant and controversial Bernier.

The campaigns of the two frontrunners differed in style, substance, and strategy. Bernier's campaign was edgy and generated headlines. It succeeded in raising more money and signing up more members than any of the others, while pitching a libertarian transformation of the Conservative Party. Scheer took a more low-key approach, attempting to exploit the preferential ballot system by securing votes from members whose preferred candidates had been eliminated. He obtained more caucus support than anyone and was careful not to aggressively attack the other candidates, despite ample opportunity to do so given some of their rhetoric about values and immigration issues.[11] Scheer, though a social conservative, sought to project an image as the unifier of a big-tent Conservative Party. The campaign designed for him by manager Hamish Marshal attempted to avoid the negative attention drawn to other campaigns that were overtly recruiting social conservatives. He nevertheless assured social conservatives that, in him, they had a welcoming candidate once their first or second choice was dropped from the ballot. The strategy succeeded, but not without lingering consequences for the general election campaign.

Of particular relevance was an interview Scheer conducted with the pro-life advocacy organization RightNow, in which he coyly stated he supported freedom of conscience among his MPs, allowing them to speak about matters that are important to them. Continuing, he was careful to not use the word "abortion" when stating: "Our party policy is clear on that and I think in order to maintain unity of our caucus it's important that the prime minister respects that."[12] He did, however, reiterate that he had always voted pro-life as an MP. The transparently evasive attempt to court social conservatives but not alienate centrist voters illustrated a pattern that would undermine Conservative efforts throughout the general election campaign. But it succeeded in the CPC leadership contest as social conservative candidates were eliminated from the contest. Saskatchewan backbencher Brad Trost placed fourth and played a significant role in the eventual outcome. Considered a fringe candidate by many, Trost became the go-to candidate for large numbers of social conservatives. After initially receiving a respectable 8.35 percent on the first count, Trost maintained his support levels until the ninth count, when he got a 50 percent boost after another social conservative favourite, Ontario's Pierre Lemieux, was eliminated. When Trost was eliminated, more than half of his support went to the eventual victor. Social conservative activists immediately took credit for Scheer's victory and just as immediately began demanding a return on their investment, ensuring social conservative issues such as limiting access to abortion would remain on the agenda even if the Conservatives' opponents didn't put them there.[13]

Despite the obligatory show of unity among all the candidates immediately following the leadership campaign, it didn't take long for Bernier to sow irreparable divisions between himself and his caucus colleagues. He continued to savage the Canadian agriculture supply management system long after the leadership campaign had been decided, and he derided Scheer's supporters as "fake Conservatives," mere puppets of the powerful Canadian dairy lobby.[14] Scheer immediately removed Bernier as critic for innovation but, despite considerable pressure from Conservative MPs, did not expel him from caucus. On the eve of the Conservatives' national convention later that summer, Bernier took matters into his own hands and resigned from the party. In a blistering speech he accused the Conservatives under Scheer of being unprincipled, of "abandoning conservatives," of having nothing of substance to offer, and of being "too intellectually and morally corrupt to be reformed."[15] By September Bernier had established his own party. Post-election analysis indicated that, even under assumptions of perfect transference, Bernier's Peoples' Party cost the Conservatives a maximum of six seats.[16]

THE CAMPAIGN TEAM

The Leader

Upon winning the Conservative leadership and being sworn in as official opposition leader, Scheer proved to be a steady if not inspiring parliamentary presence. He succeeded in holding the government accountable, particularly when it stumbled during the prime minister's ill-fated 2018 trip to India and during the SNC-Lavalin controversy in early 2019. He consistently chastised the government over its environment policies, taking every opportunity to deride the federal carbon tax after the government's provincial consensus broke down when cooperating governments in Ontario, Alberta, and the Maritimes were defeated. He did, however, endure considerable criticism for not immediately presenting Canadians with an alternative climate action strategy,[17] preferring instead to keep his powder dry until the spring of 2019 when he released five speeches under the umbrella of *My Vision for Canada: The Andrew Scheer Keynotes*.[18] Together, the five keynote speeches were well-written and reasonably detailed, and the issues addressed were well articulated. The first, "Limited Government, Limitless Potential," covered the main plank of the Conservative election platform: affordability. It centred on cancelling the federal carbon tax, spurring international investment in Canada, achieving energy independence by 2030, and reinstating a series of Harper-era tax credits. It also introduced voters to the Conservative's main campaign narrative: that Justin Trudeau is a wealthy elitist, out of touch with average Canadians' economic realities, and is actively dismantling the Harper legacy of economic prosperity. Included was a snappy juxtaposition of Conservative and Liberal values regarding the size and scope of government, and it concluded by attempting to spin the Conservatives as the party of "yes," in particular with regard to major resource projects, and the Liberals as the party of "no." He attempted to reiterate this message on the campaign trail but it never resonated with voters.

Subsequent speeches included a "unity-in-diversity" address that was designed to inoculate the Conservatives against accusations they were anti-immigration. Under Harper the Conservatives had built considerable support within Canada's diverse and burgeoning ethnic communities but lost much of their credibility during the 2015 election campaign when they were outflanked by the Liberals on immigration levels, their perceived lack of compassion for refugees, and their abysmal messaging about Canadian values, including proposing a "barbaric cultural practices" hotline.[19] Scheer attempted to rebuild their image and counter opponents' branding of them as intolerant by telling supporters who did not accept the idea that immigration is important to Canada or who displayed any forms of intolerance, racism, and extremism: "There's the door." His "Foreign Policy and Defence: A Stronger Canada in a Turbulent World" keynote speech chided the Trudeau record on international affairs and included a critique of the renegotiated NAFTA deal that drew a rebuke from Ambrose, who had worked with the government during negotiations.[20] He defended the Harper record on supporting Israel and not compromising values when dealing with China, support for oppressed LGBTQ individuals in other countries, and his maternal and child health initiative, which tied international development to Canadian values. The keynote speech titled "A Closer and Freer Confederation" was peppered with platitudes about respecting constitutional jurisdiction, reconciliation with Indigenous peoples, and chastising the Trudeau record on both, but the focus was his proposal for a national energy corridor.

Undoubtedly, the most anticipated of the five keynote speeches was "A Real Plan to Protect Our Environment." Scheer had endured considerable criticism for deriding the Liberals' approach to the environment, particularly its carbon tax, while not providing Canadians with a plan of his own.[21] The manifesto opened with an attack on the Liberals' failures to effectively meet Kyoto and Paris targets and a promise to repeal the tax. Scheer's preference was to use technology in taking the climate fight global. He argued that exports of lower-emission Canadian fossil fuels and carbon capture technology would allow Canadians to make a meaningful contribution to CO_2 reductions. Overall, the environment plan previewed what would follow during the campaign, offering scant detail in primary areas of importance, while littering the issue space with dozens of other proposals to avoid discussion of issues where the party was vulnerable to legitimate critique.

The Conservative environment strategy was based on the goal of reinforcing the idea that no party's plan would solve the global issue or even meet current Canadian commitments,[22] thereby inoculating the party against accusations that it had no plan at all.[23] No attempt was made to recruit voters whose primary concern was climate change; rather, it was designed to shield the Conservative campaign, allowing it to move back to its primary narrative. But even "sixty pages – eleven thousand words within fifty-five specific proposals," as Scheer boasted in his address, did little to shield Conservatives against the near-universal accusation they were environmental laggards. Unfortunately, Conservatives did more to reinforce opponents' negative narrative than counteract it. A pre-campaign example emerged when Scheer and his caucus refused to support the Liberals' climate emergency motion in the House of Commons. Although equipped with effective talking points about Trudeau being a "high carbon hypocrite" because of the number of flights he takes, opposing the motion allowed detractors to frame the Conservatives as the only party not willing to take climate change seriously, a charge Scheer also had to defend against when he refused to attend any climate strike rallies during the campaign. As with other aspects of the Conservatives' 2019 campaign, their actions and communications strategies neutralized the impact of having pithy talking points or voluminous policy documents.[24]

The Candidates

The Conservatives were the first party to nominate a full slate of candidates, having all 338 in place by Labour Day. The party employed a standard screening process that largely worked, given that it was not designed to screen out social conservatives but simply those who could potentially embarrass the party during the campaign. Several such nevertheless achieved nominations, including one Manitoba candidate who stepped down after his Islamophobic social media posts were uncovered. But Scheer stuck by others, understanding that if he had to remove all social conservatives who had made questionable comments, attended politically divisive events, or had unsavory associates he would potentially be replacing dozens. The process was nevertheless called into question after it was revealed that one of its Ontario candidates cleared CPC vetting but had been deemed unacceptable by the provincial Progressive Conservatives because of her controversial social media posts. When the Liberals launched a blitzkrieg of exposure-attacks on specific Conservative candidates during the first week of formal campaigning, all were allowed to remain as candidates so long as they retracted, apologized, and specifically recognized the party position on the issue at hand. Only one Conservative candidate was banished after the nominations closed.[25]

The party succeeded in attracting a number of high-profile candidates, including former Olympic synchronized swimming medalist Sylvie Fréchette in Quebec, former Canadian Football League player Peter Dyakowski in Ontario, and country music crooner George Canyon in Nova Scotia. None were elected. Flushing out the ranks were former journalists, members of Canada's military, small business owners, former provincial MLAs, and former CPC MPs. The roster boasted 105 female candidates, a record for the party, and considerable ethnic and religious diversity, including "indigenous Canadians, LGBTQ+ Canadians, Muslims, Sikhs, Jewish Canadians, Christians, Hindus, Buddhists, and new Canadians."[26]

The National Campaign Team and Organization

The Conservative national campaign team was led by a core group of campaigners plucked from Scheer's successful CPC leadership bid and the party organization.[27] Few, however, had previously served in senior national campaign positions. Hamish Marshal, an experienced political consultant and former Harper-era staffer, was appointed campaign chair. He had known Scheer since they both arrived on Parliament Hill as Canadian Alliance junior staff members after the 2000 election.[28] Marshal became manager of strategic planning in Harper's PMO and served as the party's pollster during the 2008 election campaign. After that he pursued private-sector projects through his consulting firm Torch Agencies, including organizing the successful 2015 No referendum campaign to defeat metro Vancouver's proposed TransLink tax.[29]

Joining Marshal were two deputy campaign managers. Dustin Van Vugt managed the party's 150-person war room in Ottawa. Van Vugt held several staff positions in Harper's governments before being appointed executive director of the party with responsibilities for overseeing the election that saw Scheer selected as leader. Joining the leader on tour was Chief of Staff Marc-André Leclerc, who got to know Scheer after he left the speaker's job and who had been recruited to help organize the Quebec arm of his leadership campaign. Long-serving Scheer loyalist and principal secretary Kenzie Potter also travelled on the tour. Scheer's director of communications, Brock Harrison, assumed primary responsibility for messaging. Harrison was recruited to Ottawa after serving five years in Alberta provincial politics. He was assisted by Simon Jefferies, who interacted with reporters on a daily basis, and Cory Hann, the party's communications director, who ran a war room rapid response communications team tasked with responding to the news of the day.[30] Stephen Taylor, who ran *NewsHubNation.com* with former Conservative MP Monte Solberg, was responsible for running Scheer's digital campaign.

CAMPAIGN FINANCING, LOGISTICS, AND OUTREACH

Financing the 2019 Conservative campaign was not an issue as the party continued to out-fundraise all the other parties over the course of the 42nd Parliament. As the data in table 3.2 demonstrate, increased contributions from supporters adequately compensated for lost per-vote allowances as they were phased out by Harper. During election years, contributions increased from just under $23 million in 2011 to approximately $30 million in 2015. The party surpassed that milestone with nearly $31 million collected by the end of 2019. Its constituency associations were also financially well-equipped. Although amounts varied wildly between the flush western ridings and the anemic Quebec ones, together they held $24.2 million in net assets at the end of 2018 compared to approximately $19 million in 2014.[31]

The Conservatives ramped up advertising in 2018 as they attempted to introduce Scheer to Canadians, spending nearly $2.2 million, primarily on television ($1.2 million), with lesser amounts on radio ($565,134) or print and other media ($397,124).[32] These patterns would be replicated during the 2019 campaign. Social media would play a role but would not be relied upon for either advertising or for voter identification and contact. As outlined by CPC director of digital strategies Stephen McCreary, social media can be a powerful tool but, because of its expense and wasted reach beyond the borders of any single constituency, not to the extent local campaign activists believe.[33]

Voter identification and contact were managed through the Conservatives' Constituent Information Management System (CIMS) as updated with its Go Mobile canvassing application (C2G), which allowed volunteers to record information about potential voters at the doorsteps. Information was aggregated at the party's war room in Ottawa and supplemented with data from various rounds of mass text messaging, allowing voters to be ranked according to their likelihood of supporting the party; supporters were prompted to vote, donate, or order lawn signs.[34] However, reliance on direct contact at voters' doorsteps proved difficult. Campaign chair Marshal decided against implementing a large phone campaign, arguing that the decline in landline subscriptions and voters penchant for call screening meant phoning was not efficient. But without a significant supporting phone campaign many local campaigns found themselves lacking sufficient information to execute effective get-out-the-vote strategies. Problems were particularly acute in Manitoba, where Conservative volunteers had just completed a successful provincial campaign, and in the Atlantic Provinces, where membership was sparse. Rebelling against national campaign directives, some local candidates took matters into their own hands and established their own phone banks late in the

Table 3.2
Conservative Party revenue: National party annual averages, 2003–19 (thousands)

	2003–05	2006–07	2008–10	2011–14	2015–18	2019
Contributions	14,379	17,813	18,767	19,553	22,588	30,878
Number of contributors	88	108	103	92	100	197
Mean dollar value per contributor	164	165	182	212	225	157
Transfers (from candidates, associations, leadership contestants)	132	190	79	1,817*	598*	47
Total contributions and transfers	14,512	18,002	18,845	21,370	23,186	30,925
Allowances	7,623	9,803	10,407	7,824	–	–
Total contributions and allowances	22,134	27,806	29,252	29,120	23,186	30.925

* Including 1,732,821 from leadership contestants in 2016 and 2017.
Source: Elections Canada, www.elections.ca.

campaign. The labour-intensive door-knocking efforts also reduced the number of volunteers available to attend Scheer's tour events, an outcome Conservative strategists recognized but denied was a problem until the media began reporting on the small size of Scheer's crowds compared to Trudeau's.[35] By mid-campaign, local volunteers were ordered to cease door-knocking on days Scheer was in their vicinity in order to pack his events.[36]

The Conservatives organized a conventional leader's tour that made stops in all provinces. Demonstrating the campaign's belief it could win the election, efforts were concentrated in areas the Conservatives needed in order to make gains. The clear focus was Ontario, where Scheer made nearly half of his more than seventy stops, and in Quebec, where he made fifteen visits. He also made as many trips to Atlantic Canada, ten in total, as he did to British Columbia, where he made nine stops. Prior to the final weekend, he made only five stops on the Prairies, correctly assuming those campaigns needed little help from their leader.[37] Scheer typically announced one of the party's campaign commitments each day of the tour. These were supported by news releases, social media posts, e-mail notices, and other promotions designed to buttress the overall advertising campaign.

Conservative campaign advertising relied heavily on video, distributed through paid television ads and other media, including its nearly decade-old YouTube channel. The focus was twofold: (1) continue to introduce Scheer to voters by way of ads featuring him explaining his "It's-time-for-you-to-get-ahead" platform and (2) further discredit Trudeau by way of the "not-as-advertised" narrative. On its own the ad campaign may have been effective, but it was routinely undermined by a variety of deficiencies. The party's economic message about Canadians not being able to get ahead and being concerned for their jobs was undercut by the reality of a national economy that was performing well, including registering historically low unemployment levels. The "not-as-advertised" attack on Trudeau was discredited by Scheer's evasiveness about his social conservatism, his dual Canada-USA citizenship, and the campaigns' repeated embellishments or outright fabrications about what a Liberal government would do if re-elected.

The Conservative campaign tried to keep all advertising contracts and agencies confidential, understanding that some of the contracting firms' associations with other clients would be controversial. Examples emerged late in the campaign when it was revealed that ONE Persuasion Inc., the firm that campaign chair Marshal established with a number of other former Conservative operatives, was executing election advertising contracts for both the Conservatives and the Canadian Association of Petroleum Producers (CAAP). Conservative spokespeople attempted to dismiss the matter using standard talking points, stating "we don't comment on vendors."[38] However, given that CAAP was registered with Elections Canada as a third party, and that Scheer, Marshal, and CAAP president Tim McMillan had attended an April meeting in Alberta to discuss strategies, the campaign was quickly accused of collusion. Scheer's attempt at damage control only served to amplify his credibility gap. Elections Canada contradicted his claim that it had provided a formal ruling clearing the party of any collusion, stating it had provided only "guidance" and had included a warning about perceived collusion.[39]

Scheer stuck to the nondisclosure talking points on the final weekend of the campaign when faced with accusations he had hired well-known ex-Liberal Party strategist Warren Kinsella's Daisy Group consulting firm to conduct opposition research on Bernier's People's Party. Documents obtained by the media clearly indicated the project was designed to discredit Bernier and to ensure that he was not invited to participate in the official leaders' debates. The plan developed by Daisy Group included a sinisterly named "seek-and-destroy" phase, and it was clearly designed to be covert, to ensure the client was not named, and, if possible, to avoid Elections Canada third-party regulations.[40] The covert nature of this operation fuelled the salacious interest of journalists, who peppered Scheer with questions, which he refused to answer, nearly two dozen times in one encounter. It forced the campaign off-message, again, and furthered the negative narrative that Scheer was not being forthcoming with voters. When Scheer stood his ground in defending the questionable claims it only served to prolong the amount of time he would spend off-message and further instill an image of disingenuousness.[41]

THE CONSERVATIVE 2019 PLATFORM

Timidly, late in the day on the Friday before Thanksgiving, with only a week remaining in the campaign, the Conservatives finally released their full platform. The timing of the release revealed two primary concerns. First, it suggested a lack of confidence in Scheer's ability to defend the platform during the leaders' debates. Second, the party was concerned that the program cuts it contained, small by most objective measures, would nevertheless be used by their opponents to reinforce the narrative that Conservatives would make reckless cuts similar to those contained in the first budget of the Doug Ford government in Ontario. The federal Conservatives were already doing everything possible to distance themselves from Ford, and strategists determined they could not afford to fuel that narrative. The strategy largely failed. Given that most of the planks had been announced during the first four weeks of the campaign, holding back the full platform until very late in the campaign did nothing to blunt their opponents' attacks. Rather, it furthered the increasingly widespread impression that the Conservatives were not being completely forthcoming with Canadians, a narrative that had been solidified by Scheer's performance at the leaders' debates.

The platform was divided into six main sections: (1) more money in your pocket, (2) more good jobs, (3) more innovation to fight climate change, (4) more help at home, (5) more strength abroad, and (6) a fiscal overview, including a costing from the parliamentary budget officer. The first plank promoted the Conservatives' most important positive campaign position. "More Money in Your Pocket" was aimed at three targets: *for you, for your kids, for your retirement. For you* included twelve promises, five of which were tax reductions, including its planned signature measures, a universal income tax cut, and repeal of the carbon tax. It also promised to remove the GST from home energy bills, reinstate a green public transit tax credit, and provide more tax help for volunteers and the disabled. The remainder focused on home ownership. *For your kids* contained five commitments, all of which were tax initiatives. Four commitments were outlined in the *for your retirement section*, including a tax reduction by increasing the age credit. The rest dealt with pension protections.

The second section, "More Good Jobs," was designed to serve as the Conservatives' main attack plank against the government's economic record, a curious choice given the historically low unemployment rates achieved during the Liberals' first mandate. It opened by promising to stop *Justin Trudeau's attacks on small business*, including repealing the government's tax changes to professional corporations, reducing red tape, and appointing an expert panel to review the tax system for fairness and competitiveness. The second section featured what was originally envisioned to be the party's signature economic nation-building policy, *creating a national energy corridor*. The proposal had been previously announced but had failed to gain traction as a galvanizing issue due in no small part to how long it would take to implement, jurisdictional complexities, and the growing perception that it was little more than an oil and gas pipeline plan. Recognizing the weaknesses, the Conservatives argued that it would also enable Ontario and Quebec hydroelectricity to have access to new markets, provide Atlantic Canadians with vital telecommunications infrastructure, and engage Indigenous rights holders. Despite the nods to other economic interests, when packaged with a promise to repeal Bill C-69, known derisively in Alberta as the "no more pipelines act"; a promise to end the ban on shipping off the north coast of British Columbia; a commitment to build the Trans Mountain pipeline; and a declaration that a Conservative government would assert federal jurisdiction by declaring infrastructure projects "for the general advantage of Canada," the energy corridor was largely characterized as an attempt to force pipelines on recalcitrant provinces, particularly Quebec, where opposition was most intense.[42] The industrial support provisions demonstrated a significant weakness in the platform and the campaign more generally in that it offered little for Central Canadian voters.

The third section was designed as a shield against attacks claiming the Conservatives were soft on polluters and had no plan for fighting climate change. Most of the provisions in the "More Innovation to

Fight Climate Change" plank focused on the technology-not-taxes theme. Included were a range of environmental issues: three of the two dozen addressed plastics waste but few provided specifics on addressing domestic CO2 reduction. A Conservative government would instead rely on "taking the climate change fight global" by exporting cleaner Canadian fossil fuels and CO2 reduction technologies, existing or not yet invented. Overall, as in the Scheer speech outlined above, the environmental plank failed to blunt opposition attacks or widespread media criticism.

Rounding out the platform was a catch-all plank entitled "More Help at Home," which included more than seventy divergent pledges in support of Canadian cultural industries, law-abiding firearms owners, veterans, immigrants, and Canada's most vulnerable. It promised support for neighbourhoods as well as for rural and remote areas. The neighbourhoods provisions alone totalled seventeen commitments, primarily law-and-order proposals designed to deal with gang violence. These were in addition to the party's proposed reforms of the criminal justice system, which merited its own section and five specific proposals. Together with its nearly two dozen proposals for foreign affairs entitled "More Strength Abroad," and its relatively scant "Fiscal Overview," the six planks of the Conservative platform were packaged together in an effort to provide a great deal of volume but few specifics on issues of interest to voters in regions where the party needed to make gains.

CAMPAIGN DYNAMICS

For Conservatives, the dynamics they would encounter throughout the campaign were previewed several weeks prior to the official writ being issued. In late August, the party unveiled its campaign theme, "It's Time for *You* to Get Ahead"; boasted about its full coffers and its full slate of candidates; and released a new suite of TV ads. But it also found itself playing defence when the Liberals launched their initial volley of attacks against the party's perceived social conservatism. Liberal cabinet minister Ralph Goodale tweeted a video of then rookie MP Scheer's 2005 speech in the Commons, in which he opposed same-sex marriage by using an awkward metaphor stating that calling a dog's tail a leg doesn't make it a leg. More substantially, he used explicitly religious language to argue that same-sex couples do not qualify to be married because they cannot "naturally" procreate.

Conservatives have long argued, with considerable evidence,[43] that their leaders face a double standard on the same-sex marriage issue. Indeed, Goodale himself had twice voted against same-sex marriage equality in the 1990s. But the Conservative campaign refused to reference this or any other examples, believing the best way to overcome its own vulnerabilities was through avoidance and denial. In short, despite recognizing that they understood a double standard existed, Conservatives did nothing to diffuse it as a campaign issue. They delayed having Scheer publicly address the same-sex marriage controversy for nearly a week as headlines echoed the Liberal narrative. When they finally placed Scheer in front of the media, he refused to acknowledge his personal beliefs and unconvincingly stated Conservatives would protect all rights. Conservative strategists believed that, because former leader Stephen Harper had successfully managed the same-sex marriage issue for nearly a decade in power, they could also do so. After Harper had been plagued by the same issue in the 2004 campaign he made a tacitly adroit but risky gambit on the opening day of the 2006 campaign by promising a free vote on the issue. That strategy, designed to neutralize the issue as an ongoing discussion point during that campaign, succeeded.[44] However, the 2019 Conservative campaign did nothing similar and repeatedly reinforced the negative imaging through its own actions.

The stench of the social conservative albatross around Scheer's neck would only intensify as the summer drew to a close.[45] At the same time he was ineffectively dealing with the same-sex marriage issue, his chief Quebec campaign organizer, Conservative MP Alain Rayes, claimed that Scheer's position on abortion choice had changed since his election as leader and that he would not allow "even one of his backbench MPs to present an anti-abortion bill."[46] Rayes was backed by star candidate Fréchette, who claimed the commitment was a deal breaker for her becoming a Conservative candidate.[47] Rayes immediately recanted, and Scheer defended MP independence on conscience issues by reaffirming their right to introduce such motions. He then refused to answer follow-up questions about how he would vote should they do so, simply repeating his refrain that a Conservative government would not reopen the debate and that as prime minister he would govern for all Canadians.[48] Conservative strategists appeared blissfully unaware that they were building for themselves the same trap in which Preston Manning had been ensnared during the Reform Party's first Parliament. Manning simultaneously tried to mollify social conservatives while assuring mainstream voters they had nothing to fear from him or his party.[49] The strategy failed for Reform in the last century, and the flurry of critical headlines should have alerted Conservatives that it was failing them two decades later. The approach undermined the Conservative campaign's most important narrative – that Justin Trudeau is *not as advertised* but that Canadians could trust Andrew Scheer to be genuine, down to earth, and authentic. Rather, the evasiveness contributed to an impression of Scheer as inauthentic and therefore untrustworthy.

Scheer launched the Conservatives' formal campaign in Quebec, where the party was anticipating making gains. Conservatives knew they would need to recruit former Bloc supporters to their cause if they were going to improve on the twelve seats the party won in 2015. They followed past CPC campaign practices in organizing a distinct Quebec campaign and Quebec-specific messaging. Scheer promised not to intervene in the Quebec government's secularization law. With a nod to the potential threat that Bloc leader Yves-François Blanchet represented, he argued that no matter who the Bloc leader was, the Bloc could not replace Justin Trudeau or put more money in Quebecers' pockets. Invoking an aggressive tone not seen since the height of the SNC-Lavalin scandal, Scheer then pivoted to his main target, accusing Trudeau of lies and cover-ups, including blocking witnesses from testifying to the RCMP.[50] Although criticized for overplaying his hand earlier in the year by demanding Trudeau's resignation immediately after the SNC-Lavalin story broke, Conservative strategists believed that he needed to become even more aggressive in reinforcing their main campaign message that voters should reject Trudeau because he was "not as advertised." Taking this forceful position on the first day of the campaign, in Quebec where Trudeau's position on SNC-Lavalin was not unpopular, was designed to demonstrate Scheer's courage and strength of character. It succeeded only in putting Quebecers on notice that there were limits to how far Conservatives would go in accommodating that province's distinct character.

The forcefulness of Scheer's attacks on Trudeau was based on Conservatives' belief that Canadians had changed their perspectives about the prime minister. In 2015 they believed that Trudeau was not disliked enough to aggressively attack him and risk reinforcing their mean-spirited image. By 2019 they believed he was vulnerable. Rather than temper his approach, Scheer became increasingly aggressive in his attacks on Trudeau's character as the campaign unfolded, to the point at which they appeared shrill and at times undignified. The strategy was grounded in the belief that most of what the Conservative campaign needed to do was to amplify issues that would allow the government to defeat itself. This approach reached a crescendo during the only English-language debate in which Trudeau participated, where Scheer opened by bluntly stating that Trudeau was a "fraud and a phony" who did not deserve to govern Canada.[51] However, the success of the strategy was at least partially dependent on Scheer's ability to project a leadership style opposite to that with which Conservatives were portraying Trudeau: Scheer needed to be genuine, authentic, and credible. Understanding they still had plenty of work to do introducing Scheer to voters, that their opponents would attempt to fill unknowns with negatives, and that their efforts to date were not sufficient, Conservatives determined he needed to be more aggressive. Indeed, at the start of the campaign fully one-fifth of voters did not know enough about Scheer to even provide an evaluation.[52] Further, his negative evaluations outweighed his positives. But the new aggressiveness did little to improve his evaluations, and, over the course of the campaign, Scheer's authenticity and credibility deficits increased, severely undercutting his ability to advance the party's narrative about Trudeau.

Scheer's handling of the Liberals' exposure of Conservative candidates' past indiscretions combined with his own intractableness to further the steady decline in his credibility. During the prime minister's darkest days of the campaign, when he was apologizing for appearing in blackface, Scheer found himself playing defence instead of reinforcing the "not-as-advertised" narrative. After requiring apologies from his candidates when their indiscretions had been exposed, when faced with questions about why he would not meet even this minimal standard and apologize for his prior statements against same-sex marriage, he refused, offering no retraction and indicating no regret.[53] Hence, in what could have been a positive turning point in the campaign for the Conservatives, Trudeau's blackface troubles led to no noticeable changes in the Liberals' support levels.[54] Another example of the Conservatives damaging their own credibility emerged when Scheer found himself with no option but to pivot after taking a severe beating over abortion rights in the first French-language debate. After repeatedly refusing to acknowledge his personal pro-life position during the debate,[55] he reversed course the following day by acknowledging his pro-life position, but he also claimed that he had "always answered this question openly and honesty" – as if no one, including the inquiring reporters, had witnessed the previous evening's spectacle. The incident betrayed a considerable level of cynicism and contempt not only for the journalists making inquiries but also for voters at large.

The campaign went on to commit a number of additional "unforced errors." Scheer was accused of having embellished his resumé by claiming he had been an insurance broker before entering politics, when in fact he had not been accredited.[56] Even more damaging, when his dual Canadian-American citizenship was revealed, his response that he hadn't made that revelation himself because nobody had asked him about it, and that it wasn't a big deal anyway, appeared disingenuous and contemptuous.[57] When grilled by reporters about why he would be the only party leader not attending a global climate strike event, he blamed his tour schedule; meanwhile, he was making a campaign announcement supporting better automobile commutes in Vancouver, a city in which one of the 140 climate march events across the country was being held.[58] He panned the Trudeau-renegotiated NAFTA deal but said he would ratify it anyway.[59] He criticized the Liberal approach to safe injection sites but offered no plan to address the problem.[60] Each of these incidents demonstrated a lack of authenticity and furthered the impression that he was not being as transparent as he could be – or as he believed others should be.

Towards the end of the campaign the Conservatives stooped to a new low of embellishment that generated a slew of negative headlines and reinforced their credibility gap. They falsely accused the Liberals of planning to decriminalize all drugs,[61] increase the GST,[62] and tax Canadians' profits from the sale of their principal residences.[63] All of these claims were quickly debunked by an increasingly critical media. In justifying their plan to reduce Canada's foreign aid commitments, the Conservatives claimed Canada was sending foreign aid to Russia, North Korea, and Iran, when at best those countries were receiving Canadian help by way of international aid agencies.[64] They made broad claims that carbon taxes have been proven to not reduce CO_2 levels, despite the assertions of experts who argued otherwise to any journalist who was looking to fact-check the claim.[65] The aggressiveness, evasiveness, and fabrications repeatedly took the party off-message and contributed to its inability to promote its own platform.

In a sign that even Conservative supporters were sensing trouble, some began to openly campaign for a leadership change before votes had even been cast.[66] Undeterred, Scheer boasted that the party was solidly behind him, continued to assert it would win, and claimed the right to form a government even if it did not achieve a majority.[67] When that claim was disputed by constitutional experts and a media corps that had become accustomed to challenging every Conservative utterance with increasingly hostile headlines, Scheer remained intransigent.[68] Soldiering on, he released a "100-day Action Plan" for what he would do immediately after being sworn in as prime minister,[69] and he bemoaned the media's preoccupation with secondary issues while he was trying to campaign positively, announcing new policy proposals on a daily basis. However, his boutique policy announcements, aptly described by one critical journalist as "a medley of some of Stephen Harper's greatest hits,"[70] could not compete with the Conservatives' own penchant for generating negative headlines for themselves. In what captured the essence of the Conservative campaign, Scheer spent the final weekend refusing to answer questions about the party's hiring of Kinsella's Daisy Group and preparing an election-night victory speech.[71]

CONCLUSION

The 2019 election was a disappointment for Conservatives given their high expectations after Liberal support floundered in the year leading up to the vote. Despite winning more votes than the party had earned since merging the Reform/Alliance and PC parties – more than 6 million, equalling 34.4 percent of the total votes cast – and outpacing the Liberals by nearly a quarter-million votes, they failed to win an election that many Conservatives were convinced was eminently winnable. Conservatives gained votes in all provinces except Quebec and Ontario, the two provinces where they most needed to make gains. Nationally, the party elected 121 members, a gain of twenty-six from dissolution and twenty-two more than they elected in 2015. Only four incumbent Conservative MPs lost their reelection bids, most notably deputy leader Lisa Raitt.[72] Seventy-eight incumbent Conservatives retained their seats while thirty-eight, nearly one-third, of the new Conservative caucus would be parliamentary rookies. Twenty-two female Conservatives were elected; this was more than the seventeen they elected 2015 but fewer than the twenty-eight elected in 2011.[73]

The Conservatives improved their seat representation in seven of ten provinces but were shut out of Newfoundland and Labrador, Prince

Edward Island, and all three Northern territories. They lost ground in Quebec, winning ten seats compared to the dozen they picked up in 2015. Although they won three additional seats in Ontario, they fell far short of expectations, winning only thirty-six, three more than they won in 2015 and far short of what was required to achieve victory. More substantial gains were made in each of the western provinces. The Conservatives won thirty-three Alberta seats, losing only one to the NDP. Conservative candidates swept Saskatchewan, winning all fourteen seats, including Regina-Wascana, where they handily defeated Liberal stalwart Ralph Goodale. The party won seventeen of British Columbia's forty-two seats, but only five of the twenty-one seats in the Lower Mainland, and none in Vancouver or on Vancouver Island. Conservatives won three additional seats in Manitoba but were shut out of Winnipeg, contributing to a pattern of urban losses that was particularly pronounced in Ontario, Quebec, and British Columbia.[74]

The outcome satisfied few in the party. Social conservatives felt betrayed. Some blamed Scheer for abandoning them and immediately began calling for his resignation.[75] Other Conservatives blamed Scheer's pandering to social conservatism for the loss.[76] For his part, Scheer blamed the loss on poor communications, dismissed most of his senior campaign team in the weeks following the loss, and indicated his determination to fight for his leadership in the lead-up to a mandatory confidence vote he would face at the next party convention set for April of 2020. He immediately established a three-pronged review of the campaign that included: appointing former Conservative cabinet minister John Baird as chair of a committee that would complete an expedited review of the party's campaign organization strategies and performance; a visit by the leader to each province, which would include meetings with candidates; and an internal review chaired by party executive director van Vugt. But Scheer's leadership would not survive the brief two months it took Baird to submit his report. Following their meetings, defeated candidates, particularly in Quebec, were eager to publicly air their grievances about Scheer's leadership.[77] Senior operatives became increasingly vocal in their criticisms,[78] and some began to openly organize to have Scheer resign.[79] When it was revealed that Scheer had been receiving party funds for his personal expenses, including to support his children attending private schools, van Vugt was removed as executive director and Scheer announced his intention to resign as Conservative leader once the party selected

Table 3.3
Conservative Party of Canada election results, 2004– 19

Year	Result	Total votes	Percent of votes	Seats	Percent of seats
2019	Liberal minority	6,155,662	34.4	121	35.8
2015	Liberal majority	5,600,496	31.9	99	29.3
2011	Conservative majority	5,835,270	39.6	166	53.9
2008	Conservative minority	5,209,069	37.7	143	46.4
2006	Conservative minority	5,374,071	36.3	124	40.3
2004	Liberal minority	4,019,498	29.6	99	32.1

Source: Elections Canada, www.elections.ca.

a replacement. Lisa Raitt and Dan Nowlan were appointed co-chairs of a leadership selection organizing committee that established a rigorous set of criteria for potential candidates, including $300,000 in fees and a requirement that nomination forms include three thousand party members' signatures (only $100,000 and three hundred signatures were required in the 2017 contest that elected Scheer). The party also agreed to postpone its planned policy convention so the leadership process could be completed in six-months, as opposed to the eighteen months it took in 2017.

With the end of Andrew Scheer's brief tenure as leader the Conservatives will have a new leader in place to fight the next election. However, many of the divisions within the party that surfaced during Scheer's time as leader and were openly displayed during the 2019 election campaign will continue to be the focus of its deliberations going forward. Scheer's decision to resign allowed the party to avoid the nasty dispute over his leadership that was already under way and that was reminiscent of the difficulties those battles caused the federal Progressive Conservatives in the twentieth century.[80] But the dynamics that led to Scheer's difficulties remain. Importantly, the 2019 campaign revealed the difficulties the party faces in recruiting supporters beyond its base when it attempts to play both sides of the social conservative divide. Indeed, polling throughout the election demonstrated that the Conservatives had a smaller proportion of swing voters willing to consider casting a ballot for them than did any of the other major parties. Stephen Harper made great strides in uniting the warring factions of Canadian federal conservatism and establishing a healthy political organization supported by a very loyal base of votes, which could also appeal to enough centrist voters to produce electoral victories. Andrew Scheer and the 2019 Conservative campaign team did nothing to improve on that success. Rather, the party now appears more divided than it has been since its 2004 inception and suffering from a tarnished brand associated with a social conservatism that is out of touch with contemporary public opinion on a variety of gender, identity, and environment issues.[81] If the Conservatives are to unseat the Liberals and again form a national government, they will be wise to consider a leader with a more broad demographic and regional appeal, who will in turn be well advised to adopt a very different approach to those issues when structuring strategies for their next federal election campaign.[82]

NOTES

1 See Eric Belanger and Jean-François Godbout, "Why Do Parties Merge? The Case of the Conservative Party of Canada," *Parliamentary Affairs* 63, 1 (2010): 41–65.
2 Much has been written about the CPC government under Harper. For examples, see the various chapters from James Farney and David Rayside, eds, *Conservatism in Canada* (Toronto: University of Toronto Press, 2013); and J.P. Lewis and Joanna Everitt, eds, *The Blueprint: Conservative Parties and Their Impact on Canadian Politics* (Toronto: University of Toronto Press, 2017). For an introduction to and review of six book-length examinations of Harper, see Michael D. Behiels, "Stephen Harper's Rise to Power: Will His 'new' Conservative Party Become Canada's 'Natural Governing Party' of the Twenty-First Century?," *American Review of Canadian Studies* 40, 1 (2010): 118–45.
3 Tom Flanagan, *Harper's Team: Behind the Scenes in the Conservative Rise to Power*, 2nd ed. (Montreal and Kingston: McGill-Queen's University Press, 2009).
4 Stephen Harper, "The Rebirth of the Canadian Alliance: Address to the National Convention," Edmonton, 6 April 2002.
5 J.P. Lewis and Joanna Everitt, "Introduction," in *The Blueprint: Conservative Parties and Their Impact on Canadian Politics*, ed. J.P. Lewis and Joanna Everitt (Toronto: University of Toronto Press, 2017), 6.
6 See Faron Ellis, "Stephen Harper and the 2015 Conservative Campaign: Defeated But Not Devastated," in *The Canadian Federal Election of 2015*,

ed. Jon H. Pammett and Christopher Dornan (Toronto: Dundurn, 2016), 28–9.
7 See Ofer Kenig, "Classifying Party Leaders' Selection Methods in Parliamentary Democracies," *Journal of Elections, Public Opinion and Parties* 19, 4 (2009): 433–47.
8 The thirteenth and final count indicated 118,137 votes were still active, 23,225 fewer than were counted on the first ballot.
9 See Éric Grenier, "How 66 Voters Could Have Cost Maxime Bernier the Conservative Leadership," CBC News, 1 June 2017. The five ridings in which the two candidates tied were: Esquimalt–Saanich–Sooke, BC; Newmarket–Aurora, ON; Abitibi–Baie-James–Nunavik–Eeyou, QC; Montarville, QC; and Repentigny, QC.
10 See Ellis, "Stephen Harper and the 2015 Conservative Campaign."
11 Anne Kingston, "How Kellie Leitch Touched Off a Culture War," *Maclean's*, 23 September 2016.
12 RightNow Press Release, "RightNow Congratulates New Pro-life Conservative Party of Canada Leader Andrew Scheer," 27 May 2017.
13 Anna Nienhuis, "If Scheer Is Serious about Free Speech and MP Independence, He Won't Stifle Abortion Debate," *National Post*, 12 June 2017.
14 See Maxime Bernier and Martin Masse, *Doing Politics Differently: My Vision for Canada* (Toronto: Optimum Publishing International, 2018), chap. 5, "Live or Die with Supply Management."
15 Maxime Bernier's speech to reporters, Ottawa, 23 August 2018.
16 After fielding candidates in nearly every riding, the party received only 292,703 votes, elected no representatives, and saw its leader defeated in his Quebec riding of Beauce. See Lee Berthiaume, "Upstart People's Party Had Little Impact on Election Results," Canadian Press, 23 October 2019.
17 Campbell Clark, "After Two Years, Scheer Plans to Tell Us Who He Really Is," *Globe and Mail*, 6 May 2019.
18 Rachel Aiello, "Scheer to Discuss His 'Vision' for Canada in Series of Speeches," CTV News, 6 May 2019.
19 See Ellis, "Stephen Harper and the 2015 Conservative Campaign."
20 Joan Bryden, "Rona Ambrose Disagrees with Scheer's Assertion That Trudeau Caved to Trump on NAFTA," Canadian Press, 27 August 2019.
21 "Conservative Leader Andrew Scheer Promises Detailed Climate Plan by End of June," Canadian Press, 27 April 2019; and Rachel Aiello, "Where Is Your Climate Change Plan? Liberal Ministers Ask Scheer," CTV News, 29 April 2019.

22 Simon Donner, "No Party's Climate Plan Will Avoid Dangerous Global Warming Levels, *Policy Options*, 1 October 2019.
23 Gerry Nicholls, "When It Comes to Climate Change, Scheer Can't Win," *Hill Times*, 1 July 2019.
24 Jolson Lim, "Scheer to Oppose Liberal Motion on Declaring Climate Emergency," *iPolitics*, 15 May 2019.
25 Burnaby North-Seymour Conservative candidate Heather Leung was removed after video emerged of her making homophobic remarks.
26 Conservative Party of Canada news release, "Conservatives First Party to Reach Full Slate of Candidates Ahead of Election," 3 September 2019.
27 See Laura Ryckewaert, "Tried and Tested Team behind Conservative Party's Bid to Return to Government," *Hill Times*, 16 September 2019.
28 John Geddes, "Hamish Marshall's Plan to Win Election 2019 for Andrew Scheer," *Maclean's*, 8 August 2019.
29 See Jordan Bateman and Hamish Marshal, *Everyone But the People: How Everyday Taxpayers Overcame Vancouver's Elite and Defeated the TransLink Tax* (Regina: Canadian Taxpayers Federation, 2016).
30 Paul Wells, "If Justin Trudeau Loses, It Will Be Because of Andrew Scheer's Secret Weapon," *Maclean's*, 7 August 2018.
31 See Janna Smith, "Liberals, Tories Evenly Matched When It Comes to War Chests for Local Campaigns," Canadian Press, 13 August 2019.
32 Financial statements of the Conservative Fund Canada, 31 December 2018, Elections Canada, *www.elections.ca*.
33 See Stephen Maher, "Why the Liberals Are Outspending Everyone on Facebook," *Maclean's*, 25 September 2019.
34 The Conservatives also employed a controversial technology used in previous campaigns that led to accusations the party intentionally misdirected voters to the wrong polling stations. The Responsive Marketing Group's technology allows live agents to handle multiple calls at once by responding to callers' questions with prerecorded answers. See Stephen Maher, "Is That a Conservative Campaigner Calling, or a Recording?," *Maclean's*, 16 September 2019.
35 Katie Simpson, "Conservatives Say They're Not Bothered by Modest Crowd Sizes: Andrew Scheer's Team Says It Prefers to See Its volunteers Out Knocking on Doors," CBC News, 18 September 2019.
36 Giuseppe Valiante, "Tories Hold Biggest Rally of Election Campaign But Fail to Reach Desired Attendance," Canadian Press, 4 October 2019.
37 Ben Cousins, "Tracking the Leaders: Analysis Suggests Heavy Focus on Ontario, Quebec and BC," CTV News, 17 October 2019.

38 Bill Curry, "Company Co-founded by Scheer's Campaign Manager Receiving Tory and Oil Group Contracts for Election Ads," *Globe and Mail*, 8 October 2019.
39 Bill Curry, "Elections Canada Contradicts Scheer's Claim That Ruling Was Issued in Support of Conservative Advertising Practices," *Globe and Mail*, 9 October 2019.
40 Bill Curry and Tom Cardoso, "Kinsella Firm Hired to 'Seek and Destroy' Bernier's People's Party, Documents Show," *Globe and Mail*, 18 October 2019.
41 Sean Boynton, "Scheer Defends Conservative Chinese Facebook Ads Saying Trudeau Will Legalize Hard Drugs," Global News, 12 October 2019.
42 John Ivison, "Is Scheer's Ambitious Energy Corridor Just a Pipe Dream?" *National Post*, 29 September 2019.
43 Stuart Thomson, "Media Coverage about Andrew Scheer's Faith Hurt Him with Voters: Angus Reid Poll," *National Post*, 28 November 2019; and Angus Reid Institute, "The Politics of Faith: Does a Leader's Personal Religious Practice Hurt or Help with Voters? It Depends," 28 November 2019.
44 See Faron Ellis and Peter Woolstencroft, "A Change of Government, Not a Change of Country: Conservatives in the 2006 Federal Election," in *The Canadian Federal Election of 2006*, ed. Jon H. Pammett and Christopher Dornan (Toronto: Dundurn, 2006), 58–92.
45 As describe by Peter MacKay, former Harper cabinet minister and the last leader of the national Progressive Conservative Party in a post-election panel at the Washington DC-based Wilson Center. See Brian Platt, "Update: After Blistering Critique, Peter MacKay Denies He Wants Andrew Scheer's Job," *National Post*, 30 October 2019.
46 Althia Raj, "Andrew Scheer Tries to Clarify Tory Stance on Abortion But Creates More Confusion," *HuffPost Canada*, 28 August 2019.
47 Lina Dib, "Olympic Gold Medalist Sylvie Frechette to Run as Conservative Candidate in Fall Federal Election," Canadian Press, 26 August 2019; and Catherine Levesque, "Quebec Tory Lieutenant Contradicts Scheer on Abortion," Canadian Press, 27 August 2019.
48 Aaron Wherry, "Scheer Tried to Douse a Debate on Abortion, Same-sex Marriage — and Muddied the Waters Even More," CBC News, 30 August 2019.
49 Faron Ellis and Keith Archer, "Reform at the Crossroads: The 1997 Election," in *The Canadian General Election of 1997*, ed. Alan Frizzell and Jon Pammett (Toronto: Dundurn, 1997), 111–34.

50 Daniel Leblanc and Robert Fife, "Ottawa Blocks RCMP on SNC-Lavalin Inquiry," *Globe and Mail*, 10 September 2019.
51 David Lunggren and Kelsey Johnson, "Main Canadian Opposition Leader Slams PM Trudeau as a Fraud in Key Election Debate," Reuters, 7 October 2019.
52 See Éric Grenier, "Leader Meter," CBC News, 5 September 2019.
53 Mia Rabson, "Scheer's Same-Sex Marriage Comments Return to the Fore Amid Trudeau Scandal," Canadian Press, 19 September 2019.
54 Angus Reid Institute, "Liberal Momentum Softens and Centre-Left Voters Look Again to Greens, NDP," 23 September 2019.
55 Rene Bruemmer, "Leaders Come Out Swinging in French Debate, Fighting for Quebec Votes," *Montreal Gazette*, 3 October 2019.
56 Canadian Press, "Andrew Scheer Accused of Falsely Claiming He Was Once an Insurance Broker," 30 September 2019.
57 Canadian Press, "Scheer Stuck on Dual Citizenship While Promoting Tough-on-Crime Agenda," 4 October 2019.
58 Ryan Maloney, "Andrew Scheer Is the Only Major Leader Not Planning to Attend a Climate Protest Friday," *HuffPost*, 26 September 2019.
59 Canadian Press, "Scheer Intends to Ratify the New NAFTA Despite Saying Trudeau Gave Everything to Trump," 15 September 2019.
60 John Paul Tasker, "Andrew Scheer Slams 'Terrible' Liberal Approach to Safe Injection Sites," CBC News, 24 September 2019.
61 Graham Slaughter, "Truth Tracker: Conservative Ads Falsely Say Liberals Will Legalize All Drugs," CTV News, 12 October 2019.
62 Jonathon Gatehouse, "Fact Check: The Conservatives' Misleading Claims about a 'Secret' Liberal Housing Tax – An Attack Site with an Altered Document and No Hard Evidence of Changes to Capital Gains," CBC News, 8 October 2019.
63 Beatrice Britneff, "Reality Check: The Liberals and NDP Haven't Proposed a GST Hike," Global News, 18 October 2019.
64 Jonathon Gatehouse, "Andrew Scheer's Claim about Foreign Aid Deemed False: Official Figures Don't Support Idea That $2.2 Billion a Year Is Going to Rich or Undeserving Nations," CBC News, 1 October 2019.
65 See Joanna Smith, "Baloney Meter: Andrew Scheer Says the Carbon Tax 'Has Been Proven to Fail,'" Canadian Press, 25 September 2019; and Aaron Wherry, "Scheer Says British Columbia's Carbon Tax Hasn't Worked. Expert Studies Say It Has," CBC News, 2 October 2019.
66 Marieke Walsh, "Despite Leadership Questions, Scheer Says Conservatives Are United behind Him," *Globe and Mail*, 11 October 2019.

67 Marieke Walsh, Bill Curry, and Kristy Kirkup, "'Whoever Gets the Most Seats Gets the First Shot': Andrew Scheer Makes Case for Leading a Minority Government," *Globe and Mail*, 17 October 2019.
68 Joan Bryden, "'Complete Nonsense': Experts Dispute Scheer's Claims about Forming Government," Canadian Press, 19 October 2019.
69 Conservative Party of Canada, "100 Day Action Plan: Repealing Trudeau's Carbon Tax before January 1," 17 October 2019; and John Paul Tasker, "Scheer Touts '100 Day Action Plan' as He Asks Voters for a Conservative Majority," CBC News, 15 October 2019.
70 Aaron Wherry, "Why Andrew Scheer's Campaign Platform Sounds So … Familiar," CBC News, 24 September 2019.
71 Alex Boutilier and Robert Benzie, "Scheer Refuses to Deny Conservatives Hired Operative to Dig Up Dirt on Opponent," *Toronto Star*, 19 October 2019.
72 The others were Quebec MPs Alupa Clarke, Beauport-Limoiloe; Sylvie Boucher, Beauport-Côte-de-Beaupré-Île d'Orléans-Charlevoix; and Harold Albrecht from the Ontario riding of Kitchener-Conestoga. See Beatrice Paez and Palak Magnat, "Anti-Trudeau Sentiments, Vote Splits among Left, Star Power: Why 49 Incumbents May Have Lost Bids for Re-election," *Hill Times*, 24 October 2019.
73 "Canadian Parliament Primer," CBC News, October 2019.
74 Philippe J. Fournier, "A Riding-by-Riding Breakdown of the Election Results Shows the Conservatives' Biggest Weaknesses – and a Troubling Urban-Rural Divide," *Maclean's*, 27 October 2019. For a very accessible interactive map of results from every riding, see 338Canada.com.
75 Marieke Walsh, "Social Conservative Groups Call for Andrew Scheer to Resign," *Globe and Mail*, 25 November 2019. See also Jack Fonseca, "Canada Election Analysis: Scheer Compromised Beliefs, Giving Trudeau an Easy Win," *Campaign Life Coalition Newsletter*, 28 October 2019. One MP who continued to support Scheer blamed the other parties for anti-Catholic bigotry. See Rachel Aiello, "On Scheer Same-Sex Marriage Stance, Tory MP Accuses Parties of 'Anti-Catholic Bigotry,'" CTV News, 9 November 2019.
76 Rachel Aiello, "Scheer's Position on Same-Sex Marriage 'Could Be Fatal' Conservative Insiders Say," CTV News, 1 November 2019.
77 Daniel LeBlanc and Marieke Walsh, "Quebec Conservatives Criticize Scheer's Leadership at Montreal Event," *Globe and Mail*, 26 November 2019.
78 Jamie Ellerton and Melissa Lantsman, "The Conservatives Can't Be Stuck in the Past on LGBTQ Rights," *Globe and Mail*, 20 November 2019.

79 Marieke Walsh and Robert Fife, "Prominent Conservatives Set Up Non-Profit to Campaign for Leader Andrew Scheer's Removal," *Globe and Mail*, 27 November 2019.
80 George C. Perlin, *The Tory Syndrome: Leadership Politics in the Progressive Conservative Party* (Montreal and Kingston: McGill-Queen's University Press, 1980). See also Faron Ellis and Peter Woolstencroft, "New Conservatives, Old Realities:The 2004 Election Campaign," in *The Canadian General Election of 2004*, ed. Jon H. Pammett and Christopher Dornan (Toronto: Dundurn, 2004) for a discussion of the Alliance Party's decent into turmoil over its leadership following the 2000 federal election.
81 See Faron Ellis, "Twenty-First Century Conservatives Can Continue to Succeed," in *Crosscurrents: Editors' Choice*, 8th ed., ed. Mark Charlton and Paul Barker (Toronto: Nelson, 2015), 17–36.
82 Tom Flanagan, "Now More Than Ever, Peter MacKay Is the Right Choice for Conservative Leader," *Globe and Mail*, 21 January 2020.

4

Making the Best of It: Political Marketing and the Federal NDP's Fight for Relevance

David McGrane

Elections can be about expectations. The success or failure of a party is often judged not by how many seats it lost or gained but by the degree to which it met, failed to meet, or surpassed the expectations of voters, party members, the media, and competitors at the outset of the campaign. Given the difficulties of the federal New Democratic Party (NDP) and its leader in the four years preceding the 2019 Canadian federal election, the party was expected to fare poorly – to the point of possibly losing party status and becoming largely irrelevant to Canadian politics. Ultimately, the strategists of the federal NDP were able to make the best of a bad situation and ensure that the party ended up doing better than many believed that it would.

For the purposes of this chapter, political marketing is defined as the study of how parties win or lose elections.[1] In particular, it involves examining parties' activities in terms of "gathering of market intelligence through informal and formal means, developing party policies and a party brand, mobilizing party members, building relationships with stakeholders, positioning in relation to competing parties, targeting of certain segments of voters, allocating scarce resources, and communicating a party's policy offerings through paid advertising and the management of news media."[2] This chapter uses a political marketing approach to understand three fundamental elements of the federal NDP's 2019 campaign strategy: (1) its stated internal goals, (2) the tactics it used to achieve those goals, and (3) how it attempts to position itself in relationship to its competitors and in the minds of its targeted voters.[3]

Using interviews with party operatives and analysis of the party's television commercials and news releases,[4] I argue that the federal NDP's primary goal was to hang onto the seats that it had, thereby ensuring that it would remain relevant in Canadian federal politics and possibly even hold the balance of power in a minority Parliament. The tactics it devised to achieve this goal revolved around a regionalized campaign to concentrate on the areas of Canada where it held seats (Ontario, British Columbia, and Quebec) and an inexpensive air game that depended on earned media covering the leader's tour as opposed to depending heavily on paid advertising. The NDP also adopted the tactic of emphasizing the Sikh background of new leader Jagmeet Singh, rather than downplaying it, in an effort to differentiate him from other leaders and to emphasize his authenticity. The party's plan positioned itself in relation to its competitors by trying to confirm the suspicions of Liberal/NDP switchers that Justin Trudeau was not sincere and that the Liberals were not as "progressive" as they portrayed themselves. Hence, its message to its targeted voters was that the NDP had a leader who was genuine and who would advocate for bold action on issues, whereas Trudeau and the Liberals talked a good game but failed to deliver (i.e., pharmacare, cost of living, climate crisis, and higher taxes on the wealthy).

Research on the federal NDP has traditionally concentrated on its ideology, internal party organization, and its relationship with Canada's labour movement.[5] More recently, a small literature has emerged on the federal NDP's political marketing, building upon the insights of the older literature on the party while introducing new conceptual frameworks to understand the party's contemporary activities.[6] The political marketing of the federal NDP during the McDonough, Layton, and Mulcair years is analyzed in my latest book – *The New NDP: Moderation, Modernization, and Political Marketing*. By using the party's 2019 campaign as a case study, this chapter seeks to analyze the political marketing of the party under Singh's leadership. It also seeks to analyze the historical significance of the federal NDP's campaign as it marks the first time that a major Canadian political party has fought a federal election with a member of a racialized minority as its leader.

THE TRIALS AND TRIBULATIONS OF THE NDP, 2016 TO 2019

The expectations of federal NDP politicians, operatives, and rank-and-file members going into the 2015 election campaign was that their party had a realistic shot at forming a minority government, perhaps even a majority government.[7] With the loss of over half its seats on election night, there was bitter disappointment and the party slowly fell into disarray. Most of 2016 was taken up with controversies over the leadership of Thomas Mulcair and the Leap Manifesto, a document written by NDP activists centred in Toronto that advocated that the party take a hard ideological turn to the left by pursuing policies such as banning the construction of all new pipelines and eliminating free trade agreements.[8] The party's April 2016 convention ultimately voted to have a leadership race by a margin of 52 to 48 percent and to wait until the fall of 2017 to hold the contest. In a close vote, the convention also supported having riding associations use the Leap Manifesto as a basis for debate about the future ideological direction of the party (though the NDP would not officially adopt the manifesto as party policy).

Against this backdrop of questions about the NDP's leadership and ideological identity, the party was in organizational upheaval. With the loss of fifty seats in the 2015 election, hundreds of NDP staff on Parliament Hill and in constituency offices across the country lost their jobs, and several of the experienced political operatives at party headquarters left to pursue other opportunities. The per-vote subsidy, which had been a key part of funding the NDP's success in the Layton and Mulcair years,[9] was completely eliminated, and the party's fundraising slumped due to donors being disappointed with the outcome of the federal election. The party was forced to drastically cut staff at party headquarters and decided to bring in as its new national director Robert Fox, an outsider whose previous experience was as the executive director of the human rights NGO Oxfam.

The party was then thrown into a long and drawn out leadership race in the midst of uncertainty over its ideological direction and while dealing with organizational and financial difficulties. Eventually, Jagmeet Singh was elected as the federal NDP leader on 1 October 2017, winning a first-ballot victory with 53.8 percent of the vote over three experienced NDP MPs (Charlie Angus, Niki Ashton, and Guy Caron). The criminal defence lawyer and Ontario NDP MPP for Barmalea-Gore-Malton became the first member of a racialized minority to lead a major political party in Canada's history. During the leadership campaign, Singh's race was brought up repeatedly, with some party members openly questioning if Canadians were ready for a Sikh party leader who wore a turban and a beard. In the face of questions about his religion and ethnicity, Singh ran an effective campaign that focused on his slogan "Love and Courage," and he spoke frequently about the racism and discrimination that he faces as a practising Sikh. At one event, a heckler who was a member of the anti-Islamic group Rise Canada accused Singh of being a member of the Muslim Brotherhood and planning to bring Sharia law to Canada. The video of Singh responding "We welcome you. We love you. We support you ... we believe in your rights" and encouraging the crowd to chant "love and courage" went viral.[10] His media savvy and youthful persona, which included competitive mixed-martial arts fighting and wearing expensive tailored suits while riding his bespoke bicycle, led to comparisons with the public image that had made Prime Minister Trudeau popular in the 2015 federal election.[11]

Despite his convincing win, Singh's leadership got off to a rocky start. Indeed, commenting on Singh's first year as leader, NDP MP Nathan Cullen admitted that it was not the first year that Singh had hoped for.[12] The NDP leader was criticized by media pundits for what they considered to be a series of missteps, such as not immediately condemning the 1985 Air India bombing as an act of terrorism in a CBC interview, mishandling a case of sexual harassment within his caucus, not being clear on his position on pipelines, demoting one of his veteran MPs for voting against the party line (a move that he later reversed), being absent in the national media because of his decision to not immediately seek a seat in the House of Commons, and, in a media interview, being unaware of a statement made by the Chinese ambassador to Canada that the Canadian government's call for the release of two Canadians detained in China was rooted in "white supremacy."[13] Fairly or not, some in the media characterized Singh as having little substance, as being unable to control his caucus, and as generally not being ready to lead a major political party or be prime minister of Canada.[14] At the same time, the NDP's polling numbers remained static at around 15 percent (less than the 20 percent it had received in the 2015 election), the party did poorly in a series of by-elections, and quarterly returns from Elections Canada showed its fundraising numbers continued to be low.

It was in this context that Singh decided to contest a by-election in British Columbia (Burnaby South) that was eventually set for February 2019, even though he had suggested during the leadership race that he may not seek a seat in the House of Commons until the 2019 federal election. Around the same time, Singh shook up his staff, with Jennifer Howard replacing Willy Blomme as his chief of staff. Burnaby

South is traditionally an NDP stronghold, and it was vacant because the incumbent NDP MP, Kennedy Stewart, had decided to run for mayor of Vancouver. In the lead-up to the by-election, Tom Mulcair, the former NDP leader, and many in the media suggested that Singh would not be able to hold onto the NDP's leadership if he did not win.[15] Singh ended up winning Burnaby South, but the party did poorly in other by-elections held that day; in particular, it lost Mulcair's previous Montreal-area seat to the Liberals.

Jagmeet Singh entered the House of Commons only six months before the beginning of the 2019 campaign, but his leadership was solidified and the party was hoping that he would settle into his position as leader after a difficult rookie year. His performance in Question Period was well received, and he released an autobiography entitled *Love and Courage* that was praised for its honesty about his experiences with racism, an alcoholic father, and the trauma of being sexually abused when he was a teenager by his tae kwon do instructor.[16] On the other hand, the media speculated that the retirement of a large number of NDP MPs, combined with the party being slow to recruit a full slate of candidates, meant that it was facing a difficult election.[17] The NDP remained in third place in public polling, well back of the Conservatives and Liberals, and some polls even showed the Greens overtaking the NDP in national vote intention.[18] Many pundits argued that the NDP would have a hard time holding onto its Quebec seats because that province's tendency towards secularism clashed with Singh's wearing of a turban.[19] Indeed, under Bill C-21, passed by the Legault government in the summer of 2018, Singh's turban would disqualify him from being hired as a teacher, government lawyer, judge, or police officer in Quebec.

ELECTION PREPARATION

Given that the federal NDP's political operatives were hearing talk of their party not even winning official party status (twelve seats) and feeling like they were starting from behind, they were realistic when setting their internal goals. The primary goals were to get Jagmeet Singh known and popular among Canadians voters (particularly young and urban voters) and to hold on to all of the thirty-nine incumbent seats that the NDP had at the dissolution of Parliament to ensure that the party remained relevant in federal politics. The party was also hoping for a breakthrough in a very small number of targeted non-incumbent seats where the party had strong local candidates, like St John's East and Davenport. Reaching these goals would mean preserving what was left of the party's seats in Quebec, ensuring that the Greens remained a marginal force in Canadian federal politics with only a tiny caucus of MPs, and possibly holding the balance of power over a minority Liberal government.

However, achieving these goals would not be easy. When compared to the federal NDP's 2015 campaign, certain organizational realities stand out upon examining the party's 2019 effort: less money, fewer paid staff and more reliance on volunteers, less preparation, and more turnover at party headquarters.

On top of losing the per-vote subsidy, for several reasons the NDP continued to have fundraising troubles after Singh became leader: low polling numbers, the popularity of the Trudeau Liberals, infighting in the party being heavily reported in the media, and fewer staff at party headquarters devoted to fundraising. There was even one financial quarter when the Greens raised more money than the NDP, the first time that this happened since financial donations started being reported quarterly.[20] Heading into the election it became clear to operatives that the NDP would be able to spend roughly $10 million centrally in the 2019 campaign, compared to the $30 million that it spent in 2015. Spending by local campaigns would also be significantly lower than in the previous election.

With less money being raised and fewer MPs in the House of Commons, there were fewer staff to prepare for the 2019 election. The NDP's 2015 campaign had been the product of four years of intensive preparation by paid staff at party headquarters and on Parliament Hill, where the party formed the official opposition.[21] It took almost two years from the evening of the 2015 federal election to Singh's election as leader, and during this time very little election preparation took place. Once Singh was in place, the turnover of staff at party headquarters continued as Melissa Bruno replaced Robert Fox as national director. However, Bruno was not named national campaign director at the same time, meaning that her duties for election preparation were somewhat limited. In fact, it was not until Marie Della Mattia and Alexandre Boulerice were appointed as campaign co-chairs in September 2018 that election preparation began in earnest. Both were working as volunteers, and Boulerice was doing the job on top of being a sitting MP. Significant party resources were also being funnelled towards Singh's by-election. It was clear that the NDP would have less time, less money, and a smaller team to prepare its 2019 election campaign than in the previous election but the same amount of work to do.

One of the first moves made by the campaign co-chairs was to create a formal strategy document for the campaign. This plan, written by an ad hoc working group of NDP campaign professionals from around the country who were offering their services for free, outlined the party's basic tactics for achieving its goals. Given the emphasis on re-electing incumbents, the document envisioned a regionalized campaign with an emphasis on parts of the country where the NDP held seats, such as Vancouver Island, British Columbia's Lower Mainland, major cities on the Prairies, northern Ontario, southwest Ontario, and parts of southern Quebec. Instead of having a plane dedicated to party use for the entire leader's tour, the party would use a bus to tour around a specific region for several days and then charter a plane to fly between regions.

The strategy document also established how the NDP would attempt to position itself in relationship to its competitors and in the minds of its targeted voters, whom it identified as Liberal/NDP switchers (i.e., voters hesitating between the Liberals and the NDP). There was limited funding for research on the NDP brand or the Singh brand going into the election. The small number of focus groups that were held told operatives that Trudeau was not really genuine and was wearing thin on them. Moreover, while these voters did not know much about Singh, the more they saw him, the more they liked him. As such, operatives devised the tactic of contrasting Singh's warmth and authenticity to Trudeau's lack of sincerity. Trudeau was someone who said that he cared about you but really didn't. On the other hand, Singh was "in it for you," which became the NDP's slogan. It was also decided that Singh was going to talk about three issues, all of which dealt with areas where NDP operatives felt that the Liberals were promising a lot but not delivering concrete results – health care, the climate crisis, and affordability. Further, unlike the Liberals, the NDP would pay for programs in these areas by making the richest people and the richest corporations in Canada pay their fair share of taxes. In this sense, the NDP would run a leader-centric campaign based upon ensuring that the wealthy pay higher taxes to pay for the party's plans in its three priority policy areas. In contrast to 2015, when extensive private polling was used, NDP strategists in 2019 did not have funds for this, and they chose these issues based on their gut instincts and public domain polling.

Similar to the situation in federal elections going back to 2004, the federal executive was also the NDP's Election Planning Committee (EPC) in 2019. The EPC was a large group of about thirty volunteers from all over Canada, supported by party staff. It met four times in the lead-up to the election by conference call, formally approved the campaign budget, and gave feedback on the platform and messaging. However, members of the EPC played a purely advisory role and were not heavily involved in day-to-day preparation for the election. In May 2019, Jennifer Howard was finally appointed as the party's national campaign director, and Michael Balagus was named her special advisor. Both of them were volunteers. Howard was doing the national campaign director job on top of her paid employment as Singh's chief of staff, and Balagus's day job was chief of staff to Andrea Horwath, the Ontario NDP leader and leader of the official opposition at Queen's Park. They assumed primary responsibility for directing election preparation at party headquarters, and their appointment signalled an end to the large turnover in staff at party headquarters as they gradually began to place staff into the positions they would hold during the election period.

One immediate challenge that emerged for the new national campaign director and her advisor was candidate recruitment. In 2015, the party had all of its candidates in place approximately four months before the writ was dropped, and many of its candidates were in place over a year before election day. At the beginning of July 2019, the party only had 112 candidates nominated out of 338 and that number only grew to 175 by the end of August.[22] That meant the NDP had yet to nominate almost half of its candidates with only two weeks left before the campaign began. NDP operatives pointed to several reasons for the party's difficulties nominating candidates in 2019 compared to 2015. There were more spots to fill: the NDP held fewer seats in the House of Commons compared to the run-up to the 2015 election, and about one-third of the NDP caucus that was elected in 2015 was retiring. The lack of staff at party headquarters led to delays in the vetting process, and there were fewer paid regional organizers to recruit candidates. Moreover, the NDP's lower polling numbers made it difficult to convince candidates to run for the party, and its policies to ensure a diverse slate meant that nominations needed to be delayed until efforts could be made to find members of equity-seeking groups (e.g., women, racialized minorities, Indigenous people, and people with disabilities) to run for the nomination.

THE ELECTION PLATFORM

While the NDP may have lagged in getting its candidates into place, it was well ahead of its rivals when it came to the release of its platform, which was entitled *A New Deal for People*. The campaign co-chairs and the operatives in the working group made the somewhat unorthodox decision to release the NDP's platform in June, a full three months before the start of the campaign. The early release was intended to garner media attention for the NDP in order to give it momentum going into the campaign. Earned media attention was important because the party had no financial resources to run pre-election television or radio advertising (though it did do a pre-election social media ad buy to promote the platform). It was also hoped that the release of the platform would attract candidates to the party and would give existing candidates and the leader something to talk about over the summer as they met with voters. The platform was written by members of the ad hoc working group of NDP campaign professionals, who were volunteering their time, as well as some MPs from the NDP caucus. It was based on their impressions of what Canadians needed, their values as New Democrats, resolutions passed at NDP conventions, and the caucus's interaction with stakeholders over the past four years. Singh also had ideas of his own that were added, and he, as leader, had final approval of the document that was released.

Given that the process that had led to the platform's creation relied more on the gut instincts of MPs and others on the ad hoc working group than it did on polling on the preferences of swing voters, it is not surprising that NDP operatives described it as speaking to the party's base, as unabashedly progressive, and as establishing a sharp contrast between the social democracy of Singh's NDP and the centrism of Trudeau's Liberals. Indeed, *A New Deal for People* was more left-wing than were NDP platforms in the Layton and Mulcair years, which had hewed close to the commitments being made by the Liberals during those elections.[23]

The Layton and Mulcair platforms had relied on higher corporate taxes for revenue generation, eschewing any increases in personal taxes. Indeed, Layton's and Muclair's platforms tried to ensure that middle-class Canadians knew that they would not be paying any additional taxes under an NDP government, and there was even a reluctance to be seen as taxing high-income individuals to pay for increased social programs.[24] It was feared that such policies would reinforce the NDP's negative image as a "tax-and-spend party."[25] Passages that portray class politics (i.e., seeing politics as a clash between the rich and the poor) were hard to find in those earlier platforms.

In contrast, *A New Deal for People* adopted a left-wing populist discourse with hints of class politics, similar to that of Bernie Sanders in the United States or Jeremy Corbyn in Britain. The platform strongly criticized the Liberals' refusal to make large corporations and upper-class Canadians pay more taxes and committed to increasing corporate taxes *as well as* to increasing the personal income tax rate for those making over $210,000 annually; increasing capital gains taxes; putting a 12 percent tax on boats, aircraft, and expensive cars; and creating a new wealth tax on "super-rich multi-millionaires with wealth over $20 million."[26] In the news release accompanying the platform's launch, Singh says that Trudeau, who himself is a member of the upper class, choses to "help big corporations and his wealthy friends, and make everyday Canadians pay for it."[27] In contrast, Singh insisted that New Democrats would make "life better for all Canadians by having the richest of the top one per cent pay one per cent more."[28] In a nod to class politics, Singh argued that the problem with Canadian politics was that we have a prime minister who is a member of the ruling class and who refuses to sufficiently tax fellow members of that class to pay for adequate social programs that help all Canadians.

The platforms in the later Layton years contained no commitments for new universal social programs, though Mulcair had promised a pharmacare program and fifteen-dollar-a-day childcare in 2015. *A New Deal for People* reiterated Mulcair's commitments on pharmacare and childcare in order to highlight the Liberal government's slow progress in these policy areas, while adding a new pledge for dental care as part of Canadians' coverage under Medicare. On housing, the *A New Deal for People* promised that an NDP government would build 500,000 affordable units over the next decade and spend over $1 billion annually on grants to Canadians paying high rents. These budget commitments were significantly more expensive and generous than what the NDP had promised in its 2011 and 2015 platforms or what the Liberals were promising in the 2019 election.[29] Similarly, the NDP's commitments around funding to combat climate change were higher, and its targets for greenhouse gas emission levels were lower, in the party's 2019 platforms compared to its proposals in the previous two elections. More spending would mean running a deficit. Mulcair and Layton had always promised balanced budgets, whereas Singh's platform predicted a $16.5 billion deficit after four years of NDP government (a deficit that, due to the NDP's policies, which would make corporations and the wealth pay more taxes, the party claimed was lower than the one the Liberals would run). On the key issue of pipelines, Mulcair had adopted a position similar to Trudeau's: in favour of the Trans Mountain pipeline as long it passed a rigorous environmental review.[30] For his part, Singh echoed the sentiments of the Leap Manifesto by stating that the NDP opposed the expansion of the Trans Mountain pipeline and the federal Liberal government's purchase of that pipeline because of opposition by Indigenous groups and because it would hurt efforts to build a low-carbon economy.[31]

In short, *A New Deal for People* proposed more taxing measures, more regulations, and more spending than the 2011 and 2015 federal NDP platforms, creating a starker ideological divergence between the Liberals and the NDP than had existed over the last decade.

THE CAMPAIGN PERIOD

At the outset of the campaign, the party had to decide how to deal with Jagmeet Singh's religion and race, given the questions being raised in the media about whether Canadians were ready for a Sikh prime minister. There were not many examples to follow, either from Canada or around the world. The examples of candidates like American president Barak Obama, London mayor Sadiq Khan, Manitoba NDP leader Wab Kinew, and Calgary mayor Naheed Nenshi did come to the minds of the strategists, but none of these politicians were Sikhs who wore a turban and a beard. It was ultimately decided that the NDP should address Singh's race and religion directly, by accentuating how it made him different from the other party leaders *in a good way*. Singh could be portrayed as more authentic, as able to build bridges between different types of Canadians, as aware of what it is like to face injustice and overcome it. Despite having little money for market research to confirm it, operatives believed that Singh's race and religion might be able to capture the attention of media and voters and make the NDP leader stand out against his rivals. It could be an advantage as opposed to a liability. The media was very negative about the NDP going into the campaign, talking about the possibility of large seat losses due to Singh's inexperience, Canadians' wariness about a Sikh prime minister (particularly in Quebec), the party's low fundraising, and its inability to recruit candidates.[32] Given the media's grim analysis of the party's electoral prospects, the nightmare scenario was that the party would be ignored by the media and dismissed as irrelevant to the campaign, especially if the Conservatives and Liberals were seen as battling each other for a majority government.

The launch of the NDP's campaign on 11 September went smoothly and provided the first sign that the party might be able to outperform the low expectations of pundits and stay in the media spotlight. *National Post* columnist John Ivison declared that Singh had the best launch of all of the leaders, with "slick visuals of the leader and his new bride, clothing designer Gurkiran Kaur; sharp opposition research linking Liberals to their 'wealthy friends'; and a people-focused launch speech that talked of Trudeau's 'pretty words and empty promises.'"[33]

While behind the scenes the party struggled to find and properly vet candidates in all of the country's ridings over the first couple of weeks of the campaign, it did ultimately succeed in nominating a diverse slate of candidates.[34] Several events kept the NDP in the media spotlight and in front of Canadian voters. At the beginning of the second week of the campaign, *Time* published photos of Trudeau in blackface, and questions of racism became front and centre (see chapter 2, this volume). Considering that Singh was the first person from a racialized minority background to lead a major Canadian federal party and the only non-white party leader in the campaign, his reaction to the photo was heavily reported, as was Trudeau's private phone call to him to apologize. Singh's handling of the incident was widely praised in the media as he repeated his message that he did not want to focus on Trudeau's actions but on the racialized minorities who were hurt by them.[35] NDP operatives saw the blackface event as a turning point in their campaign as Canadians were able to see, many for the first time, their leader's compassion, authenticity, and grace as he spoke about the uncomfortable topic of racism in contemporary Canadian society. Singh appeared more like a statesman than a politician. Other smaller events kept the NDP leader in the news, such as the man approaching him in a market in Montreal to tell him to "cut off his turban" to look more Canadian, his insistence that he was not joking when he said that Donald Trump would be impeached, and his indignation when asked by a reporter why he was offering a "blank cheque" to Indigenous communities who did not have clean drinking water.[36] He also had some memorable moments on social media, such as a fifteen-second viral video on Tik Tok that contrasted his policies to Trudeau's, reports of his direct messages with singer Rihanna on Instagram, and the endorsement of author Rupi Kaur (who has 3 million Instagram followers). Strategists tried to use social media as a low-cost method of getting Singh known and attempted to be as innovative and humorous as possible in order to achieve maximum "organic reach" (i.e., free circulation of Singh's message through his followers liking and sharing the content that he posted).

Operatives thought that Singh also performed admirably in the two French debates, in which his strategy was to relay the following message: despite the differences in his appearance compared to most Quebecers, he was still similar to the "average Quebecer" and held the same values as the Quebec francophones who had voted in large numbers for Jack Layton in 2011. However, Yves-François Blanchet, the leader of the Bloc Québécois, outshone the federalist party leaders in the French debates.[37] Singh's moment of greatest impact came with his performance in the English leaders' debate, for which his operatives had created a strategy that consisted of his showcasing his energy and authenticity, attacking Trudeau on his failures to implement genuinely progressive policies in government, and illustrating that there were few ideological differences between the Liberals and Conservatives. This strategy appeared to work as, to many, Singh appeared approachable, likeable, and respectful by refraining from talking over the other leaders. He also had a good sense of timing, getting laughs by mentioning his "bright orange turban" when the moderator accidentally referred to him as "Mr Scheer" and landing a zinger at the end of the segment on the environment by referring to Trudeau and Scheer as "Mr Delay and Mr Deny" when it comes to climate change. The media narrative coming out of the debate was that Singh was the winner, and public domain polling illustrated that Singh had left the most positive impression with voters.[38] Further, Singh continued to have memorable moments that were reported in the mainstream media – like being mobbed by students wanting to take selfies when he visited Ryerson University, leading crowds in the "Jagmeet Jump" at the end of his rallies, and having #UpRiSingh trending on various social media platforms.

As the campaign entered its final two weeks, the NDP campaign team felt that earned media from their leader's tour and the English leaders' debate had succeed in generating momentum for their party. Reflecting his strong performance, polls showed Singh's personal popularity rising dramatically during the early part of October, especially among young voters, even if voting intentions for the NDP rose only slightly.[39] With polls showing neither the Liberals nor the Conservatives having a level of popularity that would translate into a majority government, the media began to speculate on possible minority government scenarios involving the NDP holding the balance of power. Before the campaign began, Singh had announced that the NDP would not use its votes in the House of Commons to prop up a minority Conservative government because Scheer's "disgusting prejudice against LGBTQI2S+ people" showed that the Conservatives could not trusted "to champion the fundamental rights of Canadians."[40] Operatives felt that this statement had helped solidify the NDP's left-wing credentials in contrast to the Greens, who were refusing to rule out working with the Conservatives in a minority government situation. With a little over a week to go in the campaign, just before the Thanksgiving weekend, Singh laid out six "urgent priorities," including pharmacare and a wealth tax, that would guide the NDP's negotiations with parties other than the Conservatives in the event of a minority Parliament.[41] This announcement not only kept the media talking about the NDP but also combatted strategic voting – supporting the NDP could help get progressive things done by bringing about a minority government in which the Liberals would be forced to negotiate with the NDP. Speculating about the possibility of a minority Liberal government also undermined Liberal arguments about having to vote strategically against the NDP to avoid a Scheer-led Conservative government. By voting NDP, Liberal/NDP switchers could vote for something (i.e., a Liberal minority government with the NDP holding the balance of power) as opposed to voting against something (i.e., a Conservative government).

In contrast to stories in the media prior to the campaign about how Singh's inexperience and ethnicity might hurt the party, operatives argued that he made no glaring mistakes or gaffes and outperformed everyone's expectations. Indeed, it was pointed out that, during the campaign, the national media were almost giving Singh equal air time to Trudeau and Scheer, the first time that this had happened since Singh became leader. Their leader's strong performance, along with the dynamics of the campaign (which featured debates over race and potential minority government situations) kept the NDP relevant to the campaign and squarely in front of Canadian voters. Instead of being a liability for the party, Singh's race and religion became an advantage when the campaign's narrative turned to questions of race and racism, and several national media outlets ran stories about his experiences with discrimination.[42]

ADVERTISING AND NEWS RELEASES

A more extensive examination of the NDP's strategy can be accomplished by looking closely at the party's commercials and news releases. All of the federal NDP's commercials during the campaign were coded using the Qualitative Data Analysis Software (CAQDAS) program N-vivo 10, which calculates that "percentage coverage" is based on the number of characters coded into a particular theme.[43]

Despite limited resources, the party produced three negative commercials attacking Trudeau and one positive commercial touting Singh's leadership (see figure 4.1). The negative commercials were humorous, featuring a pair of actors representing Trudeau and an average voter. As the voter expresses concerns about health care and affordability to the prime minister in a coffee shop, Trudeau is not listening because he is too busy texting CEOs of big corporations who are thanking him for their tax breaks. They end with the tag line: "Justin Trudeau: Not in It for You."

The positive commercial illustrates well how NDP operatives decided to embrace, as opposed to run away from, Singh's Sikhism. It features images of Singh interacting with voters from diverse backgrounds. Singh narrates the commercial, and it plays on how people tell him that he is "different," ostensibly because he is a Sikh who wears a beard and turban. In response, Singh says that he is "different" because, unlike other politicians, he does not work for the wealthy and he will improve health care and reduce the cost of living and greenhouse gas emissions. While the commercial does not mention Trudeau or the Liberals, Singh alludes to the prime minister when he says that politics is about "not just saying the right things, but actually doing them." The commercial ends with the tag line: "Jagmeet Singh: In It for You." There is an element of class politics and left-wing populism in the English commercials, with Trudeau being portrayed as doing the bidding of his corporate friends and Singh fighting for the real preoccupations of Canadians.

There was only one French commercial produced and it was given limited air time in Quebec (see figure 4.2). In a bid to attract earned media about the commercial and to embrace Singh's religion as a strength rather than as a weakness, Singh reveals his long hair under

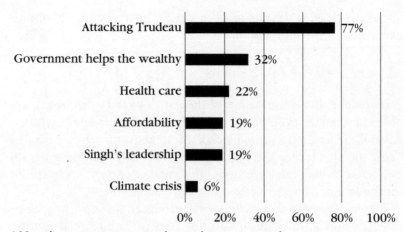

* Note that percentages may total more than 100 percent because some passages were coded twice if they implied two different themes.

Figure 4.1 Percentage coverage of themes in NDP English TV ads (2019 election)

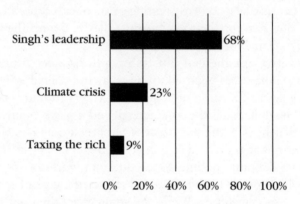

* Note that percentages may total more than 100 percent because some passages were coded twice if they implied two different themes.

Figure 4.2 Percentage coverage of themes in NDP French TV ads (2019 election)

his turban at the beginning of the commercial, something that he had not done before publicly and something that it was hoped would demystify his turban for Quebecers who knew little about the Sikh religion. Further, the commercial shows Singh practising mixed martial arts, riding his bespoke bike, and going to Montreal's Gay Pride Parade with Alexandre Boulerice. Singh narrates the commercial, and he plays on the French expression that Quebec "n'est pas une province comme les autres" by saying "Je ne suis pas comme les autres. Comme vous, mon identité, c'est ma fierté." The intention of the commercial was to signal to Quebecers that, despite his turban, Singh was similar to them. Just as Quebecers have battled against discrimination due to speaking Canada's minority official language, Singh has battled against discrimination as a member of a racialized minority group. Ultimately, Quebecers and Singh share the same experiences and same values when it comes to the climate crisis and taxing the wealthy (in particular, oil companies, whom Singh mentions). The intended message is that, since Singh is like Quebecers, he will fight for them, and the commercial ends with the tag line "NPD: On se bat pour vous."

Table 4.1 uses the same inductive coding technique as do figures 4.1 and 4.2 to analyze the news releases of the NDP during the campaign. Overall, it depicts three interesting elements of the NDP's strategy. First, reflecting the party's focus on Liberal/NDP switchers, the main emphasis of NDP party headquarters' media relations throughout the campaign was to attack Trudeau and the Liberals. Scheer and the Conservatives are infrequently mentioned, and when they are mentioned it is usually to say that the Liberals and Trudeau are similar to them. The Bloc Québécois or its leader were not mentioned because operatives thought that the NDP was more threatened by the Liberals in Quebec and they did not really see the Bloc's surge coming. The NDP did attack the Greens a couple of time during the campaign over May's apparent willingness to work with the Conservatives in a minority government and her willingness to allow free votes for Green MPs on abortion; they did not want to attack the Greens too much because doing so would give the fledging party creditability, but they did want to portray the Greens as being to the right of the NDP and comfortable with a Scheer government.

Second, the three issues that operatives had identified prior to the beginning of the campaign (climate change, affordability, and health care) are ever present and take up a lot of the space in the news releases. Given the goal of getting Singh well known, and the tactic of running a leader-centric campaign, it is not surprising that the news releases consistently laud his leadership, particularly in Week 4 (the week following the English leaders' debate). Another important theme, particularly in the last week of the campaign, was the need to stand up to the wealthy and to impose higher taxes on the rich and big

Table 4.1
Percentage coverage of themes in federal NDP press releases by week

Week 1 (11 September–22 September)	Week 2 (23 September–29 September)	Week 3 (30 September–6 October)	Week 4 (7 October–13 October)	Week 5 (14 October–21 October)
Attack Trudeau and LPC: 41%	Attack Trudeau and LPC: 60%	Attack Trudeau and LPC: 80%	Attack Trudeau and LPC: 45%	Attack Trudeau and LPC: 63%
Affordability: 16%	Affordability: 25%	Indigenous issues: 30%	Singh's leadership: 42%	High corporate profits but low taxes on the wealthy: 46%
Singh's leadership: 15%	Climate crisis: 30%	High corporate profits but low taxes on the wealthy: 15%	Affordability: 17%	Indigenous issues: 30%
Health care: 15%	Health care: 17%	Health care: 14%	Health care: 16%	Singh's leadership: 20%
High corporate profits but low taxes on the wealthy: 14%	Indigenous issues: 9%	NDP team: 12%	Climate crisis: 10%	Jack Layton's legacy: 14%
Climate crisis: 12%	Money laundering: 6%	Childcare: 11%	NDP Team: 10%	Women's rights: 13%
NDP team: 10%	Women's rights: 6%	Northern Ontario issues: 11%	Women's rights: 7%	Quebec issues: 12%
Creating jobs: 9%	Attack Scheer and CPC: 5%	Gang crime: 5%	Attack May and Greens: 3%	Attack Scheer and CPC: 4%
Attack Scheer and CPC: 8%	Gang crime: 5%	Singh's leadership: 5%	Electoral reform: 2%	LGBTQ rights: 1%
Indigenous issues: 7%	NDP team: 5%	Attack Scheer and CPC: 10%	Attack Scheer and CPC: 2%	Health care: 1%
Childcare: 4%	Singh's leadership: 2%	Affordability: 9%	Fiscal responsibility: 1%	Affordability: 1%
	Create jobs: 2%	Create jobs: 3%	Childcare: 0.28%	Climate crisis: 1%
	High corporate profits but low taxes on the wealthy: 1%	Quebec and federalism: 3%	Indigenous issues: 1%	Assisted suicide: 0.36%
	Attack May and Greens: 0.38%			

* Note that percentages may total more than 100 percent because some passages were coded twice if they implied two different themes.

corporations in order to fund social programs that would help everyday Canadians. This theme is similar to those of class politics and left-wing populism that were contained in the party's commercials. While Indigenous issues were barely mentioned in the NDP's news releases during its campaigns from 2000 to 2015,[44] they figured prominently in the party's news releases in 2019. In particular, the party used the prevalence of boiled water advisories on Indigenous reserves as a symbol of the Trudeau government's lack of real action on reconciliation, in contrast to the prime minister's frequent comments about how much he cared about Indigenous issues. It is interesting to note that issues like electoral reform, labour rights, and LGBTQ rights did not come up in the NDP's news releases, despite being often associated with the party.

Finally, while the places that Singh visited are not included in table 4.1, there is evidence of the party's regionalized campaign. Singh spent the first twelve days of the campaign in southwest Ontario and, to a lesser extent, Quebec, and we can see the emphasis on affordability and health care as the issues that the operatives felt were important to potential Liberal/NDP switchers in those two provinces. The rise in prominence of the issue of the climate crisis in Week 2 coincides with Singh spending seven consecutive days campaigning on Vancouver Island and the Lower Mainland of British Columbia, where the Greens were threatening to take votes away from the NDP. The virtual disappearance of mentions of the climate crisis in Week 3 happened when Singh spent a day in Saskatoon and time in northern Ontario. Singh spent the last couple of weeks in British Columbia and Ontario, with a couple of events in Quebec, and this interlude coincides with NDP news releases emphasizing his leadership, Quebec issues, affordability, and making the rich pay more taxes – issues that operatives identified as setting up a good contrast between Singh and Trudeau for Liberal/NDP switchers in these three crucial regions.

Overall, Singh spent the vast majority of his time during the campaign touring southern Ontario and southern British Columbia by bus, with some time also spent in the north of Ontario, in and around Montreal, and Ottawa (due to the debates being held there).[45] He visited Nova Scotia and New Brunswick on the same day and visited Saskatchewan and Manitoba only once. He did not visit Alberta, Prince Edward Island, Newfoundland and Labrador, northern parts of Quebec, or any of the territories. As opposed to trying to get even coverage for Singh's tour throughout the country, the emphasis was clearly on the incumbent seats that the NDP believed they could hold on to. This geographical distribution deviated from Mulcair's and Layton's campaigns, which attempted to go to most parts of Canada during the election, and was a return to how Alexa McDonough campaigned in 2000 when the NDP decided to run its campaign like a series of simultaneous by-elections in the party's niches of support, which were concentrated at that time in certain parts of Nova Scotia, Ontario, Manitoba, Saskatchewan, and British Columbia.[46]

The political activity of the Canadian labour movement has become increasingly independent of the federal NDP since the changes to party financing laws in 2004 that banned federal parties from accepting union donations.[47] The 2019 federal election saw the continuation of this trend. The primary goal of the Canadian Labour Congress (CLC) in 2019 was to prevent a Conservative government, and its secondary goals were to protect NDP incumbents and to take advantage of a few opportunities for the NDP to win new seats. The passage of Bill C-76 in 2018 had resulted in a number of amendments to the Canada Elections Act, introducing stiff penalties for collusion and coordination between political parties and third parties (i.e., business groups and unions) during the writ period and in the three months ahead of the writ period. The new rules forced the CLC to remove its representative from the NDP's EPC and cut off almost all communication between the NDP and the CLC starting on 30 June 2019 until the end of the election campaign. As such, the CLC had to pursue its primary and secondary goals with very minimal communication between itself and NDP headquarters. Indeed, NDP operatives reported that the CLC and unions played no role in devising and operationalizing the party's strategy in 2019. This situation was a marked deviation from elections during the second half of the twentieth century when the NDP was the "political arm of labour" and unions funded a large portion of the party's campaigns, played an important role in determining the party's strategy, and seconded staff to run the party's day-to-day campaign activities.[48]

In 2019, the CLC adopted a "digital first strategy" that eschewed running television and radio commercials (though some individual unions, like Unifor, did run commercials linking Scheer to Doug Ford). The crux of the CLC's strategy was to use issue-based digital advertising to identify voters concerned with pharmacare, gender-based violence, pensions, creating jobs, and making Canada more inclusive. If these voters were in ridings that the CLC had identified through regional and riding-level polling as ones that could potentially go to the Conservatives, they would be sent e-mails and other electronic messages informing them of the issues of the campaign as the CLC saw them and eventually encouraging them to get out and vote. The focus on issues allowed the CLC to pursue its goals in the campaign without explicitly advising voters to vote NDP or telling them to vote strategically for the Liberals. The idea was to use digital organizing tools to push progressive voters to the polls in key ridings to prevent Conservative victories and lead, it was hoped, to the NDP winning more seats. As permitted under the new rules, the CLC also encouraged local union activists to volunteer their time to help NDP candidates win key ridings. However, as in elections since 2004, unions were not permitted to second their paid staff to NDP campaigns.

ANALYSIS OF RESULTS

Table 4.2 compares the average popular vote and seat total of the NDP from 1962 to 2008 to the NDP's performances in 2011, 2015, and 2019. It allows us to take both a long-term and short-term perspective on the party's 2019 election results.

When compared to the last two federal elections, the NDP's 2019 results were very disappointing for the party. The party's popular vote and seat count is lower in every province when one compares its performance in 2019 with its historic breakthrough in 2011. The NDP is now the fourth party in the House of Commons and a long way from being the official opposition and government-in-waiting. Indeed, the NDP's popular vote is now half of what it was in 2011 (30.6 to 15.9 percent). If we compare the NDP's performance in 2019 to the 2015 election, there is similarly little good news for the party as its popular vote dropped from 19.7 to 15.9 percent, and it lost almost half of its seats, going from forty-four seats to twenty-four seats.

Comparing the seat totals and popular vote by province between 2015 and 2019 also reveals few bright spots. The party saw its popular vote increase slightly in Newfoundland and Labrador, Nova Scotia, and Manitoba. But these small increases in popular vote produced only two additional seats, with the party also winning the single seat in Nunavut – the first time it has done so since the riding was created in 1997. The party's popular vote stayed essentially the same in Ontario, Alberta, and British Columbia, resulting in a loss of five seats in those provinces compared to 2015. The NDP saw its vote decline

Table 4.2
NDP electoral results in 1962–2008, 2011, 2015, and 2019

Province	NDP average vote (1962–2008)	2011 NDP vote	2015 NDP vote	2019 NDP vote	NDP average seat total (1962–2008)	2011 NDP seat total	2015 NDP seat total	2019 NDP seat total
NL	12.3%	32.6%	21.0%	23.9%	0.1	2	0	1
PEI	7.0%	15.4%	16.0%	7.6%	0.0	0	0	0
NS	16.9%	30.3%	16.4%	18.9%	1.1	3	0	0
NB	12.0%	29.8%	18.3%	9.4%	0.4	1	0	0
QC	6.9%	42.9%	25.4%	10.7%	0.1	59	16	1
ON	17.5%	25.6%	16.6%	16.8%	7.3	22	8	6
MB	24.0%	25.8%	13.8%	20.7%	3.3	2	2	3
SK	30.0%	32.3%	25.1%	19.5%	3.2	0	3	0
AB	9.7%	16.8%	11.6%	11.5%	0.1	1	1	1
BC	28.1%	32.5%	25.9%	24.4%	7.9	12	14	11
Territories	25.2%	27.8%	25.3%	25.6%	0.6	1	0	1
National	15.9%	30.6%	19.7%	15.9%	24.1	103	44	24

dramatically in Quebec, New Brunswick, and Prince Edward Island, and to a lesser extent in Saskatchewan. While the NDP had no seats to lose in New Brunswick and Prince Edward Island, it lost all three of its seats in Saskatchewan and all but one of its sixteen seats in Quebec. The Orange Wave that swept over Quebec in 2011 was reduced to a ripple.

The main beneficiaries of the NDP's electoral misfortune in the 2019 election were the Bloc Québécois in Quebec and the Conservatives in the rest of Canada. If one looks at the seats that the NDP won in 2015 but lost in 2019 outside Quebec, the Conservatives won seven of those seats, the Greens won one, and the Liberals one. In Quebec, the Bloc Québécois won eleven seats that the NDP won in 2015 and the Liberals four. The Liberals might have been able to squeak out a majority government had they done better in seats won by the NDP in 2015, particularly seats the NDP won in Quebec.

Looking at the NDP's 2019 results in a long-term perspective, it is hard to escape the conclusion that the party's performances in 2011 and 2015 were historic aberrations. What is most striking about table 4.2 is that the NDP's popular vote and seat total in 2019 matches *exactly* its average popular vote (15.9 percent) and average seat total

(24.1 seats) in elections from 1962 to 2008. The party's progress in 2011 and 2015 has essentially been wiped out. When one looks at the NDP's electoral results since its founding at the beginning of the 1960s, the party's 2019 results are "par for the course." It neither underperformed nor overperformed on its pre-2011 historical averages for votes and seats. Upon seeing the national results at the bottom of the television screen for the first time, one older volunteer arriving late to the NDP's election night gathering in Saskatoon after counting votes in polls in the north end of the city remarked to me: "Oh, that is usually where we end up." She was exactly correct.

CONCLUSION

NDP strategists were obviously unhappy with losing half of their party's seats and being virtually wiped out in Quebec. They were also disappointed with being unable to pick up new seats in downtown Toronto, Brampton, and Surrey, where Singh spent quite a bit of time during the campaign and where there are large new Canadian populations. They regretted the party's lack of preparation in terms of having lots of turnover in staff at party headquarters, starting late in organizing the central campaign, and having many candidates being nominated close to or during the writ period leading to weak local campaigns. They were also frustrated that the party did not have the financial resources to buy paid advertising to capitalize on the momentum Jagmeet Singh developed in the English leaders' debate.

Nonetheless, the professionals' evaluation of their campaign can be summed up as follows: it could have been much worse. Despite all of the challenges that the NDP was facing going into the campaign, the goals, tactics, and positioning that they developed for the party were able to make the best of a bad situation. Nightmare scenarios of losing party status, of the Greens eclipsing the NDP, of Singh performing badly and the party being thrown into another leadership race, were all averted. The NDP avoided falling into irrelevance in Canadian federal politics as it did after disappointing results in the 1993 and 2000 federal elections; in those cases, a tiny NDP caucus, without a permanent leader, was facing off against a large majority Liberal government. Singh's leadership is now unquestioned by the caucus, party members, and the public. Indeed, a poll taken after the election showed that 87 percent of NDP voters from the 2019 election wanted Singh to stay on as leader.[49] Most important, the Liberal minority government ensures that the activity of the federal NDP will remain relevant and in the media spotlight. What the NDP does and what it says will matter in Canadian politics.

In terms of political marketing, it is interesting to note that the party's operatives were quietly satisfied with their strategy. Given the party's lack of preparation and financial resources, they feel that they adopted the right tactics and positioning at the outset of the campaign to run a regionalized campaign, to focus on earned media coverage of Singh's tour to generate momentum, and to emphasize class politics in terms of taxing the rich and advocating universal social programs. Indeed, they reported changing very little in their strategy as the campaign progressed.

The 2019 NDP campaign marked the first time that a party had a member of a racialized minority as its leader in a Canadian federal election. It is likely, however, that there will be more racialized leaders in Canadian elections in the future as the country's population continues to become more and more ethnically diverse. The historical significance of the NDP's 2019 campaign might be that it was able to prove that what some in the media and in the party perceived as a weakness – having a leader from a racialized minority who wears religious symbols – could actually be a strength. As the NDP's French and English television commercials attest, the party did not run away from the differences in Singh's appearance but embraced them. Instead of advising Singh to never talk about race, the NDP's strategists encouraged him to talk about uncomfortable topics like the existence of racism in Canadian society. They felt that Singh's differences uniquely positioned him to talk about certain issues in a way that white political leaders could not. In the words of one, they "let Jagmeet be Jagmeet," and his popularity rose consistently throughout the campaign to the point at which polls showed him being more popular than his party.[50] With growing diversity in Canadian politics, the NDP's 2019 federal election campaign might be looked upon as a blueprint for how politicians from racialized minorities might do politics in our country. If so, the NDP 2019 campaign could prove to be an important moment in Canadian political history.

NOTES

1 David McGrane, *The New NDP: Moderation, Modernization, and Political Marketing* (Vancouver: UBC Press, 2019), 5.

2 David McGrane, "Political Marketing and the NDP's Historic Breakthrough," in *The Canadian Federal Election of 2011*, ed. Jon Pammett and Christopher Doran (Toronto: Dundurn, 2011), 77–8.
3 For a discussion on the relationship between political marketing and campaign strategy see McGrane, *New NDP*, 124–7.
4 I conducted semi-structured interviews with NDP operatives working the party's central campaign. In order to ensure that the interviewees could be candid, I took handwritten notes as opposed to recordings. These interviews are used to ascertain an overall sketch of the party's goals, tactics, and positioning in relation to the electorate, and to find out how the operatives evaluated the success of their campaign strategy. As such, the information contained in several sections of this chapter was obtained by telephone interviews with NDP officials from 31 October 2019 to 1 December 2019. An agreement was made with informants to publish their names but not to attribute any exact quotations or information to a particular person. The following NDP officials graciously agreed to be interviewed: Jennifer Howard (national campaign director), George Soule (senior media advisor), Marie Della Mattia (campaign co-chair and political advisor on leader's tour), Mathieu Vick (party president), Brett Farrington (director of political action for the Canadian Labour Congress), and an NDP war room staffer who wished to remain anonymous.
5 See Walter Young, *The Anatomy of a Party: The National CCF, 1932–1961* (Toronto: University of Toronto Press, 1969); Alan Whitehorn, *Canadian Socialism: Essays on The CCF-NDP* (Toronto: Oxford University Press, 1992); David Laycock and Lynda Erickson, *Reviving Social Democracy: The Near Death and Surprising Rise of the Federal NDP* (Vancouver: UBC Press, 2015).
6 Alex Marland, "Amateurs versus Professionals: The 1993 and 2006 Canadian Federal Elections," in *Political Marketing in Canada*, ed. Alex Marland, Thierry Giasson, and Jennifer Lees-Marshment (Vancouver: UBC Press, 2012), 59–75; Jared Wesley and Mike Moyes, "Selling Social Democracy: Branding and the Political Left in Canada," in *Political Communication in Canada: Meet the Press and Tweet the Rest*, ed. Alex Marland, Thierry Giasson, and Tamara Small (Vancouver: UBC Press, 2014), 74–91; McGrane, *New NDP*.
7 David McGrane, "From David McGrane, from Third to First and Back to Third: The 2015 NDP Campaign," in *The Canadian Federal Election of 2015*, ed. Jon Pammett and Christopher Doran (Toronto: Dundurn, 2016), 85–116.
8 McGrane, *New NDP*, 319–22.

9 Ibid., 4.
10 Graham Slaughter, "Jagmeet Singh Shuts Down Heckler with 'Love and Courage,'" CTV News, 8 September 2017, https://www.ctvnews.ca/politics/jagmeet-singh-shuts-down-heckler-with-love-and-courage-1.3581894.
11 Adam Radwanski, "Jagmeet Singh Brings Swagger to the NDP," *Globe and Mail*, 23 September 2017.
12 Gary Mason, "Singh Has a Won a House Seat: Now, the Hard Part Begins," *Globe and Mail*, 27 February 2019.
13 Canadian Press, "For NDP's Jagmeet Singh, the Pressure Rises as the Votes Draw Closer," *National Post*, 14 January 2019, https://nationalpost.com/pmn/news-pmn/canada-news-pmn/for-ndps-jagmeet-singh-the-pressure-rises-as-the-votes-draw-closer.
14 For an example, see Stephen Maher, "Jagmeet Singh's Rookie Blunders" *Maclean's*, 7 December 2017, https://www.macleans.ca/politics/ottawa/jagmeet-singhs-rookie-blunders/.
15 Rachel Gilmore, "Singh's Leadership Days Likely Numbered if He Loses Byelection: Mulcair," CTV News, https://www.ctvnews.ca/politics/singh-s-leadership-days-likely-numbered-if-he-loses-byelection-mulcair-1.4247166.
16 Zi-Ann Lum, "Jagmeet Singh Book Purposefully Light on Political Content, NDP Leader Explains," *Huffington Post*, 28 May 2019, https://www.huffingtonpost.ca/2019/04/28/jagmeet-singh-book-love-and-courage_a_23718371/.
17 Éric Grenier, "Jagmeet Singh's NDP Is Losing Incumbents and That Could Hurt in 2019," CBC News, 29 August 2019, https://www.cbc.ca/news/politics/grenier-ndp-incumbents-1.4801888.
18 Phillippe J. Fournier, "What's Wrong with Jagmeet Singh's NDP?," *Maclean's*, 27 May 2019, https://www.macleans.ca/politics/ottawa/whats-wrong-with-jagmeet-singhs-ndp/.
19 Alex Ballignall, "Will Jagmeet Singh's Identity Be a Campaign Issue?," *Toronto Star*, 4 September 2019, https://www.thestar.com/politics/federal/2019/09/04/will-jagmeet-singhs-identity-be-a-campaign-issue.html.
20 Between April and June 2019, the Green Party raised $1,437,722, beating the NDP's $1,433,476.
21 See David McGrane, "Election Preparation in the Federal NDP: The Next Campaign Starts the Day after the Last One Ends," in *Permanent Campaigning Canada*, ed. Alex Marland, Thierry Giasson, and Anna Lennox Esselment (Vancouver: UBC Press, 2017), 145–83.
22 Catharine Tunney, "NDP Struggling to Nominate Candidates as Election Call Draws Nearer," CBC News, 30 August 2019, https://www.cbc.ca/news/politics/ndp-nomination-candidates-1.5263840.

23 For an analysis of Liberal and NDP platforms in Canadian federal elections from 2000 to 2015 see McGrane, *New NDP*, 187–96.
24 McGrane, *New NDP*, 138–74.
25 Ibid., 147.
26 New Democratic Party of Canada, *A New Deal for People* (Ottawa: New Democratic Party of Canada, 2019), 108.
27 New Democratic Party of Canada New Release, "Singh's New Deal for People: Expanding Health Care to Cover You from Head to Toe," 16 June 2019.
28 Ibid.
29 In 2015, the NDP promised to build ten thousand new affordable housing units and "protect" 350,000 existing affordable housing units. In 2011, the party vaguely promised to provide "significant new funding for affordable and social housing." See New Democratic Party of Canada, *Building the Country of Our Dreams* (Ottawa: New Democratic Party of Canada, 2015), 18; New Democratic Party of Canada, *Giving Your Family a Break* (Ottawa: New Democratic Party of Canada, 2011), 6.
30 Peter O'Neil, "NDP leader Thomas Mulcair Throws Pipeline-Policy Punches," *Vancouver Sun*, 8 June 2014, http://www.vancouversun.com/news/leader+thomas+mulcair+throws+pipeline+policy+punches/10078481/story.html.
31 New Democratic Party of Canada News Release, "Jagmeet Singh: Liberal Government Must Abandon Trans Mountain Expansion," 22 February 2019, https://www.ndp.ca/news/jagmeet-singh-liberal-government-must-abandon-trans-mountain-expansion-0.
32 For example, see Adam Radwanski, "Low Budget, High Stakes: NDP Hopes Singh's Campaign Shift Isn't Too Late," *Globe and Mail*, 2 September 2019.
33 John Ivison, "Jagmeet Singh's Campaign Benefits from the Blessing of Low Expectations," *National Post*, 12 September 2019, https://nationalpost.com/opinion/john-ivison-jagmeet-singhs-campaign-benefits-from-the-blessing-of-low-expectations.
34 The party reported its candidates being 49 percent women, 24 percent racialized, 12 percent LGBTQ2, 12 percent under thirty years of age, 8 percent Indigenous, and 5 percent people living with disabilities.
35 Abigail Bimman, "Analysis: Behind-the-Scenes with Jagmeet Singh as the Brownface Story Broke," Global News, 19 September 2019, https://globalnews.ca/news/5932228/jagmeet-singh-justin-trudeau-brownface-story/.
36 David Thurton, "Is Canada racist? Jagmeet Singh Says 'No Question' – Then Pulls His Punches," CBC News, 13 October 2019, https://www.cbc.ca/news/politics/jagmeet-singh-racist-canada-1.5316318.

37 See chapter 5, this volume.
38 See John Ibbitson, "Andrew Scheer Fought Hard in the Leaders' Debate, But the Night Belonged to Jagmeet Singh," *Globe and Mail*, 7 October 2019, https://www.theglobeandmail.com/politics/article-andrew-scheer-fought-hard-in-the-leaders-debate-but-the-night/; and Abacus Data, "Election Poll: Singh Impresses at Debate While Trudeau and Scheer Break Even," 10 October 2019, https://abacusdata.ca/english-debate-who-won-election-2019-canada-poll/.
39 For instance, Angus Reid reported that Singh's favourability among voters had shot up by twenty points in early October. See Angus Reid Institute, "Singh Sizzles in English Debate, But Will NDP Momentum Solidify, or Ultimately Fizzle?," 10 October 2019, http://angusreid.org/election-2019-post-english-debate/.
40 CTV News, "Singh Would Not Support Conservatives If NDP Holds the Balance of Power after Fall Election," 22 August 2019, https://www.ctvnews.ca/politics/singh-would-not-support-conservatives-if-ndp-holds-the-balance-of-power-after-fall-election-1.4561260.
41 CBC News, "NDP Leader Jagmeet Singh Begins to Lay Out Minority Scenario Priorities," 10 October 2019, https://www.cbc.ca/news/politics/ndp-singh-priorities-minority-1.5315981.
42 For example, see Denise Balkisson, "Jagmeet Singh and the Costs of Being Canadian," *Globe and Mail*, 3 October 2019.
43 QSR International, *Nvivo 9 Basics* (Doncaster, AU: QSR International, 2010), 54.
44 McGrane, *New NDP*, 130, 135, 141, 149, 156, and 167.
45 Of the forty days of the campaign, Singh spent approximately 40 percent of his days in Ontario, 30 percent in British Columbia, 15 percent days in Quebec, and 10 percent in other provinces (Nova Scotia, New Brunswick, Manitoba, and Saskatchewan).
46 McGrane, *New NDP*, 129.
47 Ibid., 40–89.
48 Ibid., 45–6.
49 Angus Reid Institute, "Leadership Litmus Test: Conservative Voters Evenly Divided over Whether Scheer Should Stay or Go," 6 November 2019, http://angusreid.org/post-election-cpc-leadership/.
50 See Angus Reid Institute, "Singh Sizzles in English Debate."

5

The Battle for Quebec

Eric Montigny

Quebec is rarely a real battleground for four federal parties, as it was in the 2019 election. According to a compilation by Yannick Dufresne's Chaire de leadership en enseignement des sciences sociales numériques at Université Laval,[1] the leader of the Liberal Party of Canada (LPC) participated in twenty-seven events in Quebec compared to nineteen for his Conservative (CPC) counterpart and seventeen for the New Democrat (NDP) leader.[2] From Laurier to Trudeau Sr, Quebec almost always gave a large contingent of MPs to the Liberal Party. The Mulroney era marked one of the few Conservative interludes. Then, the failure of the Meech Lake Accord gave rise to the Bloc Québécois (BQ), which dominated until the NDP Orange Wave of 2011. Following the 2015 election, as Bélanger and Nadeau put it,[3] Quebec's representation in the House of Commons had the colours of the rainbow. In 2019, the four main parties fully integrated Quebec into their election strategy. And for a good reason: the Quebec electorate is very volatile. There is now little partisan identification and seventy-eight seats to win.

Nothing happened as expected in Quebec. Justin Trudeau was counting on the collapse of the NDP in the province to maintain a majority in the House of Commons. The Liberal campaign plan was clear: to make gains to offset any losses it might have elsewhere in the country. Instead, they lost five seats. Andrew Scheer anticipated a significant breakthrough in Quebec. He issued multiple messages of openness towards many Quebec government policies, while recruiting a team of well-established candidates. The Conservatives lost two seats. Jagmeet Singh began his campaign by proposing to conduct a new round of constitutional negotiations to correct the historical error of patriating the Canadian Constitution without Quebec's signature. His party lost fifteen seats. It was the Bloc Québécois that caused the surprise. Led by Yves-François Blanchet, it gained twenty-two seats.

How can we explain this rebirth of the Bloc Québécois when many counted it as dead a few weeks earlier? Does this reflect a strong return of the independence issue? From a Quebec perspective, what will we remember of the 2019 election? What were the main issues? What was the influence of the leaders' debates? These are the main questions that I try to answer in this chapter.

To this end, it is first essential to situate the federal election in the context of Quebec's realigning provincial election of 2018. This pivotal event was marked by a government formed by a party that had never been in power and by a Parti Québécois that had slipped to fourth in the National Assembly. Only by examining this election will it be possible to explain the particular dynamics that played out in Quebec in 2019.

Later in this chapter, I also analyze the Quebec campaigns of the six parties accredited by the Leaders' Debate Commission.[4] The Liberals quickly found themselves on the defensive. The Conservative campaign was sealed by the social conservatism of its leader. The Bloc Québécois abandoned independence to launch an autonomist campaign. The leader of the NDP was not able to translate his debate success into votes. The Greens missed an opportunity to break through, while Maxime Bernier lost his bet. With a minority government, the election campaign doesn't seem to be over.

A NEW ERA IN QUEBEC:
THE DECLINE OF THE YES-NO CLEAVAGE

Quebec is a society distinct from the rest of Canada, and it has a distinct party system. The presence of the Bloc Québécois, a party that only runs candidates in the seventy-eight Quebec ridings, contributes to making its political dynamic more complex. In addition to being able to provoke fourfold struggles in some constituencies, its presence reinforces the centre-periphery cleavage on issues related to the centralization or decentralization of the federation.

Francophone media coverage also forms a parallel universe to the English-language press situated outside Quebec. If the issues covered are sometimes the same, they are regularly different. The same applies to their framing. This media asymmetry was illustrated by Justin

Trudeau, who agreed to participate in two debates in French and a single debate in English. In addition to the English and French debates of the Leaders' Debate Commission, which brought together six party leaders, the *Quebecor* consortia held its own debate with only Messrs Blanchet, Singh, Scheer, and Trudeau. Similarly, it is important to note that, normally, very little attention is paid to federal politics. Quebecers are first and foremost interested in Quebec politics. They follow the National Assembly more closely than they do the House of Commons. Their eyes turn to the federal scene only when an election comes up or when there is an important crisis.

The lack of attention paid to federal politics could also provide a partial understanding of the high electoral volatility of Quebecers at the federal level since 2008. After years of Bloc domination, the 2011 Orange Wave gave the NDP fifty-nine seats. As figure 5.1 illustrates, Quebecers have been quite volatile in their vote choices.

Since 2008, there have been significant variations in the number of seats won by each party. In the last four elections, Quebecers have not shown significant partisan loyalty on the federal scene. In fact, only the LPC in Montreal and the CPC in the greater Quebec City area could claim to have a relatively strong geographical base.

This electoral volatility has been accompanied by the erosion of the Yes-No cleavage on independence that had structured the Quebec political debate since the birth of the Parti Québécois. On the Quebec scene, this cleavage was manifested as follows:

> A fraction of the new middle class now supports the Liberal Party, which advocates profitable, more or less renewed federalism, and another fraction (intellectuals, artists, professors, some members of the liberal professions, etc.) supports the Parti Québécois, which advocates Quebec's political sovereignty with an economic association with the rest of Canada. It is therefore a primarily political split within a new middle class that supports, in essence, the same neo-capitalist project with some variations depending on whether the focus is on private enterprise with the Liberal Party or on the state and the cooperative sector with the Parti Québécois.[5]

This Yes-No split on independence emerged on the federal scene in the wake of the 1982 unilateral repatriation of the Constitution and the failure of the Meech Lake Accord. From 1993 to 2008, it was

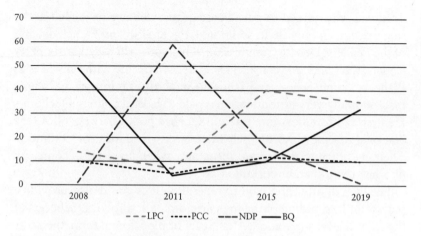

Figure 5.1 Number of seats by party in Quebec, 2008–19

essentially expressed through a confrontation between the Bloc Québécois and the Liberal Party. However, from election to election, the decline of the sovereigntist movement gradually eroded this structuring cleavage.[6] In 2019, this erosion was clearly illustrated by the candidacy of a former PQ health minister under Pauline Marois who chose to run for Justin Trudeau's Liberals.[7] Without the federalist-independentist benchmark, the Quebec vote has become much more volatile.

The decline of the prominence of the independence issue in Quebec is well documented. According to Simon Langlois, it began the day after the 1995 referendum,[8] and it is particularly relevant to new generations of voters.[9] This led to major challenges within the Parti Québécois.[10] Some go so far as to predict its disappearance in connection with the replacement of generations.[11] The decline of this Yes-No divide was reflected in 2018 with the election of a Coalition avenir Québec government. This realignment election allowed a political party that had never governed to win seventy-four of the 125 seats in the National Assembly,[12] and it ended fifty years of alternation between the Liberal Party of Quebec and the Parti Québécois. The latter was even overtaken by Québec solidaire, a new radical left-wing party, in terms of number of seats. The Coalition avenir Québec and Québec solidaire define themselves more along left-right lines, on environmental vison as well as cultural issues. With the end of a two-party system, Quebec is experiencing a reconfiguration and fragmentation of partisan lines. In the same spirit, the new premier, François Legault, fully embraces an autonomist vision of Quebec within the Canadian federation.

Autonomy should be understood as a third path between the federal status quo and independence, where Quebec claims more powers and respect for its jurisdiction within the federal system.[13] With Louis-Hyppolite Lafontaine, this political trend has its roots in the nineteenth century.[14] It reappeared under Maurice Duplessis and Daniel Johnson Sr, as well as under Jean Lesage and Robert Bourassa. The autonomist vision is based on the national character of the Quebec state. This implies that the Quebec premier is the heir of New France and must protect a francophone national culture in North America. Even though the Yes-No divide has been eroded, this is not the case for Quebec nationalism. It is now based on pride in its international economic and cultural successes and on the integration of newcomers into a French-speaking host society.[15]

It is in this context that we must understand the importance of the issues associated with immigration and secularism for Quebec society, which were important in the election. Since the Quiet Revolution, Quebec has gone from a society in which religious power was omnipresent to one of the least religious societies in the world. Quebec has developed its own model of integration and of how to live together, halfway between the Anglo-Saxon multiculturalism model and the full French secularism model. Empirically, studies show that Quebec-style interculturalism would give better results than these two models.[16] Looked at from this perspective, most Quebecers do not understand the attacks of English Canadian elites on Quebec's model. At best, they see it as a lack of understanding; at worst, they see it as Quebec bashing.

In this context, how can we then understand the Quebec results of 21 October 2019? How could an independentist party like the Bloc Québécois have been successful despite the decline of the Yes-No divide? Its management of the campaign, combined with the autonomist stance it adopted, helps to explain this comeback.

A PARALLEL CAMPAIGN IN QUEBEC

The two Canadian solitudes fully expressed themselves in this election campaign. In Quebec, Premier François Legault intervened frequently, while remaining neutral by prohibiting his MNAs from supporting any candidate.[17] The issues discussed in Quebec and the rest of Canada were very different, as was the media coverage. Similarly, there was a before and an after the TVA debate, when the Bloc Québécois began rising and the Conservatives fell. At the beginning of the campaign, "Mr. Legault decided to focus more closely on four demands underlying the fundamental principle that Quebec should form a distinct nation and be free to make its choices in all areas related to its existence."[18] More specifically, these four demands for the federal party leaders were:

- that Quebec obtain more immigration powers to decide alone on the number of immigrants in each category, choose the conditions required before granting permanent residence (including an assessment of the level of French and an assessment of knowledge of Quebec values), and fully manage the temporary foreign worker program
- respect for the Law on State Secularism (Bill 21) and a commitment by the federal government that it not participate in any legal challenge
- application of the Charter of the French Language to companies under federal jurisdiction
- implementation of a single income tax return managed by the government of Quebec, as opposed to two separate returns.

This strategy of a Quebec premier making a list of demands is not new: Liberal premier Jean Charest also used it in 2008. At the time, he claimed cultural sovereignty for Quebec in response to federal cuts in this sector.[19] By forcing the federal parties to take a stand on these issues, François Legault set the tone of the campaign from the start. It should be noted that, according to Angus Reid, with an approval rating of 64 percent, he was then the most popular premier in Canada.[20] Not having to deal with the interests of the rest of Canada and having no chance of forming the government, the Bloc Québécois quickly answered yes to all these requests. Andrew Scheer was open to three out of four, as was Jagmeet Singh. Scheer rejected the application of the Charter of the French Language to federally chartered companies, while Singh opposed the introduction of a single tax return. In the last leaders' debate in French, Justin Trudeau said he was in favour of Quebec administering a values test to immigrants.

Most important, however, was the issue of secularism and the federal government's possible challenge to Bill 21. The Conservative and NDP leaders had spoken out against the law, while respecting the jurisdiction of the National Assembly. The Bloc Québécois has taken up this issue by including it in its ads, which stated: "La laïcité, c'est nous." Only Justin Trudeau did not close the door to potential federal involvement in a court challenge. The day after the debate in English, François Legault reprimanded him, reminding him that this law had the support of 70 percent of the Quebec population: "I find it quite special that a leader comes to say that he is prepared to challenge the popular will of Quebecers."[21]

The Quebec media analyzed the main promises made by the federal parties prior to the first leaders' debate from the perspective of constitutional jurisdictions. We rarely see the editorial writers of *La Presse* and *Le Devoir* on the same page with regard to denouncing the high number of federal party promises in areas of Quebec jurisdiction.[22] This argument was also repeated by the leader of the Bloc Québécois during the only debate in English. Empirically, a study of electoral promises by area of constitutional jurisdiction confirmed this perception.[23] An analysis of forty-eight press releases issued before the first leaders' debate shows that the LPC made six commitments that fell under provincial jurisdiction, compared to five that fell under federal jurisdiction. In the case of the NDP, there were nine commitments on the provincial side and six on the federal. Only the CPC had the opposite ratio, with three on the provincial side and twelve on the federal. It almost seemed as if the Liberal and NDP promises were more focused on themes that are usually found in a provincial election campaign. Some of the promises made were purely local, such as new ferries in British Columbia or a hospital in Brampton, Ontario.

Tax measures generally do not interfere with provincial jurisdiction, which is why the Conservative total is lower. However, this was not the case with the new social measures put forward by the LPC and the NDP. In the case of the Liberals, these promises may signal a return to a more centralizing approach towards federalism. For the NDP, however, we must recall its recognition of asymmetrical federalism. By allowing Quebec to withdraw from pan-Canadian social programs, it could claim respect for the powers of the National Assembly. As John Ibbitson pointed out, one of Stephen Harper's strengths in regard to national unity was his respect for constitutional jurisdiction.[24] This

Table 5.1
Number of electoral promises by issue area

	Economy	Social programs	Environment	Justice	Taxation and purchasing power	Transportation
Liberal Party of Canada	1	5	4	1	3	0
Conservative Party of Canada	4	1	2	2	9	1
New Democratic Party	0	8	2	2	2	1
Total	5	14	8	5	14	2

Source: https://policyoptions.irpp.org/magazines/october-2019/une-campagne-electorale-vraiment-federale/.

hands-off approach, and his small federal government vision, previously took oxygen away from the Bloc Québécois. In this campaign, in terms of federal proposals to intervene in what many saw as Quebec's jurisdiction, Justin Trudeau did a lot to give the Bloc fresh life.

THE TVA DEBATE

The first debate in French on TVA gave the Bloc Québécois the opportunity to once again become a credible option for Quebec voters. As figure 5.2 shows, this was the most important event of the campaign in Quebec, a real turning point in voting intentions.[25] Until 2 October, the Liberals and Conservatives had been fighting for first place, according to Léger's data. In June, Andrew Scheer's party had even surpassed Justin Trudeau's in the minds of Quebecers. The Bloc Québécois was at the same level as it was in 2015, when the NDP and the Greens were fighting for fourth place.

Quickly put on the defensive over the abortion issue (see chapter 3, this volume), the Conservative leader missed his first chance to make a good impression in front of a large Quebec audience. Relatively unknown to Quebecers, he appeared hesitant and nervous. His opponents did not hesitate to define him as a social conservative, a position that has no political space in Quebec. Conservative support then began to fall sharply, costing the Conservatives about ten percentage points

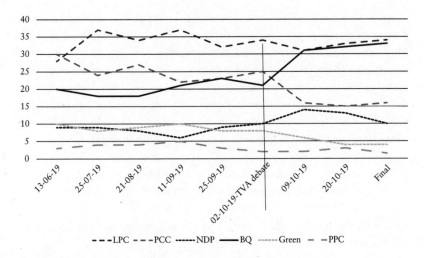

Figure 5.2 Léger polls in Quebec from June to 20 October 2019

Source: https://leger360.com/wp-content/uploads/2019/10/Politique-fédérale-20-oct-2019.pdf.

within a few days. The Conservatives' prospects of winning any substantial number of seats declined.

On the other hand, the debate allowed the leader of the Bloc Québécois to stand out. Yves-François Blanchet has regularly participated in television debates. Before running for the leadership of the Bloc Québécois, he was on the most popular program of the RDI information network, *Les Ex*. With former MNAs Marie Grégoire and Yollande James, this program, on a daily basis, brings together three former parliamentarians who discuss the issues of the day. During the debate, Blanchet did not mention independence at all; instead, he echoed the Legault government's autonomist measures and demands. A new two-man battle then emerged between the Bloc Québécois leader and his Liberal opponent. At the beginning of the campaign, Quebecers had been receptive to the Conservative message and were listening to get to know Andrew Scheer. As for Jagmeet Singh, his Quebec campaign never took off in terms of voting intentions. Even though there was some recovery after the debates, he finished where he started, around 10 percent. This left the Bloc Québécois a free pass to oppose Justin Trudeau and translated into a large increase of 12 percent for them in public opinion.

As we have seen, Quebec experienced a very different election campaign than was experienced elsewhere in Canada. François Legault's ghost was omnipresent. The Conservatives and the Bloc were even fighting over his friendship. The question of Quebec's autonomy was clearly raised in the campaign. It took different forms: the Secularism Act, respect for constitutional jurisdiction, increased powers for Quebec. Quebec nationalism is back in force because it now, for the most part, rests on more consensual issues than independence.

THE LIBERAL CAMPAIGN: ON THE DEFENSIVE FROM THE START

Justin Trudeau originally intended to sweep Quebec to keep his majority. However, he was the architect of his own misfortune because he relied on a campaign plan that was not well adapted to Quebec's specific characteristics. Paradoxically, in 2015, Liberals opted for a targeted election campaign made specially for Quebec. Even the election signage was distinct. This was not the case in 2019. Unlike the 2015 election, Justin Trudeau's Liberals seemed to take Quebec for granted. They felt the weakness of the NDP and the Bloc would allow them to make gains in most regions of the province. Therefore, at the beginning of the campaign, the main opponent targeted was the Conservatives. The first days of the campaign were characterized by attacks on Andrew Scheer's social conservatism and the austerity that would result from the election of a Conservative government. While the attacks on the Conservative leader over his personal positions on abortion hurt him politically, the attacks on the Ford government's austerity program in Ontario had no resonance in Quebec.

Trudeau made the choice not to appoint a political lieutenant for Quebec. In doing so, he broke with the tradition of his predecessors, who ensured that Liberals had a strong and visible voice in the Quebec media ecosystem. This did not prevent the federal government from making government announcements in the weeks leading up to the election call. During this operation, it was the member of Parliament for St-Maurice-Champlain, François-Philippe Champagne, who acted as spokesman. It should be noted that the government of Quebec took great care to distance itself from this operation.

When he responded to a question from a journalist when the election was called on 11 September, Justin Trudeau had no idea that a few words would haunt his entire campaign in Quebec.[26] He was responding to a question on Bill 21, the Quebec law on secularism, which provides that state representatives in a position of authority (judges, police officers, prison guards, teachers) who do not have a vested right right may not wear a religious symbol in the course of their work. By saying that, "for the time being" he did not exclude federal intervention in legal proceedings brought by citizens against Bill 21, Justin Trudeau was closing the door on the possibility of making gains in Quebec. This one remark quickly led to a drop in Liberal voting intentions. There were hasty attempts to explain. One of the party's star candidates, Réjean Hébert, who had been minister of health under the Parti Québécois government, had participated in the introduction of an even more extensive bill in 2013 and had to justify himself. Justin Trudeau also had to justify his position when meeting electors.[27] Twice, Premier Legault intervened to remind people of the Quebec consensus on secularism.[28] This was particularly the case after the English-speaking debate, in which Justin Trudeau appeared to be the only leader to try to score politically with his opposition to Bill 21.

The Liberal campaign also had a false start in Quebec in terms of organization. The first controversy revolved around the French version of its campaign theme song. Ridiculed by the media and on social media for several days for the poor quality of its French translation, the song quickly became the symbol of the party's disconnection from the Quebec electorate.[29] The chorus used the words "La main haute," which has absolutely no meaning in French, even though it was presumably supposed to mean "One Hand Up," the title of the party's English song. The fact that this song was played fed into the accusations of the former Quebec lieutenant and former mayor of Montreal Denis Coderre that the campaign was being run from Toronto and did not have any sensitivity to the reality of Quebec. After a few days, the party had no choice but to withdraw this version of the song.[30] In Quebec, this controversy had much more negative resonance for the Liberal campaign than did the "blackface" controversy.

"Blackface" (see chapter 2, this volume) illustrated the existence of the two solitudes.[31] Although the "scandal" provoked aggressive journalistic treatment in the English-speaking world, the French-speaking press showed restraint. On the first day of the controversy, the news did not even make the headlines in most francophone daily newspapers. The same phenomenon was observed at the political level. The leader of the Bloc Québécois even defended Justin Trudeau. Since they have not been exposed to the realities of segregation in the United States, it is important to specify that francophone Quebecers do not have the same cultural references as do anglophones on this issue. For many, this episode reinforced Justin Trudeau's pronounced taste for disguise, illustrated by his trip to India.

At the same time, internal conflicts associated with local ridings were making headlines. One was the case of a nominated candidate, Hassan Guillet, a well-known imam whom the party withdrew because of publications deemed anti-Semitic. Guillet defended himself and announced that he would run as an independent. A quarrel also broke out when the party refused to confirm the candidacy of a sitting member of Parliament, Éva Nassif. In response, the local association didn't want to release campaign funds to the candidate imposed by the party.[32] In another sign that not everything was running smoothly on the organizational level, the Liberals also had difficulties completing their Quebec team of candidates.[33]

The environmental issue, especially the fight against climate change, was a key focus of the Liberal campaign. In Quebec, this positioning was essentially based on the recruitment of a star candidate, the well-known and highly publicized environmentalist Steven Guilbeault. In a rare development, Guilbeault had even obtained the right to dissent from the party's stance on the Trans Mountain pipeline, which Trudeau had nationalized. The Liberal leader also promised, unlike the Conservatives, not to impose a pipeline on Quebec territory.[34] In terms of image, Trudeau's meeting with the young environmental activist Greta Thunberg while she was in Montreal to participate in a climate march helped to "greenwash" his leadership.[35] The march, held during the campaign, brought together hundreds of thousands of demonstrators in the streets of Montreal.

In response to the rise of the Bloc Québécois, the Liberals were forced to change their message at the end of the campaign. Aiming at Quebecers now willing to vote for the Bloc, Justin Trudeau invited voters to send "strong Quebecers to government, not in opposition."[36] He added that this would also avoid a Conservative government. This new positioning, a few days before the vote, was an admission that the initial campaign plan had not worked and that nothing had gone as planned.

THE CONSERVATIVE CAMPAIGN: DERAILED BY SOCIAL CONSERVATISM

As Léger's survey data indicate (see figure 5.2), the Conservatives won the pre-campaign in Quebec. Andrew Scheer, while still little known, was able to start the campaign in the lead. For the first time since Brian Mulroney, Quebec Conservatives had reason to hope for significant gains; instead, they ended up with two fewer seats. To discern what happened we need to look back at the highlights of a campaign that never took off; instead, it was overshadowed by the leader's social conservatism and by a radical change in strategy at the end of the campaign.

The Conservative leader appointed one of his primary supporters as a Quebec lieutenant. Alain Rayes refined a Quebec election platform and had been travelling around the province for months to build a real organization and recruit a team of quality candidates, including several elected municipal officials. These included the former mayor of Trois-Rivières and the former president of the Fédération québécoise des municipalités, who ran against Maxime Bernier in Beauce. Several former elected officials of the National Assembly had also agreed to run under the Conservative banner. A few days before the launch, Rayes even announced the candidacy of an Olympic star, Sylvie Fréchette. Hopes were high, as were expectations. It was with this background that the party's Quebec campaign was launched in Trois-Rivières.[37]

Then things started to go wrong. The message of the first week of the campaign was marred by conflicting positions on abortion. For the Quebec lieutenant, it was clear that the Conservative Party would not reopen this debate. Andrew Scheer in effect then rebuked his lieutenant by taking the position that MPs could introduce such bills on their own behalf. Alain Rayes took the blame, saying that he had misrepresented his party's position.[38] Even before the campaign began, Andrew Scheer had taken his Quebec lieutenant offside. Scheer's inability to get out a clear message on abortion undermined his whole campaign in Quebec. It was the subject of the first question asked of him in the TVA debate, and the Conservative leader's uneasiness on this issue was exposed to the Quebec electorate. Unable to answer one day, the next day he said he was pro-life, while also saying he would not reopen the debate. After that, a large part of the Quebec electorate simply stopped listening to what Andrew Scheer had to say.

One of the Conservatives' initial challenges was to connect with Quebecers. It was from this perspective that they recruited their team of Quebec candidates and developed a program to respond to François Legault's autonomist vision. Their concept of an energy corridor through which both western oil and Quebec hydroelectricity would pass was also intended to generate more social acceptability for a pipeline project.[39] However, the controversy over abortion and candidate statements about social conservatism,[40] along with anti-Quebec declarations,[41] destroyed these efforts. These controversies had a much more devastating impact in Quebec than did the Conservative attacks on the Montreal-based company SNC-Lavalin.[42] On the environmental issue, Scheer's decision to ignore the Montreal climate march also illustrated a misreading of Quebec society.[43]

Initially, from a communication point of view, the Conservative strategy was based on two axes. The first was to tackle the Liberal record by insisting on Justin Trudeau's lack of coherence. A series of negative ads was broadcast on French-language television networks and on the internet. At the same time, a more positive advertising campaign was broadcast to spread the message that a Conservative government would "put money back into the pockets" of Quebecers. For example, the party proposed to abolish the GST on electricity bills. The Conservatives' main message to Quebecers was essentially the same as the one they addressed to all voters (see chapter 3, this volume).

Halfway through the campaign, when critics were voicing their concerns about the leader's performance in Quebec,[44] there was a change of tone. This was apparent at the second debate in French, in which Andrew Scheer attacked the Bloc Québécois and associated it with the Parti Québécois. Negative ads recalling Yves-François Blanchet's sovereigntist allegiance were also broadcast. A few days before the vote, in La Prairie, the Conservative leader also delivered an important speech on his vision of Quebec within Canada.[45] In this more personal speech, he indicated that he would respect Quebec's autonomy, while positioning himself as the most open federal interlocutor to the Quebec government's proposals. While the reception of this speech was positive, many wondered why it had not been delivered at the beginning of the campaign. If this had happened, the Conservatives would have had a better chance of making gains as they would have adopted a consistent message of support for Quebec's autonomy.

THE BLOC: AN AUTONOMIST CAMPAIGN

The Bloc Québécois has come a long way. Under threat of disappearing following the 2011 and 2015 elections, it no longer had the status of a recognized party in the House of Commons. It then experienced a lot of turbulence at the top. The former president of the Société St-Jean-Baptiste, Mario Beaulieu, was elected leader in 2014 with the intention of making his party "the driving force behind the relaunch of the independence movement."[46] He quickly gave up his place to former leader Gilles Duceppe, who was called upon to take over the reins of the 2015 campaign. Martine Ouellet, a Parti Québécois MNA, succeeded Duceppe in 2017, and, while remaining an independent MNA in Quebec City, she gave the Bloc Québécois a resolutely *indépendantiste* and anti-system profile. This break with Gilles Duceppe's strategy led to the break-up of the caucus and the departure of the majority of its MPs in 2018.[47] Disavowed by the party's militants a few months later, it was Martine Ouellet's turn to resign.

It was in this context that Yves-François Blanchet, former minister of the PQ government, took over as Bloc leader. First, he worked to unite his troops and define a repositioning for the Bloc Québécois. Without formally renouncing independence, the strategy he adopted became resolutely autonomist, with the focus of his campaign on issues raised by the government of Quebec. In a post-election interview with a media outlet in his riding, Blanchet reminded Bloc MPs that he was directing them to work in agreement with their counterparts in the CAQ. He said, "I tell them that we are here to protect the jurisdictions of the Quebec Assembly."[48]

The Bloc Québécois was ultimately the only party able to maintain its strategy and targets throughout the campaign. It positioned itself as the only party able to represent the interests and values of Quebecers, highlights being a defence of Quebec's secularism law (Bill 21) and attacks on Liberal federal intrusions into Quebec's jurisdiction.[49] It is from this perspective that we must understand the Bloc's campaign slogan: "C'est nous [It is us]." At the same time, Blanchet targeted Andrew Scheer, saying that the Conservative leader would defend the west's interests first and foremost.

The Bloc's campaign began under the radar. Ignored by the other party leaders, Blanchet's daily announcements still made their way into the news bulletins. By giving the Bloc Québécois back its relevance, several analysts declared Yves-François Blanchet the winner of the first debate.[50] He then took advantage of the collapse of Andrew Scheer. A few days later, following the debate in English, the Bloc leader supported François Legault's decision to attack Justin Trudeau's attitude towards Quebec's secularism law.[51] The campaign then took another direction. By the last leaders' debate, the Bloc had become the main target of the Liberal and Conservative leaders.[52]

The leader of the Bloc also had to deal with some controversies. The first was initiated in the English-speaking press and had little resonance in the French-speaking ecosystem. Some considered his last remarks during the TVA debate to be racist: he said that voters should elect "men and women who look like you."[53] A few days before the vote, the party found itself truly and for the first time on the defensive. Comments deemed Islamophobic were reportedly shared by candidates on social media,[54] but their apologies were accepted by their leader. One of those candidates even filed a complaint to the Press Council in the aftermath of the election.[55]

The last days of the campaign were also marked by discussions over what meaning to give to the Bloc Québécois' potential strong return to the House of Commons. Stating that he did not want to form a coalition like the one attempted in 2008, the Bloc leader said that, in the event of a minority government: "Whatever the scenario, if what the government is proposing, whatever it is, is good for Quebec, the Bloc Québécois will work together. If it is bad for Quebec, the Bloc Québécois will oppose it."[56] While Andrew Scheer and Justin Trudeau attacked the Bloc Québécois the day before the vote, accusing it of working with the Parti Québécois to prepare independence, Yves-François Blanchet replied that the mandate he was seeking from Quebecers was "linked to what the National Assembly was carrying" and that even the Bloc Québécois activists had accepted the fact that it did not include, for the moment, the independence of Quebec.[57] In short, what the National Assembly was currently conveying was autonomism, not the nationalism of independence.

THE NDP: THE END OF THE ORANGE WAVE

With Jack Layton, Thomas Mulcair was at the heart of the NDP's success in Quebec and the 2011 Orange Wave. At the beginning of the 2015 campaign, now NDP leader, Mulcair already saw himself as prime minister and thought that Quebec NDP MPs would be easily re-elected. In the end, he did not survive the vote of confidence that took place after his defeat (see chapter 4, this volume), and, from that moment on, Quebec survivors of the Orange Wave knew they were in danger. Given that he had the support of his entire Quebec caucus, Thomas Mulcair's rejection at the Edmonton convention has been seen as the rejection of a Quebecer and of Quebec's perceived over-representation in that party.[58]

The arrival of Jagmeet Singh as NDP leader a few months later would not simplify the task of reconstruction. Unknown in Quebec, but having mastered the French language well, he was especially noticed for the wearing of a religious symbol – his turban. Not elected to the House of Commons, he also spent most of his time preparing to win his by-election in British Columbia. His first campaign message in Quebec: an advertising video introducing himself to Quebecers, in which we saw him remove his turban and explain his love for the French language and Quebec culture.[59] An English-speaking NDP elector in Montreal even advised him to remove his turban to win more votes.[60]

In terms of policies, with regard to Quebec issues, Singh chose to maintain the position developed by Jack Layton.[61] In addition to proposing the application of the Charter of the French Language to companies under federal jurisdiction in Quebec, Jagmeet Singh also opened the door to reopening the Constitution to include Quebec. He insisted on Quebec's right to withdraw from federal programs in areas of provincial jurisdiction. He also committed to being a partner with the government of Quebec on immigration matters,[62] and he promised not to interfere in the courts on the issue of Quebec secularism.[63]

The NDP's electoral message in Quebec, as elsewhere, was mainly focused on social and environmental commitments. Despite "un succès d'estime," in which many Quebecers discovered that he shared several social values with them,[64] his campaign never turned approval into votes. In his Quebec strategy, Jagmeet Singh appointed MP Alexandre Boulerice as deputy leader.[65] Boulerice's face was even featured alongside Singh's on national posters in Quebec. After 21 October, Boulerice was the sole NDP MP returned from Quebec. This 2019 result marked the end of the Orange Wave initiated by Jack Layton.

THE GREENS: A MISSED OPPORTUNITY

At the time of the 2019 election, the environmental issue had been in the headlines in Quebec for several months. Young people sporadically participated in Friday marches to fight climate change. The Green Party welcomed its first Quebec MP as a former NDP MP, Pierre Nantel, announced that he was joining the Green Party and would run under this label. Elizabeth May was no longer alone in the House since her party had won a by-election in a neighbouring riding. Environmental activist Greta Thunberg even invited herself into the campaign. The stage seemed set for Green Party gains. However, the party only ended up with 4.5 percent of the vote in Quebec.

How can this missed opportunity be explained? Seen from Quebec, the Greens' campaign plan seemed to be concentrated in British Columbia. Elizabeth May's poor command of the French language was certainly a major communication barrier. Beyond language, the messages received in Quebec were problematic on three fronts and made it difficult for voters to consider the Green option. A first controversy broke out because of Elizabeth May's support for the continued development of Alberta's oil sands a few weeks before the election was called. This quickly led to divisions and criticism from the leader of the Green Party of Quebec.[66] A second controversy arose when Elizabeth May opened the door to figures in her party holding anti-abortion positions.[67] Finally, her reaction to the sovereigntist statements of her new Quebec MP really had an impact. For the Greens, this is the episode that received the most coverage in the French-language media. When Pierre Nantel called on Quebecers to achieve independence as soon as possible, she quickly found herself on the defensive.[68] She initiated a confusing semantic debate in which she explained that being a sovereigntist does not necessarily mean being a separatist, a view that illustrated a fundamental misunderstanding of Quebec politics. Absent from the first French-speaking debate, she was quickly put out of the game.

It should also be noted that the Bloc Québécois, the Liberals, and the NDP had integrated the environment issue into the core of their campaign message. This had the effect of depriving the Greens of political oxygen while dividing the Quebec environmental movement. This division was accentuated by the Liberal candidacy of star environmentalist Steven Guilbeaut, which led the leaders of the Pact, a citizen movement to fight climate change supported by nearly 300,000 signatories, to take a stand in favour of the Liberals.[69]

THE PEOPLE'S PARTY: MAXIME BERNIER'S FAILURE

It is not every day that we see the birth of a new political party. It is even rarer to see it being invited to participate so quickly in a leaders' debate. This was the case for Maxime Bernier, leader of the People's

Party, Parti populaire in French.[70] The decision of the Leaders' Debate Commission to invite him to its two debates was controversial as the party did not clearly meet its criteria. These two debates could have been great opportunities for Maxime Bernier to reach a broader electorate. The French debate was also seen as a tool for him to keep his seat in Quebec. His national campaign had a bad start when he had to apologize for personal attacks on the young activist Greta Thunberg.[71] In addition, he claimed to be the victim of a Rhinoceros Party manoeuvre that presented another Maxime Bernier running against him.[72] His father, a former MP who had won three elections, including once as an independent, supported him, but this was not enough to enable him to keep his seat.[73] It is important to note that the Conservatives didn't spare any effort to see him defeated.[74]

Maxime Bernier's party did less well in Quebec than elsewhere, despite its Quebec origins. With only 1.5 percent of the votes in Quebec, the People's Party had fewer percentage votes than it did in Ontario, New Brunswick, British Columbia, Saskatchewan, or Alberta. Of the 63,203 votes cast for his party in Quebec, more than a quarter of them were concentrated in his riding.[75] This did not prevent him from losing it by 10 percent. When he left the Conservative Party and bet on right-wing populism, he demonstrated that there was no real political space for such a movement in Quebec.

CONCLUSION

The volatility of the Quebec electorate has once again made this election a real surprise. Like the Orange Wave of 2011 and the Liberal breakthrough in 2015, few people had anticipated the rebirth of the Bloc Québécois. Quebec has become a real electoral battleground.

The Liberals assumed that they would make gains in Quebec, without developing a targeted campaign. Justin Trudeau's position on Quebec's secularism law tripped them up. The Conservative campaign also experienced significant failures. To use Senator Claude Carignan's analogy, several Quebec Conservatives have the impression that Alain Rayes delivered a Formula 1 car to Andrew Scheer and that he put water in it instead of gasoline. His social conservatism quickly drove his campaign message off the rails. Many Quebecers simply stopped listening to him and considering his option.

At the end of the campaign, the Bloc Québécois had hopes of having the balance of power, but this did not materialize. With its result, the

Bloc Québécois will fully partake in only one of the missions it established when it was founded: to represent Quebec's interests. Unlike his father, Justin Trudeau will not be able to claim to speak for Quebecers. Pierre Elliott Trudeau could make this argument because his party had more Quebec seats in the House of Commons than René Lévesque's had in the National Assembly. However, with its autonomist campaign, the Bloc Québécois does not have an independence mandate. This will focus attention on the balancing act that Yves-François Blanchet will have to conduct between the electorate, his MPs, and his activists.

Orange in 2011, rainbow in 2015, and, with the Bloc's return to prominence in 2019, no one can predict the outcome of the next federal election in Quebec. Until then, there is a risk that the parties will remain in permanent campaign mode. Incidentally, Justin Trudeau chose to appoint Pablo Rodriguez as political lieutenant for Quebec in his new cabinet.[76] The battle for Quebec doesn't seem to be over.

NOTES

1 Report, Chaire de Leadership en Enseignment Sciences Sociales Numérique, Université Laval, https://www.fss.ulaval.ca/sites/fss.ulaval.ca/files/fss/Documents%20utiles/Recherche/Fiche_CLE-sciences_sociales_numériques_web.pdf.
2 These data were disseminated on the twitter account of this research chair. See https://twitter.com/CLESSN_UL. It also shows that the leader of the Quebec Bloc participated in 120 events in Quebec and one in Ontario. The leader of the People's Party also spent most of his time in Quebec, in particular to try to keep his seat in Beauce.
3 Eric Bélanger and Richard Nadeau, "The Bloc Québécois in Rainbow-Colored Québec," in *The Canadian Federal Election of* 2015, ed. Jon H. Pammett and Christopher Dornan (Toronto: Dundurn, 2016), 117–39.
4 Leaders Debates Commission, "Interpretation of Presentation Criteria for the Leaders' Debates," https://debates-debats.ca/en/interpretation-participation-criteria-leaders-debates/interpretation/.
5 Réjean Pelletier, *Partis politiques et société québécoise* (Montréal: Québec/Amérique, 1989), 362.
6 Marie Grégoire, Eric Montigny, et Youri Rivest, *Le cœur des Québécois* (Québec: PUL, 2016).

7 Simon Olivier Lorange, "La fin des étiquettes politiques?," *La Presse*, 17 September 2019, https://www.lapresse.ca/elections-federales/201909/17/01-5241546-la-fin-des-etiquettes-politiques-.php.
8 Simon Langlois, "Évolution de l'appui à l'indépendance du Québec de 1995 à 2015," dans *La démocratie référendaire dans les ensembles plurinationaux*, dir. Amélie Binette et Patrick Taillon (Québec: Presses de l'Université Laval, 2018), 55–84.
9 Yannick Dufresne, Charles Tessier, and Eric Montigny, "Generational and Life-Cycle Effects on Support for Quebec Independence," *French Politics* 17, 2 (2019): 1–14.
10 Eric Montigny, *Leadership et militantisme au Parti québécois: De Lévesque à Lisée* (Québec: PUL, 2018).
11 Valérie-Anne-Mahéo and Éric Bélanger, "Is the Parti Québécois Bound to Disappear? A Study of the Current Generational Dynamics of Electoral Behaviour in Quebec," *Canadian Journal of Political Science* 51 (2): 335–56.
12 Youri Rivest, "Le réalignement électoral de 2018: L'impact politique des Z," in *La Révolution Z: Ces jeunes qui transformeront le Québec*, ed. Eric Montigny and François Cardinal (Montréal: Les éditions La Presse, 2019), 157–67.
13 Adrien Cloutier and Eric Montigny, "Alberta and Other Provinces Are Taking a Page Out of Quebec's Book in Asking for More Power: The Trend Could Change Canada," *Policy Options*, IRPP 2019, https://policyoptions.irpp.org/magazines/october-2019/as-the-push-for-provincial-autonomy-spreads-where-will-it-lead/.
14 Louis Balthazar, *Nouveau bilan du nationalisme québécois* (Montréal : VLB, 2013).
15 Alec Castonguay, "CAQ: Le pari de la fleur de lys," *L'actualité*, March 2016, https://lactualite.com/politique/caq-le-pari-de-la-fleur-de-lys/.
16 Jeffrey G. Reitz, Patrick Simon, and Emily Laxer, "Muslims' Social Inclusion and Exclusion in France, Québec, and Canada: Does National Context Matter?" *Journal of Ethnic and Migration Studies* 43, 15 (2017): 2473–98.
17 Radio-Canada, "François Legault interdit à ses ministres et députés de participer à l'élection fédérale," 4 September 2019, https://ici.radio-canada.ca/nouvelle/1286766/ottawa-scrutin-quebec-canada-caquistes-.
18 Quebec, "Québec dévoile ses priorités et annonce la réouverture du Bureau du Québec à Ottawa," 17 September 2019, https://www.quebec.ca/en/premier/actualites/detail/

quebec-devoile-ses-priorites-et-annonce-la-reouverture-du-bureau-du-quebec-a-ottawa/.
19 Antoine Robataille, "Charest réclame une souveraineté Culturelle," *Le Devoir*, 13 September 2008, https://www.ledevoir.com/politique/quebec/205467/charest-reclame-une-souverainete-culturelle.
20 Angus Reid Institute, "Premier Tracker," http://angusreid.org/premier-approval-september2019/.
21 Hugo Pilon-Larose, "Laïcité: Legault accuse Trudeau de s'opposer à la volonté des Québécois," *La Presse*, 8 October 2019, https://www.lapresse.ca/elections-federales/201910/08/01-5244587-laicite-legault-accuse-trudeau-de-sopposer-a-la-volonte-des-quebecois.php.
22 François Cardinale, "La fin des campagnes électorales fédérales?," *La Presse*, 2 October 2019, https://www.lapresse.ca/debats/editoriaux/201910/01/01-5243644-la-fin-des-campagnes-electorales-federales-.php.
23 Eric Montigny, "Un campagne électorale vraiment fédérale?," *Policy Options*, IRPP, 2019, https://policyoptions.irpp.org/magazines/october-2019/une-campagne-electorale-vraiment-federale/.
24 John Ibbitson, *Stephen Harper* (Toronto: Penguin Random House, 2016).
25 It should be noted that the controversy over the photos of Justin Trudeau in blackface did not have the same resonance in Quebec as it did elsewhere in Canada.
26 Joëlle Girard, "Trudeau ne contestera pas la loi québécoise sur la laïcité pour l'instant," Radio-Canada, 1 September 2019, https://ici.radio-canada.ca/nouvelle/1295864/trudeau-laicite-signe-religieux-enseignants-cour-elections-elections-canada-2019.
27 Philippe-Vincent Foisy, "En tournée au Québec, Justin Trudeau est interpellé sur la loi 21," Radio-Canada, 14 September 2019, https://ici.radio-canada.ca/nouvelle/1301144/laicite-quebec-elections-federales-justin-trudeau-tim-hortons.
28 Valérie Boisclair, "Immigration: Justin Trudeau reconnaît le droit du Québec d'imposer un test," Radio-Canada, 10 October 2019, https://ici.radio-canada.ca/nouvelle/1341233/test-quebec-justin-trudeau-francois-legault-debat.
29 Philippe-Vincent Foisy, "*Une main haute*: La chanson de campagne des libéraux critique," Radio-Canada, 15 September 2019, https://ici.radio-canada.ca/nouvelle/1301774/chanson-parti-liberal-reactions-reseaux-sociaux.
30 Philippe-Vincent Foisy, "Nouvel enregistrement de chanson pour le PLC," Radio-Canada, 13 September 2019, https://ici.radio-canada.ca/nouvelle/1302315/parti-liberal-chanson-campagne-nouvel-enregistrement.

31 Christian Noël and Louise Blouin, "Justin Trudeau en 'blackface': Une controverse, deux solitudes?," Radio-Canada, 19 September 2019, https://ici.radio-canada.ca/nouvelle/1308899/justin-trudeau-brownface-blackface-controverse-solitudes-reactions-ontario-quebec.
32 La Presse Canadienne, "La candidate libérale qui a été parachutée dans Vimy est privée de fonds," Radio-Canada, 27 September 2019, https://ici.radio-canada.ca/nouvelle/1321316/elections-canada-laval-parti-liberal-fonds.
33 Phillipe-Vincent Foisy, "Les libéraux n'ont pas encore tous leurs candidats," Radio-Canada, 26 September 2019, https://ici.radio-canada.ca/nouvelle/1318506/candidatures-circonscriptions-nominations-bilan.
34 Radio-Canada, "Pas d'oléoduc au Québec, promet Trudeau," 11 October 2019, https://ici.radio-canada.ca/nouvelle/1342972/elections-federales-petrole-energie.
35 Valérie Boisclair and Phillipe-Vincent Foisy, "Marche pour le climat: Justin Trudeau chahuté par des manifestants," Radio-Canada, 27 September 2019, https://ici.radio-canada.ca/nouvelle/1320240/montreal-marche-climat-greta-thunberg-justin-trudeau.
36 Radio-Canada, "Campagne lancée ou non, les conservateurs sauteront dans la mêlée mercredi," 9 October 2019, https://ici.radio-canada.ca/nouvelle/1292734/conservateurs-elections-campagne-lancement-trois-rivieres-ontario.
37 Radio-Canada, "Trudeau réclame des 'Québécois forts' au gouvernement," 16 October 2019, https://ici.radio-canada.ca/nouvelle/1347800/parti-liberal-tournee-quebec-bloc-npd-conservateurs.
38 Althia Raj, "Avortement: Alain Rayes, lieutenant québécois de Scheer, admet avoir mal présenté la position du parti," *Huffington Post*, 26 August 2019, https://quebec.huffingtonpost.ca/entry/avortement-alain-rayes-position-parti-conservateur_qc_5d6472d6e4b0d2fa2dafc3aa.
39 Radio-Canada, "Non à un oléoduc au Québec, répète Legault à Scheer," 18 September 2019, https://ici.radio-canada.ca/nouvelle/1306115/pipeline-quebec-competence-environnement-federal-provincial-corridor-energetique.
40 La Press Canadienne, "Sylvie Fréchette apprécie que les conservateurs laissent les candidats s'exprimer," Radio-Canada, 17 September 2019, https://ici.radio-canada.ca/nouvelle/1304857/parti-conservateur-avortement-candidats-controverse-homophobie-racisme.
41 Louis Blouin, "Une autre candidate conservatrice met Andrew Scheer dans l'embarras," Radio-Canada, 14 September 2019, https://ici.radio-canada.ca/nouvelle/1301120/justina-mccaffrey-parti-conservateur-video-journalistes-kanata.

42 François Messier, "Scheer ramène sur le tapis l'affaire SNC-Lavalin et l'intégrité de Trudeau," Radio-Canada, 26 September 2019, https://ici.radio-canada.ca/nouvelle/1318231/enquete-snc-lavalin-grc-confidentialite.
43 Louis Blouin. "Andrew Scheer sera absent de la grande marche pour le climat à Montréal," Radio-Canada, 22 September 2019, https://ici.radio-canada.ca/nouvelle/1312117/andrew-scheer-chef-conservateur-absent-grande-marche-climat-montreal.
44 Louis Blouin and Daniel Thibeault, "Andrew Scheer va devoir 'se retrousser les manches,' selon des conservateurs," Radio-Canada, 24 September, https://ici.radio-canada.ca/nouvelle/1314136/parti-conservateur-chef-andrew-scheer-style-campagne.
45 Daniel Blanchette Pelletier, "Andrew Scheer tend la main au Québec," Radio-Canada, 15 October 2019, https://ici.radio-canada.ca/nouvelle/1347283/discours-entrevue-andrew-scheer-parti-conservateur-pcc-quebec.
46 Universite de Sherbrooke, "Élection de Mario Beaulieu au poste de chef du Bloc Québécois," 14 June 2014, http://bilan.usherbrooke.ca/bilan/pages/evenements/24104.html.
47 Radio-Canada, "Les députés dissidents du Bloc québécois claquent la porte," 28 February 2018, https://ici.radio-canada.ca/nouvelle/1086276/rencontre-chef-deputes-bloc-quebecois-dissension.
48 Martine Veillette, "L'heure est à l'action pour Yves-François Blanchet," La Journal, 6 November 2019, https://www.journaldechambly.com/lheure-est-a-laction-pour-yves-francois-blanchet/.
49 Radio-Canada, "Le Bloc québécois sur la ligne de depart," 11 September 2019, https://ici.radio-canada.ca/nouvelle/1296896/debut-campagne-elections-bloc-quebecois-canada.
50 Fannie Olivier, "Trois des quatre chefs s'en sont bien tirés lors du debate," Radio-Canada, 3 October 2019, https://ici.radio-canada.ca/nouvelle/1328960/debat-chefs-federal-tva-analyse-fannie-olivier.
51 François Messier, "Laïcité: Blanchet et Legault se braquent contre Trudeau," Radio-Canada, 8 October 2019, https://ici.radio-canada.ca/nouvelle/1336823/quebec-contestation-judiciaire-bloc-quebecois-yves-francois-blanchet.
52 François Messier, "À la veille du dernier débat, Trudeau et Scheer s'en prennent au Bloc Québécois," Radio-Canada, 9 October 2019, https://ici.radio-canada.ca/nouvelle/1338139/parti-liberal-justin-trudeau-changements-climatiques-conservateurs.
53 Catherine Levesque, "Une déclaration de Blanchet perçue comme raciste fait débat au Canada anglais," Le Soleil, 3 October 2019, https://www.lesoleil.

com/actualite/elections-2019/une-declaration-de-blanchet-percue-comme-raciste-fait-debat-au-canada-anglais-25c88e6c556ca958a2f8d72da7a9bbe5.

54 François Messier and Valérie Boisclair, "Blanchet s'excuse des propos anti-islam de candidats bloquistes," Radio-Canada, 10 October 2019, https://ici.radio-canada.ca/nouvelle/1340424/caroline-desbiens-lizabel-nitoi-valerie-tremblay-claude-forgues.

55 Simon-Olivier Lorange, "Une ex-candidate bloquiste en croisade contre le *Journal de Montréal*," La Presse, 5 November 2019, https://www.lapresse.ca/actualites/politique/201911/05/01-5248458-une-ex-candidate-bloquiste-en-croisade-contre-le-journal-de-montreal.php.

56 Marc-Antoine Ménard, "Le Bloc québécois ne participera à aucune coalition," Radio-Canada, 13 October 2019, https://ici.radio-canada.ca/nouvelle/1344201/bloc-quebecois-yves-francois-blanchet-gouvernement-minoritaire-coalition.

57 Marc-Antoine Ménard, "Yves-François Blanchet se défend d'avoir un objectif souverainiste secret," Radio-Canada, 20 October 2019, https://ici.radio-canada.ca/nouvelle/1353655/yves-francois-blanchet-bloc-quebecois-souverainete-attaques-trudeau-scheer.

58 Mélanie Marquis, "NDP: Le caucus québécois se porte à la défense de Thomas Mulcair," La Presse Canadienne, n.d., https://www.lenouvelliste.ca/actualites/politique/npd-le-caucus-quebecois-se-porte-a-la-defense-de-thomas-mulcair-8497782264a6172ff28cdd815902e1e6.

59 Christian Noël, "Jagmeet Singh sans turban pour séduire le Québec," Radio-Canada, 3 September 2019, https://ici.radio-canada.ca/nouvelle/1285491/publicite-jagmeet-singh-turban-quebec-election.

60 François Messier, "Jagmeet Singh interpellé au sujet de son turban à Montréal," Radio-Canada, 2 October 2019, https://ici.radio-canada.ca/nouvelle/1327729/nouveau-parti-democratique-racisme-systemique-marche-atwater.

61 Radio-Canada, "'Je veux être un allié du Québec,' dit Jagmeet Singh," 15 September 2019, https://ici.radio-canada.ca/nouvelle/1301171/npd-quebecois-jack-layton-elections-vote.

62 Radio-Canada, "'Jagmeet Singh se pose en partenaire du Québec dans le dossier de l'immigration," 7 September 2019, https://ici.radio-canada.ca/nouvelle/1291127/npd-jagmeet-singh-immigration-quebec-drummondville.

63 Marc-Antoine Ménard, Joëlle Girard, and Bernard Barbeau, "Jagmeet Singh entretient l'ambiguïté sur la contestation de la loi sur la laïcité," Radio-Canada, 8 October 2019, https://ici.radio-canada.ca/nouvelle/1335972/jagmeet-singh-npd-loi-laicite-contestation-gouvernement-federal.

64 Radio-Canada, "Singh et Blanchet cherchent à séduire à *Tout le monde en parle*," 23 September 2019, https://ici.radio-canada.ca/nouvelle/1312576/npd-bloc-quebecois-valeurs-environnement.
65 Giuseppe Valiante, "NDP's Jagmeet Singh Names Montreal MP Alexandre Boulerice as Deputy Leader," *Globe and Mail*, 11 March 2019, https://www.theglobeandmail.com/politics/article-ndps-jagmeet-singh-names-montreal-mp-alexandre-boulerice-as-deputy/.
66 Catherine Lévesque, "Le chef du Parti vert du Québec critique Elizabeth May," La Presse Canadienne, 29 May 2019, https://www.lapresse.ca/actualites/politique/201905/29/01-5228045-le-chef-du-parti-vert-du-quebec-critique-elizabeth-may.php.
67 Radio Canada, "Elizabeth May n'empêchera pas ses députés de rouvrir le débat sur l'avortement," 9 September 2019, https://ici.radio-canada.ca/nouvelle/1292848/droit-avortement-parti-vert-deputes-elizabeth-may.
68 La Presse Canadienne, "Un Pierre Nantel souverainiste ne pourrait pas représenter le Parti vert," Radio-Canada, 11 September 2019, https://ici.radio-canada.ca/nouvelle/1296498/pierre-nantel-souverainete-quebec-parti-vert.
69 Marc-Antoine Ménard, "Appel au vote stratégique environnemental auprès des signataires du Pacte," Radio-Canada, 17 October 2019, https://ici.radio-canada.ca/nouvelle/1350196/appel-vote-strategique-signataires-pacte-transition-laure-waridel.
70 In French, this name is reminiscent of the Bloc populaire, a party that was active at both the federal and Quebec levels between 1942 and 1947. It promoted a Canadian nationalism and was anti-conscription. Young Pierre Elliott Trudeau was a member. A forgotten part of history, no reference was made to it during the campaign.
71 Jérôme Labbé, "Maxime Bernier s'excuse d'avoir qualifié Greta Thunberg de 'mentalement instable," Radio-Canada, 4 September 2019, https://ici.radio-canada.ca/nouvelle/1287138/parti-populaire-canada-militante-suedoise.
72 La Presse Canadienne, "Maxime Bernier contre Maxime Bernier dans la circonscription de Beauce," Radio-Canada, 10 September 2019, https://ici.radio-canada.ca/nouvelle/1294908/maxime-bernier-parti-populaire-rhinoceros-beauce.
73 Émilie Dubreuil, "Les Bernier en Beauce, un 'deux pour un' qui dérange," Radio-Canada, 7 October 2019, https://ici.radio-canada.ca/nouvelle/1333930/maxime-bernier-gilles-fils-pere-elections-federales-beauce.
74 Valérie Boisclair, "Tirs croisés entre Scheer et Bernier dans la région de Québec," Radio-Canada, 18 October 2019, https://ici.radio-canada.ca/

nouvelle/1352111/andrew-scheer-conservateur-maxime-bernier-populaire-beauce.
75 Elections Canada, "Election Results," 21 October 2019, https://enr.elections.ca/Provinces.aspx?lang=f.
76 Radio-Canada, *Rodriguez, lieutenant du Québec* (video), 31 January 2019, http://ici.radio-canada.ca/info/videos/media-8183016/rodriguez-lieutenant-quebec.

6

The Climate Referendum? The Greens, the Others, and the Politics of Climate Change

Sarah Everts and Susan Harada

It was nearly midnight when incumbent environment minister Catherine McKenna stepped up to the podium to address cheering supporters who had assembled at Lansdowne Park's Craft Brewery Market in her Ottawa Centre riding.[1] By the end of the count, McKenna would glean 49 percent of the votes after a rocky first term in Parliament and at Trudeau's cabinet table.[2] She had been plagued throughout her tenure and the 2019 campaign by misogynist slurs from social media trolls, neighbourhood stalkers, and Conservative politicians, many of whom seemed willing to vent their frustration with the Trudeau government's climate change policies with sexist tropes.

When former Saskatchewan Conservative MP Gerry Ritz nicknamed her "Climate Barbie" in 2017, it was just one example of how McKenna was simultaneously subjected "to the smouldering resentments that still cling like barnacles to powerful women, and to the seething tensions around climate change," wrote *Maclean's* Shannon Proudfoot.[3] As McKenna addressed her election night supporters, however, she focused less on her detractors and more on celebrating her environmental portfolio. "I am so happy that climate change is finally a top election issue," McKenna said. "I am heartened that what we are seeing tonight is that more than two-thirds of the votes cast today were for parties that believe and were committed to climate action."

McKenna was almost accurate. According to the final tally, the Conservative Party, whose environmental platform was panned widely as being vague at best, won 34.4 percent of the popular vote, leaving 65.6 percent, just under two-thirds of the vote, to everyone else. But McKenna's general argument was solid: in 2019, a vast majority of Canadians voted for individuals or parties with environmental platforms at least as progressive as that of the Liberals. Arguably for the first time in Canadian election history the environment was consistently a priority issue for voters from the beginning of the five-week campaign until its bitter end. The Green Party's Elizabeth May framed it as a "referendum on the climate emergency."[4] A long-time Conservative communications consultant, Stephen Carter – who had run past campaigns for Calgary mayor Naheed Nenshi and Alberta premier Alison Redford – called it the "climate change election."[5] And if it all began with Andrew Scheer's Conservatives putting the Liberals on the defensive about their federal carbon tax, it ended with the Greens, NDP, Bloc, and Liberals vying for the position of *greener than thou*.

No longer a marginal issue, the environment became entirely mainstream – a harsh reality for the Conservative Party, which failed to adequately acknowledge and address the environmental anxiety blowing across the country, and a bittersweet turn for the Green Party, which failed to adequately capitalize on it. In spite of pre-campaign climate-related eruptions such as the Liberals' 2018 pipeline purchase, which had sharpened the divisions between parties and kept the climate issue in the headlines, the Green's Ottawa Centre candidate Angela Keller-Herzog, for example, languished well behind the environment minister come 21 October with 7.4 percent of the vote.

Even as McKenna's election night supporters toasted her victory over glasses of artisanal India pale ale, across the street a two-and-a-half-metre-high election billboard belonging to Conservative candidate Carol Clemenhagen shuddered in the October wind. A partial graffiti moustache defacing Clemenhagen's smiling photo might have distracted passersby from reading the list of her top priorities were it not for the fact that one of them – "climate action" – was even more incongruous on a Conservative billboard than the graffiti. (The other priorities, "fiscal responsibility" and "health," were more on-brand.)

A cynic might suspect that Clemenhagen hoped to pull environmentally minded votes away from the incumbent environment minister. But the Conservative candidate said she put climate action on her sign "because I believe in it," adding that she had voted Green in the past. Motivations aside, it is hard to imagine how Clemenhagen might have fulfilled her "climate action" promise had she won a seat in Parliament, given that her party did not supply the electorate with a robust environment platform – it was "thin gruel," as one former Conservative flak put it. "People were disappointed," Clemenhagen acknowledged. "They wanted to hear a practical action plan that was going to be well regarded by science and people who were acknowledged experts in climate action."[6]

Yet the Conservatives' strategic error of sidelining climate change ultimately had an unexpected benefit for Canada's environment writ large: namely, a minority government headed by the more environmentally progressive Liberals and propped up by political parties with more ambitious green policies. Of all the trajectories the 2019 election might have realistically taken, this one worked out as best as possible for the environment.

THE GREENEST OF THEM ALL

If there ever was a time when conditions were favourable for the Greens to gain political relevance – to attain the ability to prop up power, if not hold it themselves – the 2019 campaign was it. Just two days after the election call, Nanos Research found that Canadians had singled out the environment in general as being a top priority, with approximately 22 percent identifying it as "the most important national issue of concern," well above jobs (15.5 per cent) and health care (9 percent).[7] A late-September poll conducted by the Hope Not Hate foundation found that climate change in particular was the top concern of Canadians and that half of 1,599 Canadian respondents did not think the federal government was doing enough to address climate change.[8] And throughout the months leading up to the election – on the heels of a federal by-election victory in May 2019 that sent their second MP to Parliament – the Greens hovered at approximately 10 percent in national polls. Support grew to 15 percent in July largely due to voters surveyed in British Columbia – at 31.9 percent in that province, the Greens were even outpolling the Liberals and NDP, and they were hard on the heels of the Conservatives.[9]

More tangibly, the Greens had established a significant presence at the provincial level – three Green MLAs holding the balance of power in BC's NDP government, eight MLAs sitting as the official opposition in PEI, three MLAs in New Brunswick, a Green MPP in Ontario. It was evidence, if Canadians needed it, that a Green vote was not necessarily a wasted vote, at least provincially.

So when May launched the national campaign from her Saanich-Gulf Islands riding, it felt different, according to Deputy Campaign Manager Debra Eindiguer. For one, she said, the Greens were not automatically relegated to the sidelines in the media and were even called "one of the 'major parties.'" She continued: "Those are words that had never been used before this election ... That's incredible for us. We were 'fringe' how many years ago?"[10]

It was inevitable that with more media attention would come greater scrutiny, and there were widely reported political missteps and misunderstandings, large and small: for example, how exactly would the party handle any potential debate over abortion? How exactly would the party vet its candidates (controversies embroiling three of them had May on the defensive right from the start)? And what, exactly, were the Greens thinking when they altered a photo of May to show her holding a reusable cup and straw?[11]

It wasn't until well after the votes were counted that May finally got out in front of one issue that, left unchecked, could have overshadowed the party's post-election agenda – her continuing leadership. She had spent much of 2019 – between February and July – holding town halls in thirty-five communities across every province and in Yellowknife: meeting Canadians, listening to their concerns, selling her party and policies. It was all in anticipation of the fall election, and in the end it seemed largely for naught. Exactly two weeks after election day, May announced she was stepping down as party leader immediately (although she stayed on as an MP and took on the new title of parliamentary leader, which meant she would lead the Green caucus in the House of Commons). "I want to choose my own time of going," she told assembled journalists in Ottawa. "I want to choose a time when we've done better than we've ever done before."[12]

The accuracy of her read of the party's overall results is debatable, but Greens can be forgiven for grasping at silver linings, given May's claim that the election was a referendum on climate change. The logical extension – that it was also a referendum on a party most closely identified with all things climate – meant that the Green Party's electoral results were mixed at best, with few victories amidst the setbacks. The party's gains were eclipsed by its losses in numerous post-election headlines: "Greens' Historic Eastern Win Undermined by Western Disappointments"; "The Green Party Seemed to Be Surging: So What Happened?"; May's Greens Evaluating Campaign Tactics after Disappointing Election Results."[13]

Disappointing? On the one hand, Canadians sent three Green MPs to Ottawa – the largest federal Green caucus ever. It was a hard-won achievement for a party whose support – sprinkled as it is across the country – has historically provided little chance of electing MPs in a first-past-the-post system. On the other hand, the Greens once again failed to land anywhere near official party status, which would have ensured the resources and guaranteed voice in the House that comes with winning twelve seats. And only one new MP was added to their pre-writ roster. Jenica Atwin took her Fredericton riding with a narrow 3.3 percent margin over the second-place Conservative candidate, joining incumbents May and Paul Manly, who first won his Nanaimo-Ladysmith seat on Vancouver Island in a 2019 by-election. While Atwin's win planted the federal party's flag in Atlantic Canada, it remained the sole victory in a region of the country already primed to vote Green provincially. And framed against the overall election results was a larger disappointment. May got her wish for a Liberal minority government – "please God you don't get a majority government this time around," she told Justin Trudeau[14] – but her hopes that the Greens would hold the balance of power in the 43rd Parliament were dashed.

Other markers of Green successes and disappointments emerged with the post-election data. Across the country, more than 1 million Canadians voted Green – in sheer numbers, it was the largest show of support in the party's history in Canada and the first time it cracked the 1 million mark. Still, as a percentage of the total number of votes cast, it did not top the Greens' 2008 results. May's first campaign as Green leader that year resulted in what remains the party's high point of 6.8 percent, compared to 6.5 percent in 2019.

Further sifting through the numbers shows a similar pattern of disappointments laced with silver linings. Forty-nine Green candidates earned at least 10 percent of the vote in their individual races in 2019, which means they are eligible for a partial reimbursement of their election expenses – not an insignificant factor when the party begins recruiting potential candidates for future campaigns. It was a clear gain over 2015, when only nine edged into the 10 percent plus category. But go back again to the Green numbers of 2008, and the 2019 results can be viewed as nothing more than the party reclaiming lost ground: 14.5 percent of the Green candidates earned a spot in the reimbursement category in 2019 compared to 13.5 percent in 2008 – a difference of only 1 percent. The geography of this reclaimed territory also looked different in 2019 compared to 2008: this time support pooled at either side of the country and largely evaporated in Alberta and Saskatchewan.

Other than the fact that they won another seat, perhaps the most unambiguous evidence that the federal Greens are gaining political ground on geological timescales is in their number of second-place finishes and in the variance between those second-place Green candidates and the first-place winners. In 2008, with May as their new leader, five Green candidates placed second, with an average variance of approximately 45 percent. In 2015, the Greens were largely sidelined during a campaign that pitted Stephen Harper's Conservatives against Justin Trudeau's Liberals; they only registered one second-place finish, but at least the variance in that instance was trimmed to 10 percent. In 2019, there were seven second-place Green candidates with an average variance of approximately 13 percent. Taken in isolation, this indicates solidifying support for the Green Party. But read against the larger context of a "climate referendum" election, the Greens failed once again to make significant political headway, ceding environmental ground to the other political parties in the process.

GROWING ENVIRONMENTAL ANGST

On 8 October 2018 – a year to the month before the 2019 federal election – the Intergovernmental Panel on Climate Change released its most disquieting assessment of climate change scenarios to date.[15] The special report assessed the goals established in the Paris Agreement of 2015, when 195 nations (including Canada) had committed, at the 21st Conference of the Parties to the United Nations Framework Convention on Climate Change, to specific targets for fighting the threat of climate change, namely, "holding the increase in the global average temperature to well below 2°C above pre-industrial levels and pursuing efforts to limit the temperature increase to 1.5°C above pre-industrial levels." Specifically, then prime minister Stephen Harper's Conservative government committed to reducing Canada's annual greenhouse gas emissions by 30 percent below 2005 levels by 2030 in order to help keep global temperatures to no more than – but not well below – 2°C above pre-industrial levels.[16]

In its analysis of the Paris targets, the Intergovernmental Panel on Climate Change (IPCC) report argued that the agreed-upon 2°C limit was not a get-out-of-jail-free achievement for the environment. The report also argued the case for focusing more seriously on the Paris Agreement's aspirational 1.5°C goal – a global temperature ceiling that, in itself, would not preclude large-scale environmental catastrophe either. To illustrate the urgency, the report noted that "Coral reefs would decline by 70–90 percent with global warming of 1.5°C, whereas virtually all (> 99 percent) would be lost with 2°C." Focusing on limiting rising temperatures to 1.5°C would save not just coral reefs but people too: the reported noted that the 1.5°C goal would keep 420 million people from exposure to severe heat waves.

As for more Canada-centric warmings, the IPCC analysis predicted that by 2100 the "global sea levels rise would be 10 cm lower with global warming of 1.5°C compared with 2°C." Furthermore, the report predicted the Arctic Ocean would be alarmingly free of sea ice in the summer once per decade with global warming of 2°C but only once per century with a rise of 1.5°C. Even more worrisome, further analyses revealed the planet was actually on a path to a 3°C rise above pre-industrial temperatures by 2100, which United Nations secretary general António Guterres called "a recipe for catastrophe."[17]

The IPCC's 2018 report put a damper on the Liberal government's carbon tax, the Greenhouse Gas Pollution Pricing Act, which had been passed in June of that year and which would be enacted in 2019 – election year. Hailed by Trudeau as the main policy tool for putting the country "on track" for reaching the Paris commitment,[18] the carbon tax's objective was the less ambitious 2°C ceiling originally set by Harper. If the government wished to refocus on a 1.5°C ceiling, it would need to limit emissions to 45 percent below 2010 levels by 2030 instead of the planned 30 percent below 2005 levels.[19]

Furthermore, within a few months the news would emerge that the carbon tax was only likely to get the country about two-thirds (63 percent) of the way to the 2°C ceiling, according to the government's own analysis.[20] Even as federal environmental assessments pronounced the Liberal carbon tax subpar for reaching the Paris commitments, Conservative premiers in Alberta, Saskatchewan, Manitoba, and Ontario banded together with federal Conservative leader Andrew Scheer to argue the tax was burdensome, unnecessary, and would hurt the pocketbooks of average Canadians.[21]

Meanwhile, April 2019 saw the publication of a government report crafted by Environment and Climate Change Canada that documented the status of Canada's changing climate. Alarmingly, the report noted that, on average, Canada's North is warming "at more than double the global rate." *Canada's Changing Climate Report* also predicted that warming would lead to an increased risk of inland flooding, ocean acidification, harms to marine ecosystems, heatwaves, droughts, and wildfires.[22]

Within a few weeks, the report would prove prognostic in New Brunswick: the St John River rose beyond flood-lines for the third year in a row, and beyond its record 2018 levels. Throughout the summer and fall forest fires would once again burn through western Canada, destroying some 1.8 million hectares of land in Alberta. In the August run-up to the election call, some 30,901 fires blazed in the Amazon rainforest, raising fears about biodiversity loss and increased atmospheric carbon.[23] These and other alarming environment stories helped reinforce a trend of cultural eco-anxiety, what the American Psychological Association calls the stress resulting from "watching the slow and seemingly irrevocable impacts of climate change unfold, and worrying about the future for oneself, children, and later generations."[24] Personifying this anxiety was Swedish teenager Greta Thunberg, who had started skipping school in 2018 to protest her government's inaction on climate change in the wake of wildfires and heatwaves in Sweden.[25] By the time she sailed across the Atlantic and appeared at a mid-election climate march in Montreal, Thunberg had spawned a youth climate strike movement in Europe and abroad called Fridays for Future; she had addressed the United Nations Climate Change Conference in Poland (along with Sir David Attenborough) as well as the United Nations General Assembly in New York; and she had appeared glowering on the cover of news magazines worldwide as part of her mission to turn eco-anxiety into righteous anger.[26] In a commentary published by the *Guardian*, Thunberg wrote: "Adults keep saying we owe it to the young people to give them hope. But I don't want your hope, I don't want you to be hopeful, I want you to panic."[27]

For their part, Canadians were also succumbing to eco-anxiety. Some 315,000 Canadians joined Thunberg for a climate march in Montreal, while many more marched simultaneously in eighty-five communities across the country.[28] At a meeting with Trudeau, Thunberg accused him and his government of paying climate lip service, noting that his climate action was on par with that of her home country Sweden: "just empty words."[29]

A late-summer poll by Abacus Data suggested Thunberg's environmental alarm resonated with Canadians. "There is a sweeping consensus that climate action should be a priority, as signs of Earth's duress dominate the news," said Abacus chairman Bruce Anderson. According to his research, melting ice in Greenland and rainforest wildfires in the Amazon were "at the top of the list of drivers of demand for action," but other extreme weather-related incidents around the world, including in Canada, also fed "public expectations for action." However, while the Abacus poll found more than seven in ten Canadians thought action on climate change should be a priority for the next federal government, six in ten believed oil and gas development should also be high on the to-do list of the 43rd Parliament.[30] Trying to achieve both of these goals simultaneously during the 42nd Parliament had already landed Justin Trudeau's government in hot water.

PIPELINE PROBLEMS

Earlier in the summer of 2019, Environment Minister Catherine McKenna had put forward a motion to call climate change "a real and urgent crisis, driven by human activity,"[31] as part of getting a parliamentary promise to hit Canada's 2°C Paris commitment. That was on 17 June. The very next day, Prime Minister Justin Trudeau announced that the Trans Mountain pipeline, which the government had already purchased for $4.5 billion, would be expanded.

"The timing is ironic for sure," said Cat Abreu, executive director of Climate Action Network. "We're continuing to have a conversation about addressing climate change in Canada while skirting around the elephant in the room, which is emissions from oil and gas."[32] Trudeau's Liberals, with their commitment to expand a bitumen pipeline during what they declared was a climate emergency, banked on Canadians believing that this seeming cognitive dissonance was not inconsistent environmental policy but, rather, "a grand bargain." As CBC political columnist Aaron Wherry wrote in *Promise and Peril*, "Yes, there would be a price on carbon, but there would also be a pipeline. [Trudeau] would seek to reduce emissions for the long term even as he sought to maximize profits for the oil and gas industry in the short term."

According to Wherry's analysis, Trudeau's argument in a nutshell was:

> For however long oil is being used somewhere in the world, some of it might as well be Canadian. For however long Alberta is going to be producing oil, the province might as well get the best price for it. Meanwhile, if you're going to reduce greenhouse gas

emissions, the most efficient way to do so is by putting a price on those emissions – a price that will both take into account the environmental cost of these emissions and encourage the market to make cleaner decisions.[33]

It was a policy approach fastened to the hope that sufficient Canadian voters would place their faith in this aspirational framing: that action on climate change need not disrupt the fossil fuel status quo, that Canadians could have their cake and eat it too. This meant convincing them that Canada could increase profit margins by getting Alberta's bitumen to Asian markets via an expanded TMX pipeline and then invest in new green technologies using the anticipated increase in profits. But not everyone thought Trudeau's grand bargain was palatable. "That's like saying we need to keep selling cigarettes to have money to fight cancer," said Eugene Kung, lawyer with West Coast Environmental Law and lead on the First Nations case against the pipeline.[34]

If Trudeau thought buying a pipeline might also help him seduce Alberta voters, it was a failed strategy. "He has worked himself into an odd spot where he bought a pipeline and the people, for whose benefit he bought that pipeline, despise him," Wherry said.[35] There is a sense in Alberta, *National Post* columnist John Ivison added, that "regardless of the fact that 4.5 billion dollars of taxpayers' money was spent on a pipeline, that [the Liberal government] is not on their side."[36] In short, Albertans worried, and continue to worry, that the pipeline, although purchased, does not have enough federal backing or political will to overcome the pipeline's opponents, which include environmental and Indigenous activists as well as BC premier John Horgan, whose minority NDP government is propped up by the provincial Greens.[37] As Alberta energy minister Sonya Savage expressed in a Tweet, "The federal government must step up and assert clear authority over interprovincial pipelines. 'Death by delay' cannot be allowed to succeed."[38]

If spending $4.5 billion did not buy Trudeau any votes in Alberta, the purchase also hurt Trudeau's green credibility with environmental activists and his reconciliation credibility with many Indigenous people and their allies. Environmental activist Tzeporah Berman, from Stand Earth, said she felt alarmed by the prospect of "a Conservative government that doesn't take climate change seriously ... But at the same time the Liberal government's current plan to allow oil and gas production to increase and in fact to even facilitate that by buying the Trans Mountain pipeline and approving LNG Canada, [reveals] an incredible lack of ambition."[39]

Despite all the furor and the fuss, the pipeline and its expansion were never truly up for debate during the campaign. Although the NDP and Greens expressed adamant opposition to government ownership and expansion of the pipeline, neither was expecting to win sufficient votes to form a government; at best, they were aiming to hold the fate of a Liberal minority government in their hands. Meanwhile, both the Conservatives and Liberals supported the TMX, raising the possibility that the two most powerful parties might find themselves unusual allies should the government's pipeline face any existential threats in Canada's 43rd Parliament.

THE GREEN PLATFORMS

Climate change gained new urgency during the 2019 campaign, but it has had a political presence, albeit a more minimal one, since the late 1980s, when "Canada joined the climate change bandwagon" under then prime minister Brian Mulroney's Progressive Conservative government. The Mulroney government went on to introduce the first "green plan" in 1990. According to scholar Heather Smith, the plan was "consistent with what would become the standard Canadian policy tools to address climate change," with its largely ineffective focus on "information provision and encouraging voluntary actions."[40] Although the major parties acknowledged the environment as an issue of concern to Canadians, it wasn't until the 1990s that "climate change" emerged, somewhat sporadically, alongside the "environment" as an issue. As noted by political scientist Fay Farstad, the two can be viewed as substantially different, "with different incentives for political parties. The decarbonization of the global economy entails a more fundamental restructuring of markets and more severe regulation of behaviour than addressing any other environmental problem."[41]

In addition, Canadians did not consistently identify the environment, let alone climate change, as a top priority: polling found that "the percent of Canadians citing the environment as the most important problem in that country varied from 0.6 to 6% between 1995 and 2006."[42] There was a surge of environmental concern in 2007, and in the run-up to the 2008 federal campaign an EKOS poll found that 63 percent of those Canadians surveyed identified global warming as the most important issue facing Canada. Even so, social issues such as health and education, and economic issues pertaining to jobs and growth, were identified as the top issues for that pending campaign.[43] Seven years later, a few days before the 2015 campaign began, Nanos Research data showed the environment as being identified (unprompted) as the most important national issue of concern by only 7.7 percent of the Canadians surveyed, eclipsed by jobs and the economy (28.4 percent) and behind health care (10.5 percent). An Environics research survey found that concern specifically about climate change continued to align along party lines, with "extreme" or "definite" concern registered by the majority of NDP, Green, and Liberal supporters compared to one-third of Conservative supporters.[44]

The Conservatives

In June 2019, three months before the Liberals called the election, Andrew Scheer's Conservatives posted their environmental plan.[45] It might have behooved the party to spend those months crafting a more robust set of policies: there were no specific targets for limiting carbon or the rise of global temperatures. This was unsurprising, perhaps, given the strength of the party's support in Alberta, where climate change action was not viewed as being as important or urgent as it was elsewhere.[46] Yet Alberta's relative apathy on climate action did not indicate zero support. In 2015, an Environics poll, which found that "Albertans and Federal Conservative Party supporters continue to stand out as being less concerned about climate change and least supportive of policy actions," also found that "even among these groups opinions are divided rather than weighted heavily in opposition to climate action."[47]

One of the most concrete environmental policy promises established by the Conservative Party was that, given a mandate, it would repeal the Liberal's federal carbon tax. The argument for this, as outlined in the Conservative climate policy document, was that "Trudeau's Carbon Tax ... does nothing to protect the environment or to tackle climate change for Canada and the world ... [because] for a carbon tax to have any real effect, it will have to increase dramatically."

The statement is a blatant half-truth. It *is* true that environmental economists believe carbon taxes need to increase over time in order to successfully dampen atmospheric carbon emissions. But to argue that a carbon tax "does nothing to protect the environment or to tackle climate change" is to contradict Nobel Prize-winning environmental economists.

The 2018 Nobel Prize winner in economics, William Nordhaus, won for his work showing that "the most efficient remedy for the problems caused by greenhouse gas emissions would be a global scheme of carbon taxes that are uniformly imposed on all countries."[48] Carbon tax policy is the simplest way governments can limit atmospheric carbon levels, explained Paul Romer, who shared the Nobel Prize with Nordhaus: "If you just commit to a tax on the usage of fuels that directly or indirectly release greenhouse gases, and you make that tax increase steadily in the future ... people will see that there's a big profit to be made from figuring out ways to supply energy ... without incurring the tax."[49]

Instead of setting a price on carbon, the Conservatives said they would tax pollution-emitting industries. Scheer's party also promised to focus on supporting new clean, green technology development. This investment would be bolstered by environmental polluters who would pay in to a green tech innovation fund – but the plan gave no real details about how this would be executed. Scheer also distanced himself from the Paris commitments negotiated during Stephen Harper's government: instead of promising to hit those targets, Scheer indicated they would be aspirational. In addition, under a Conservative government, clean fuel standards would likely be left on the cutting room floor. As University of Alberta economist Andrew Leach put it, Scheer's plan was "cloaked in mystery and choked with irony." Despite claiming to have a more rigorous environmental platform than the Liberals, Leach concluded that the Conservatives' "suite of policies will, it's almost certain, increase domestic [greenhouse gas] emissions."[50]

The Greens

Elizabeth May leapt into federal politics as Green Party leader in 2006 specifically to take on the Conservative government of the day, which she described as being "the single biggest obstacle to Canadian action on climate change,"[51] after then prime minister Stephen Harper decided to ignore the 1997 Kyoto Protocol on greenhouse gas emissions (his government formally withdrew Canada from the protocol altogether in 2011). May's push for action on reducing climate emissions has been steadfast over the years even though the party's traction has been limited. In 2008, the first Green platform developed under her leadership called for a Green Tax Shift that would include a carbon tax alongside a two-stage emissions cut that would take Canada to 30 percent below 1990 levels by 2020 and ultimately 80 percent below by 2050.[52] Those proposals received little attention – a combination of the Greens' minor political party status and the headlines generated by Liberal leader Stephane Dion's proposed Green Shift, which subsumed wider discussion of the Greens' own platform.

Three campaigns later, in 2019, the Greens were calling for a 60 percent cut below 2005 levels by 2030 and an ultimate goal of net zero emissions by 2050. This was to be achieved through a variety of measures, including emission limits supported by penalties, a revenue-neutral carbon "fee" on carbon dioxide pollution sources, and the cancellation of the Trans Mountain pipeline, with funds directed instead towards a national electrical grid strategy and a transition to renewable energy sources.[53] To oversee what they said must be a concerted effort on all fronts, the Greens also proposed a "cross-party inner cabinet" so as to take the politics out of climate change solutions.

No longer the loudest voice on the climate issue, the Greens were assessed in some quarters as being ambitious but unrealistic: "practical policy beats ambition without a viable plan," according to University of Alberta economist Andrew Leach and climate scientist Katharine Hayhoe at Texas Tech University.[54] More damaging was the widely reported assessment by former parliamentary budget officer Kevin Page and the Institute of Fiscal Studies and Democracy. Initially giving the Green platform an overall failing grade for having numbers that "don't even add up,"[55] Page noted that "notwithstanding a commitment to a balanced budget over the medium term there is no strategy nor is there supporting information to guide the change in fiscal stance other than a large number of proposals."[56] After the Greens submitted additional information, Page later gave the party an overall "pass" for displaying "realistic economic and fiscal assumptions" and "transparency" but held it to a failing grade for "responsible fiscal management."[57] It was a blow to a party still fighting for credibility on the fiscal management front. Adding insult to injury, the New Democrats, who scored marginally lower overall than the Greens in Page's assessment, were given a passing grade for fiscal management.

May rejected the criticisms levelled at the Greens' plan for meeting its reduction targets. "The IPCC report said these are very difficult things to do, this will require an economic transformation, and it is global, and it will require herculean effort," she said. "It's ambitious, it will be hard to do. Yes. Yes, we say that in our documents, this will be hard to do. But it's essential if we want to survive. That part didn't come through in the election at all."[58]

The Liberals

In announcing the Liberal Party environmental platform, Trudeau promised to bring the country's net greenhouse gas emissions to zero by 2050 even as he claimed that "Canada is on track to reduce our emissions by 30% by 2030, compared to 2005 levels"[59] – a not-quite-true statement for anyone familiar with the government's own report to the contrary. At question was a seventy-nine megatonne surplus of greenhouse gas emissions, standing between the 2030 goal of 513 megatonnes and the projected reality of 592.[60] To close the gap, Trudeau hoped to rely on a variety of measures, not the least of which included a promise to plant 2 billion trees using $3 billion in profits from the controversial TMX pipeline.

But these measures were just green accoutrements to the Liberals' main plan for hitting Paris targets: the carbon tax. It was the foundation of their environmental platform and the means by which they hoped to achieve the country's emission reduction goals. The national tax on greenhouse gas-emitting fuels set the price of carbon at twenty dollars per tonne with the goal of hitting fifty dollars per tonne by 2022. In the face of a United Nations report that had named $135 per tonne as the minimum 2030 price-point for carbon pricing policies to effect change,[61] McKenna and Trudeau supplied mixed messages as to whether the Liberals might raise the price of carbon beyond 2022 to reach this goal. In the end, Trudeau pointed to 2023 as a carbon pricing re-evaluation point, given that it would likely be an election year.[62] The Liberals also proposed tax breaks for clean tech companies, infrastructure for electric cars, and a $5 billion clean power fund to improve the green profile of resource and manufacturing. They also vowed to phase out coal power by 2030 and to ban single-use plastics by 2021.

Leach and Hayhoe, analyzing the environmental policies of all the national parties for *Chatelaine*, gave the Liberals their only "A" for platform feasibility and a "B" for ambition. The Liberal environmental platform, they wrote, "builds on four years of experience, it tackles emissions across the economy, and it has measurable targets and ambitious goals."[63]

The NDP

"You do not need to choose between Mr. Delay and Mr. Deny," said NDP leader Jagmeet Singh during the 7 October English leaders' debate, in reference to Trudeau's and Scheer's climate policies, a quip he would later recycle on Twitter. "There is another option out there. We are committed to a real plan that's gonna take on the biggest polluters, take on the powerful interests, 'cause that's what we need to do."[64] Singh's strategy, at the debate and in his environmental platform, *Power to Change: A New Deal for Climate Action and Good Jobs*,[65] was to take a shot at Canada's political establishment with rhetoric from the Green New Deal movement launched south of the border by New York congressional representative Alexandria Ocasio-Cortez.

The foundation of Singh's plan was to springboard from the Liberals' existing carbon tax towards policies that would limit the global temperature rise to 1.5°C above pre-industrial marks as opposed to the 2°C plan offered by the Liberals (and inked internationally by Harper's Conservatives). As part of this, Singh's NDP promised to ensure all new buildings in Canada had a net-zero greenhouse gas profile by 2030, to do energy-efficiency retrofits on all existing homes by 2050, to subsidize low-emission vehicles and public transit, and to make all federal government vehicles electric – a set of policies that he said would create 300,000 jobs. Singh's party also promised, exclamation mark included, to "Make public transit cleaner, more convenient and more affordable – even free!"

The breathlessly enthusiastic plan was perhaps only surpassed in ambition by the Greens. However, economist Andrew Leach also took issue with the NDP platform's feasibility, noting that "Singh's plan ... is riddled with inconsistencies and short on details and, where details are given, the policies simply aren't stringent enough to meet the goals."[66]

The Bloc

Along with May, Singh, and Trudeau, Bloc Québécois leader Yves-François Blanchet joined climate marches held across the country during the election campaign. Blanchet voiced support for the country's Paris Agreement, yet made no promises to go beyond the less ambitious 2°C limit.[67] The Bloc mostly avoided carbon tax rhetoric during the campaign: it was a non-issue in the province, given that a made-in-Quebec carbon pricing scheme had been implemented years ago.[68] Although Blanchet took a firm stand against any pipelines traversing Quebec – making mention at debates of Energy East, which had long ago been panned – he said he had no qualms with pipelines outside the province.[69]

Arguably the Bloc's most interesting contribution to the campaign's environmental discussion was its proposal for what some have referred to as a national "green equalization program."[70] According to this plan, provinces that exceeded Canada's overall emission average would pay into the pockets of provinces that had lower emissions than the country's average.

THE WINNERS AND THE LOSERS

"EVERYONE WON." This ironic comment, tweeted by CBC *Power and Politics*' host Vassy Kapelos at 1:40 a.m. on election night,[71] dryly noted that many of the party leaders were giving speeches that "seemed to indicate [that] they thought they won."[72] In truth, election night brought disappointing results to many of the federal parties – the Liberals lost a majority mandate; the Conservatives failed to form any sort of government; the Greens once again fell short of expectations; and the New Democrats were reduced to one seat in Quebec. Yet if anyone – or anything – won the 2019 election, it can be argued that the environment writ large, and the issue of climate change specifically, emerged as the clear winner.

While climate change featured prominently in the Liberal, NDP, Green, and Bloc platforms, the Conservatives were the only major federal party sporting an environmental blind spot.[73] Looking back, it was clearly not the right time to do so. Although they swept Alberta and Saskatchewan, the Conservatives failed to extend their reach much beyond their base in an election that could have been theirs for the taking. There are certainly many reasons the Conservatives were unable to capitalize on a Liberal Party beset by controversy. But not having a serious environmental platform certainly did nothing to reduce the fears of centrist swing voters that Scheer might follow in the footsteps of US president Donald Trump and move backwards on climate change regulations (see chapter 3, this volume).

They might have rectified this tactical error midway through the campaign had Scheer taken his conversation with Markus Harvey to heart. Harvey – a fifty-year-old undecided New Brunswick voter who self-described as "a guy who sits on my porch, drinks whiskey and yells at the [St John] river" – was given the opportunity to discuss an issue of his choice with Scheer as part of a CBC series featuring undecided voters.[74]

Candid about being no fan of Trudeau and considering Scheer "the lesser of two evils," Harvey told the CBC that he was worried the Conservative leader was a climate denier, particularly because Scheer had not participated in any of the September climate marches as many of the other political party leaders had. "Do you understand the gravity of global warming?" Harvey asked Scheer during their recorded tête-à-tête. "For the first 40 years of my life we had four floods [on the St John River]. In the last 10 [years], we've had seven [floods]. If the water goes over the road next year, it's going to be four [floods] in four [years]." Describing the discussion to a reporter afterwards, Harvey said: "Andrew Scheer did do a bit of dancing, stumping, and politicking. I had to rein him back in and once again tell him how massive and immediate the situation [is that] needs to be addressed."

Even so, Scheer remained vague about climate policies, and Harvey cast his vote for the Greens' Jenica Atwin in Fredericton. One day after she became the party's third MP, her province's Conservative premier, Blaine Higgs, announced that he would develop a made-in-New-Brunswick carbon tax, a major about-face from his previous petulant stance on the federal carbon tax.[75] Weeks later, climate change figured prominently in the minority Liberal government's Speech from the Throne. Calling it "the defining issue of our time," the Liberals reiterated their campaign promise to reduce emissions to net zero by 2050.[76]

In response to the government rhetoric, Elizabeth May said it was imperative that the Liberals develop a more realistic plan to reach that goal: "What they say doesn't matter, what they do matters. The plan and the target we have right now will make it impossible to achieve the 2050 targets."[77] Overall reaction from the other parties was mixed: for example, Scheer wanted mention of the Conservatives' proposed national energy corridor; the NDP wanted more on climate change targets; the Bloc lauded the room it seemed to give to Quebec's hydro-electric workers.[78]

In the end, it all comes down to this: How worried are Canadians about climate change, how deeply do they believe the government must act on it, and how committed are they to push for policies that would demand the participation of all citizens as well as the political parties? As Farstad notes, "Whereas more traditional environmental issues can be considered 'valence issues' as the benefits of addressing them often accrue to the current and national population (e.g., improved air or water quality), climate change challenges parties to prioritise long-term (and often 'radical') goals over short-term gains and to altruistically think of people other than their electorates (whether people in other countries or future generations)." This, she said, combined with a left-right split when it comes to support for climate change action, points to the issue's partisan nature.[79] And if the way things played out during the campaign is any indication, the politics of climate change may prevail.

"What we got was a lot of greenwashing from the Liberals, greenwashing from the NDP, neither of whom have a target that is consistent with the science," May said. "[Given] the coverage of the issue you could fairly conclude you could vote Liberal, you could vote NDP or you could vote Green, they're all climate votes." May's fear? That the other political parties – especially in a minority government situation – will take advantage of that, do the minimum and simply kick the issue down the road. "Partisanship overtakes thought and politicians of all stripes make decisions based on what they think will advance them in six months to a year in terms of polling numbers," she said. "It's not principle, it's about winning. So if you could message something that makes it sound like you care about the environment or act on climate and not actually have to do it then that's the course that most people in politics will take."[80]

If climate continues to be a top issue for Canadians, the Greens – the party most closely identified with climate change and in fact identified as being the best to deal with the issue by 39 percent of Canadians surveyed by Ipsos prior to election day[81] – may yet have another realistic opportunity to expand its electoral success. Much depends on who the Greens choose to succeed May as party leader, a choice that will not be made until October 2020. The party's political relevance will also depend on whether it can use the post-campaign period to more effectively translate a presence at the provincial level into national support. But the Greens do not have the luxury of time. As long as climate change action remains uppermost as an issue of concern to Canadians, their political rivals will not be standing still while the Greens sort out their future. It could be that they will be shut out politically as the Liberals and NDP, and perhaps even the Conservatives down the road, fully claim the climate change space.

If that happens, it could, in a sense, return the Greens to very fundamental questions about their political identity and policy priorities – back to their beginnings as a grassroots protest party. As May put it during her first campaign in 2008, she "represent[ed] a view that survival of the planet is more important than any particular percentage of the vote for the Green party."[82] What does that look like in practical terms? In the past she mused about teaming up with the Liberals and NDP – agreeing not to run candidates against each other in ridings where that might mean defeating the climate-unfriendly Conservatives.[83] Others have raised the possibility of an outright merger with the NDP, and, given the election results, at least one commentator has already returned to that idea.[84] But that, too, would take time. In the meantime, how the Greens and the other political parties decide to meet the challenge of climate action in the immediate future will ultimately determine whether the environment – and, more specifically, climate change – was truly the winner in 2019 after all.

NOTES

1 Blair Crawford, "Incumbent Liberal Catherine Mckenna Crowned in Ottawa Centre," *Ottawa Citizen*, 22 October 2019, https://ottawacitizen.com/news/local-news/incumbent-liberal-catherine-mckenna-crowned-in-ottawa-centre.
2 All election results data in this chapter are from the Elections Canada website at https://enr.elections.ca/National.aspx?lang=e.
3 Shannon Proudfoot, "Why Would Anyone Hate Catherine Mckenna?," *Maclean's*, 4 November 2019, https://www.macleans.ca/politics/ottawa/why-would-anyone-hate-catherine-mckenna/.
4 Green Party of Canada, "This Election Is a Climate Referendum, Says Elizabeth May," 30 September 2019, https://www.greenparty.ca/en/media-release/2019-09-30/election-climate-referendum-says-elizabeth-may.
5 Kyle Bakx, "The Big Election Winner? The Carbon Tax," 22 October 2019, https://www.cbc.ca/news/business/trudeau-sheer-election-carbon-tax-1.5330829.
6 Carole Clemenhagen, former Conservative candidate in Ottawa Centre, telephone interview with Susan Harada, 15 November 2019.
7 All Nanos Research data in this chapter are from https://www.nanos.co/dataportal/.

8 Stephanie Wood, "Climate Change Number 1 Concern for Canadians, Poll Says," *National Observer*, 20 September 2019, https://www.nationalobserver.com/2019/09/20/news/climate-change-number-1-concern-canadians-poll-says.
9 Éric Grenier, "Poll Tracker - Individual Polls," 7 November 2019, https://newsinteractives.cbc.ca/elections/poll-tracker/canada/; and EKOS-Politics, "National Federal Vote Intention (Decided and Leaning Voters Only)," 3 December 2019, http://www.ekospolitics.com/wp-content/uploads/ekos_data_tables_july_6_8_2019a.pdf.
10 Debra Eindiguer, Deputy Campaign Manager, Green Party of Canada, interview with Susan Harada in Ottawa, 14 November 2019.
11 See, for example, Marieke Walsh, "Elizabeth May Clarifies Position on Abortion, Says Green Party Screens Out Candidates Who Disagree," *Globe and Mail*, 9 September 2019, https://www.theglobeandmail.com/politics/article-elizabeth-may-clarifies-position-on-abortion-says-green-party-screens/; John Paul Tasker, "Elizabeth May Says Green Party Is 'Re-Vetting' Candidates after Anti-Abortion Comments Come to Light," CBC News, 13 September 2019, https://www.cbc.ca/news/politics/green-party-re-vetting-candidates-abortion-quebec-1.5282892; Justine Hunter, "Green Party Vetting Process in Spotlight with Three Candidates Embroiled in Controversy," *Globe and Mail*, 12 September 2019, https://www.theglobeandmail.com/politics/article-green-party-vetting-process-in-spotlight-with-three-candidates/; and Kim Bellware, "Canada's Green Party Shared a Photo of Its Leader with a Reusable Cup. It Was Fake," *Washington Post*, 26 September 2019, https://www.washingtonpost.com/world/2019/09/26/canadas-green-party-shared-photo-its-leader-with-reusable-cup-it-was-fake/.
12 "Elizabeth May Steps Down as Green Party Leader," CPAC, 4 November 2019, https://www.youtube.com/watch?v=C3cs6FYaEu4.
13 Lucas Powers, "Greens' Historic Eastern Win Undermined by Western Disappointments," CBC News, 22 October 2019, https://www.cbc.ca/news/politics/green-party-election-elizabeth-may-results-1.5329778; Maura Forrest, "The Green Party Seemed to Be Surging: So What Happened?," *National Post*, 28 October 2019, https://nationalpost.com/news/politics/election-2019/the-green-party-seemed-to-be-surging-so-what-happened; and Justine Hunter, "May's Greens Evaluating Campaign Tactics after Disappointing Election Results," *Globe and Mail*, 23 October 2019, https://www.theglobeandmail.com/canada/british-columbia/article-federal-greens-learn-from-disappointing-campaign/.

14 May made the comment during the English language leaders' debate on 7 October 2019. See "Federal Leaders Debate 2019: Full Transcript," *Macleans.ca*, 8 October 2019, https://www.macleans.ca/politics/federal-leaders-debate-full-transcript/#section5.
15 All information cited in this section on the Intergovernmental Panel on Climate Change is from: Intergovernmental Panel on Climate Change, *The Special Report on Global Warming of 1.5 °C*, ed. Masson-Delmotte, V., P. Zhai, H.-O. Pörtner, D. Roberts, J. Skea, P.R. Shukla, A. Pirani, W. Moufouma-Okia, C. Péan, R. Pidcock, S. Connors, J.B.R. Matthews, Y. Chen, X. Zhou, M.I. Gomis, E. Lonnoy, T. Maycock, M. Tignor, and T. Waterfield (Incheon: KR: IPCC, 2018), https://www.ipcc.ch/sr15.
16 Margo McDiarmid, "Canada Sets Carbon Emissions Reduction Target of 30% by 2030," CBC News, 15 May 2015, https://www.cbc.ca/news/politics/canada-sets-carbon-emissions-reduction-target-of-30-by-2030-1.3075759.
17 United Nations Framework Convention on Climate Change, *UN Annual Climate Change Report 2018* (Bonn, DE: UNFCC, 2018), https://unfccc.int/sites/default/files/resource/UN-Climate-Change-Annual-Report-2018.pdf.
18 Lucas Powers, "Trudeau's Claim That Canada Is 'on Track' to Meet 2030 Climate Target Is Misleading," CBC News, 25 September 2019. https://www.cbc.ca/news/politics/trudeau-climate-change-2030-fact-check-1.5295961.
19 See note 17.
20 Environment and Climate Change Canada, Canadian Environmental Sustainability Indicators, "Progress towards Canada's Greenhouse Gas Emissions Reduction Target," 15 November 2019, www.canada.ca/en/environment-climate-change/services/environmental-indicators/progress-towards-canada-greenhouse-gas-emissions-reduction-target.html.
21 Paul Wells, "Canada's Carbon Tax Is up against a United Front of Powerful Conservatives," *Maclean's*, 7 November 2018, https://www.macleans.ca/politics/ottawa/a-carbon-tax-just-try-them/.
22 Environment and Climate Change Canada, *Canada's Changing Climate Report*, 2019, https://changingclimate.ca/CCCR2019/.
23 See the Canadian Press, "Flood Levels in New Brunswick Back at Last Year's Damaging Levels in Capital," CTV News Atlantic, 24 April 2019, https://atlantic.ctvnews.ca/flood-levels-in-new-brunswick-back-at-last-year-s-damaging-levels-in-capital-1.4390781; Ryan Flanagan, "1.8 Million Hectares of Canada Burned by Forest Fires So Far This Year," CTV Online News, 29 August 2019), https://www.ctvnews.ca/canada/1-8-million-hectares-of-canada-burned-by-forest-fires-so-far-this-year-1.4570733;

Roland Hughes, "Amazon Fires: What's the Latest in Brazil?," BBC News, 12 October 2019, https://www.bbc.com/news/world-latin-america-49971563.

24 S. Clayton, C.M. Manning, K. Krygsman, and M. Speiser, *Mental Health and Our Changing Climate: Impacts, Implications, and Guidance* (Washington, DC: American Psychological Association and Eco-America, 2017), https://www.apa.org/news/press/releases/2017/03/mental-health-climate.pdf.

25 Amelia Tait, "Greta Thunberg: How One Teenager Became the Voice of the Planet," *Wired*, 6 June 2019, https://www.wired.co.uk/article/greta-thunberg-climate-crisis.

26 See Suyin Haynes, "The Story behind Time's Greta Thunberg Cover," *Time*, 16 May 2019, https://time.com/collection-post/5588274/greta-thunberg-time-cover-portrait/; Tait, "Greta Thunberg"; and Olivia Marks, "Greta Thunberg Has a Powerful Message for Vogue Readers," *Vogue*, 31 July 2019, https://www.vogue.co.uk/article/greta-thunberg-vogue-september-2019-issue-cover.

27 Greta Thunberg, "Our House Is on Fire," *Guardian*, 25 January 2019, https://www.theguardian.com/environment/2019/jan/25/our-house-is-on-fire-greta-thunberg16-urges-leaders-to-act-on-climate.

28 Les Perreaux, "Canadians Take to Streets Calling for Action on Climate Change," *Globe and Mail*, 1 October 2019, https://www.theglobeandmail.com/canada/article-canadians-take-to-streets-calling-for-action-on-climate-change/.

29 Greta Thunberg, "Greta Thunberg, in Her Own Words, at the Montreal Climate March," CBC News, 27 September 2019, https://www.cbc.ca/news/canada/montreal/greta-thunberg-in-her-own-words-at-the-montreal-climate-march-1.5300803.

30 "Extreme Weather Spurs Demand for Climate Action." Abacus Data, 6 September 2019, https://abacusdata.ca/extreme-weather-spurs-demand-for-climate-action/.

31 CBC News, "House Passes Non-Binding Motion Declaring a National Climate Emergency," 18 June 2019, https://www.cbc.ca/news/politics/climate-emergency-motion-1.5179802.

32 Hilary Beaumont, "Canada Declares Climate Emergency, Then Approves Massive Oil Pipeline Expansion," *Vice*, 18 June 2019, https://www.vice.com/en_ca/article/wjvkqq/canada-justin-trudeau-declares-climate-emergency-then-approves-trans-mountain-pipeline-expansion.

33 Aaron Wherry, *Promise and Peril: Justin Trudeau in Power* (Toronto: HarperCollins, 2019).

34 See note 32.
35 Wherry made the comment during the Ottawa International Writers Festival "On Trudeau" event on 9 September 2019, with Aaron Wherry and John Ivison in discussion with CBC's Robyn Bresnahan.
36 Ivison made the comment during the Ottawa International Writers Festival "On Trudeau" event on 9 September 2019, with Aaron Wherry and John Ivison in discussion with CBC's Robyn Bresnahan.
37 Richard Zussman, "BC Premier Continues to Fight, Says 'It Does Not Matter Who Owns the Pipeline,'" Global News, 29 May 2018, https://globalnews.ca/news/4239419/bc-john-horgan-pipeline-federal-ownership/.
38 Sonya Savage, "Lastly, the Federal Government Must Step up and Assert Clear Authority over Interprovincial Pipelines: 'Death by Delay' Cannot Be Allowed to Succeed," @sonyasavage, 17 September 2019, https://twitter.com/sonyasavage/status/1174082907402452992.
39 Canadian Press, "Two Leading Canadian Activists Want Voters to Make Climate Change Their Main Priority," 3 September 2019, https://www.theglobeandmail.com/politics/article-two-leading-canadian-activists-want-voters-to-make-climate-change/.
40 Heather A. Smith, "Political Parties and Canadian Climate Change Policy," *International Journal* 64, 1 (2008–09): 47–66.
41 Fay M. Farstad, "What Explains Variation in Parties' Climate Change Salience?," *Party Politics* 24, 6 (2018): 698–707.
42 Quarterly Environics Focus Canada survey (1995–2006) via Canadian Opinion Research Archive, in Kathryn Harrison, "The Road Not Taken: Climate Change Policy in Canada and the United States," *Global Environmental Politics* 7, 4 (2007): 92–117.
43 "Canadians Have the Economic Jitters Now, But Worry about the Environment Longer Term," EKOS Politics, September 2008, http://www.ekospolitics.com/index.php/2008/09/election-issues-2/.
44 "Public Concern about Climate Change," Environics Institute for Survey Research, 2015, https://www.environicsinstitute.org/docs/default-source/project-documents/focus-canada-2015-canadian-public-opinion-on-climate-change/public-concern-about-climate-change.pdf?sfvrsn=b2254868_2.
45 All details about the Conservative plan in this section are from: Conservative Party of Canada, *A Real Plan to Protect the Environment*, 2019, http://s3.documentcloud.org/documents/6162205/A-Real-Plan.pdf.
46 "1 in 2 Canadians Say Action to Reduce Emissions Is 'Urgent,'" Abacus Data, 13 September 2019, https://abacusdata.ca/1-in-2-canadians-say-action-to-reduce-emissions-is-urgent/.

47 "Focus Canada 2015: Canadian Public Opinion on Climate Change," Environics Institute, 2 March 2015, https://www.environicsinstitute.org/projects/project-details/focus-canada-2015-canadian-public-opinion-on-climate-change.
48 Nobel Prize Foundation, "Integrating Nature and Knowledge into Economics," Nobel Prize Foundation, 2018. https://www.nobelprize.org/prizes/economic-sciences/2018/popular-information/.
49 Paul Romer, "Nobel Prize-Winning Economist Says Carbon Taxes Are the Solution to Climate Change," *As It Happens*, CBC Radio, 8 October 2018, https://www.cbc.ca/radio/asithappens/as-it-happens-monday-edition-1.4843029/nobel-prize-winning-economist-says-carbon-taxes-are-the-solution-to-climate-change-1.4854639.
50 Andrew Leach, "Opinion: Conservative Climate Plan Is Cloaked in Mystery, Choked with Irony," CBC News, 12 August 2019, https://www.cbc.ca/news/canada/calgary/conservative-party-climate-plan-andrew-leach-1.5240070.
51 Elizabeth May, "Why Central Nova?," (blog), 6 April 2007, https://www.greenparty.ca/en/node/5310.
52 Green Party of Canada, *Looking Forward: A Fresh Perspective on Canada's Future*, 13 October 2008, https://issuu.com/canadiangreens/docs/looking_forward.
53 Green Party of Canada, "Election Platform 2019," https://www.greenparty.ca/en/platform.
54 Katherine Hayhoe and Andrew Leach, "How the Four Federal Parties' Climate Plans Stack Up," *Chatelaine*, 3 October 2019, https://www.chatelaine.com/living/politics/2019-federal-election-climate/.
55 Alex Ballingall, "Green Party's 'Fully Costed' Platform Gets a Failing Grade from Former Parliamentary Budget Officer," *Toronto Star*, 25 September 2019, https://www.thestar.com/politics/federal/2019/09/25/green-partys-fully-costed-platform-gets-a-failing-grade-from-former-parliamentary-budget-officer.html.
56 "IFSD Fiscal Credibility Assessment: Green Party of Canada Platform 2019 Costing," Institute of Fiscal Studies and Democracy, 25 September 2019, https://www.ifsd.ca/en/blog/last-page-blog/green-2019-platform.
57 Ibid., 3 October 2019, https://ifsd.ca/en/blog/last-page-blog/green-2019-platform-2.
58 Elizabeth May, MP Saanich-Gulf Islands and former Green Party leader, interview with Susan Harada in Ottawa, 5 November 2019.
59 All details about the Liberal platform in this section are from: Liberal Party of Canada, "A Climate Vision That Moves Canada Forward,

24 September 2019, https://www.liberal.ca/a-climate-vision-that-moves-canada-forward/.
60 Environment and Climate Change Canada, *Progress towards Canada's Greenhouse Gas Emissions Reduction Target: Canadian Environmental Sustainability Indicators*, https://www.canada.ca/content/dam/eccc/documents/pdf/cesindicators/progress-towards-canada-greenhouse-gas-reduction-target/2020/progress-ghg-emissions-reduction-target.pdf.
61 Brad Plumer, "New UN Climate Report Says Put a High Price on Carbon," *New York Times*, 8 October 2018, thttps://www.nytimes.com/2018/10/08/climate/carbon-tax-united-nations-report-nordhaus.html.
62 Andrew Leach, "Liberals' Climate Balancing Act: The World Is Watching," CBC News, 25 September 2019, https://www.cbc.ca/news/canada/calgary/road-ahead-liberal-party-climate-plan-andrew-leach-1.5295477.
63 See note 55.
64 Emma Paling. "Jagmeet Singh Uses 'Mr. Delay and Mr. Deny' Nicknames to Jab at Trudeau and Scheer, *Huffington Post Canada*, 7 October, https://www.huffingtonpost.ca/entry/jagmeet-singh-mr-delay-mr-deny_ca_5d9be6a7e4b0993898053454.
65 All details about the NDP platform in this section are from: New Democratic Party, *Power to Change: A New Deal for Climate Action and Good Jobs*, https://action.ndp.ca/page/-/2019/Q2/Power-to-change-full-announcement.pdf.
66 Andrew Leach, "Opinion: NDP Climate Plan Tries (and Fails) to Carve out Middle Ground." CBC News, 13 September 2019, https://www.cbc.ca/news/canada/calgary/ndp-climate-plan-andrew-leach-1.5276006.
67 "Here Are Canada's Political Parties' Views on the Environment." the weathernetwork.com, 17 October 2019, https://www.theweathernetwork.com/ca/news/article/canada-political-party-view-on-the-environment-election-canada-liberal-conservative-party-ndp-green-party-bloc-quebecois.
68 Government of Quebec, "The Carbon Market, a Green Economy Growth Tool!," http://www.environnement.gouv.qc.ca/changementsclimatiques/marche-carbone_en.asp.
69 Federal Leaders' English Language Debate, 7 October 2019, https://www.macleans.ca/politics/federal-election-leaders-debate-2019-live-video/.
70 See note 68.
71 Vassy Kapelos, "Everyone Won!," @VassyKapelos, 10:40 p.m., 21 October 2019, Twitter.
72 Vassy Kapelos, "I Wasn't Being Serious – Just Reacting to All the Leaders' Speeches Which Seemed to Indicate They Thought They Won," @VassyKapelos, 11:07 p.m., 21 October 2019, Twitter.

73 Maxime Bernier's People's Party of Canada did not win any seats and gleaned but a tiny 1.6 percent of the vote. Had it achieved significant resonance with Canadian voters, it would have been worth noting that the party did not accept the scientific evidence for climate change.
74 All details about the CBC series and Markus Harvey in this section are from: CBC, "Undecided Voter Talks about Face to Face with Andrew Scheer," CBC Player, 2019, https://www.cbc.ca/player/play/1612680259603.
75 Jenica Atwin, As It Happens, Carol Off, CBC Radio, 2019, https://www.cbc.ca/radio/asithappens/as-it-happens-tuesday-edition-1.5330601/green-party-s-1st-mp-outside-b-c-says-flooding-made-climate-change-top-issue-in-her-n-b-riding-1.5330612.
76 "Speech from the Throne to Open the First Session of the Forty-Third Parliament of Canada," Government of Canada, 2019, https://www.canada.ca/en/privy-council/campaigns/speech-throne/moving-forward-together.html.
77 "Elizabeth May Comments on Throne Speech," CPAC 2019, https://www.cpac.ca/en/programs/cpac-special/episodes/66121190/.
78 Peter Zimonjic, "Tories, NDP Won't Support Throne Speech But Bloc Will Back Liberals' Agenda If It Comes to Vote," CBC News, 5 December 2019, https://www.cbc.ca/news/politics/tories-ndp-bloc-speech-reaction-1.5386369.
79 See note 41.
80 See note 58.
81 "Four Weeks in, Climate Change Is Fastest-Moving (29%, +4), but Health Care (35%) Still Top Issue to Make a Difference at the Ballot Box," Ipsos, 9 October 2019, https://www.ipsos.com/en-ca/news-polls/Four-Weeks-In-Climate-Change-Fastest-Moving-Health-Care-Still-Top-Issue.
82 Susan Harada, "The Promise of May: The Green Party of Canada's Campaign 2008," in *The Canadian Federal Election of 2008*, ed. Jon H. Pammett, and Christopher Dornan (Toronto: Dundurn, 2009), 162–93.
83 Susan Harada, "Opportunities and Obstacles: The Green Party of Canada's 2015 Campaign," in *The Canadian Federal Election of 2015*, ed. Jon H. Pammett and Christopher Dornan (Toronto: Dundurn, 2015). 141–62.
84 Gary Mason, "Why the Greens Should Consider Merging with the NDP," *Globe and Mail*, 7 November 2019, https://www.theglobeandmail.com/opinion/article-why-the-greens-should-consider-merging-with-the-ndp/.

7

A Close Race from Start to Finish: Polling in the 2019 Federal Election

Éric Grenier

The story of public opinion polling in the 2019 federal election is a success story. The polls did what they are supposed to do in the context of any election campaign. They informed Canadians about the general dynamics of the election and how opinion shifted over the six weeks of the campaign – particularly after a few key events. They also gave voters reasonable expectations of what was likely to occur on election day, even though their conclusions could not be exact. Furthermore, the polls – in the aggregate and individually – were quite accurate. Nearly every polling firm's final set of numbers published in the last week of the campaign put the gap in support for the Liberals and the Conservatives within the margin of error (whether applicable or otherwise). After all the votes were counted, the margin between the two parties was little more than a percentage point. Polls also informed Canadians about what their fellow citizens thought of the leaders and what issues were the most important to them in deciding how they would cast their ballot.

There was no big surprise on election night – though there were a few small upsets and some parties over- or under-performed the poll estimates. But even that was informative about what happened at the ballot box. Overall, the polls said it would be close in the popular vote. Deeper analyses of the regional data also suggested that the Liberals were more likely to win the most seats, even if they lost the popular vote, because of how their vote was distributed across the country. And, in the end, that is exactly what happened.

A CHANGING POLLING LANDSCAPE

With the media landscape continuing to change and evolve, the relationship that pollsters have with the media has shifted in concert. Before the internet, when newspapers and nightly newscasts dominated election coverage, the release of polls was an important campaign event. Polls were commissioned relatively infrequently and were quite costly, involving close cooperation between the pollsters and journalists. Reduced budgets now mean fewer media outlets have the resources to dedicate to high-quality polling. Accordingly, in some cases the cost of a poll in a formal relationship between pollster and media outlet is little more than nominal. Election polling is considered a "loss leader" for pollsters, the purpose of which is primarily promotional in nature and as a demonstration of a polling firm's capabilities, though more cost-effective methods of polling via interactive voice response (IVR) or over the internet mitigates the loss and contributes to the large number of polls published during modern campaigns. The availability of public polling (commissioned by the media or, as is increasingly common, self-commissioned by pollsters) reduces the news value of any individual poll, acting as a further disincentive for any media outlet to dedicate resources and coverage to a single poll or pollster.

The polls that were published during the course of the forty-day campaign came in all different shapes and sizes. Some pollsters retained formal relationships with individual media organizations, others had more informal arrangements, and yet others self-published their data. Polls were conducted with live interviewers over the telephone, via IVR, or from internet panels of respondents. A few pollsters also used hybrid methods, combining telephone and online samples or using both live interviewers and IVR in their telephone sampling.

Over the course of the campaign, just under 120 national polls were published, or nearly three per day.[1] This is on par with recent federal election campaigns, which have featured between 1.5 and 3.1 polls published per day.[2] In addition to these, polls for individual provinces or regions were also published – by Insights West in British Columbia and Probe Research in Manitoba, for example – along with dozens of riding-level polls conducted by Mainstreet Research for *iPolitics* and the Groupe Capitale Médias (GCM) network of French-language newspapers.

The riding polls published through *iPolitics* were largely only available through the online news site's "Election Premium" subscription and so were not freely accessible to the general public;[3] However, Mainstreet's riding polls conducted in Quebec were published in GCM's papers and websites.

In addition to Mainstreet's daily poll releases through *iPolitics*, Nanos Research also had a formal relationship with the *Globe and Mail* and CTV News and published daily results from a three-day rolling sample of four hundred respondents per day (increased to eight hundred over the final weekend). Nanos required a paid subscription for access to the full regional and demographic breakdown from its polls.[4] Ipsos, which polled for Global News, also required that users sign a terms of service agreement in order to have access to the full results. This agreement explicitly ruled out the use of the data in seat projection models. The use of subscriptions or terms of service agreements tied to polling data was a new development in this federal election campaign and forced some poll aggregators (described below) to use only the publicly available (and sometimes incomplete) data that were posted by these pollsters and/or reported in the media.

Léger worked with the Canadian Press, French-language television network TVA, and *Le Journal de Montréal* throughout the campaign. Forum Research largely released its data through the *Toronto Star* and *Montreal Gazette*, and Dart &Maru/Blue Voice Canada through the *Toronto Sun*. Abacus Data, Angus Reid Institute, Campaign Research, EKOS Research, Innovative Research Group, and Research Co. all self-published national polls during the campaign.

Another feature of the election was the presence of poll aggregators. While there were a number of websites and blogs that published polling averages and seat projections, there were two that had by far the most prominence. Throughout the campaign, CBC News operated the Poll Tracker, which was designed and maintained by the author.[5] CBC News had published a Poll Tracker in the 2015 federal election campaign as well as in the provincial elections held since then in British Columbia, Alberta, Saskatchewan, Manitoba, Ontario, Quebec, New Brunswick, and Nova Scotia. The other prominent aggregator was the website *338Canada.com*, run by Philippe J. Fournier, and whose results were published on the websites of *Maclean's* and *L'actualité*.[6] Fournier had previously published projections for provincial elections in Ontario, Alberta, and Quebec. Both sites presented weighted polling averages that combined all available polling data. Weighting factors varied according to each aggregator but included factors such as the date of a poll, the size of the sample, and the track record of each individual polling firm. These sites also presented seat projections (again, with differing methodologies but largely employing a uniform or proportional swing from the last election's results) and probability estimates for the various outcomes, including a Liberal or Conservative majority or a plurality of seats for either party. The two sites were very popular and widely cited during the campaign. On election day, *338Canada.com* received over a million hits and the CBC's Poll Tracker peaked at over a million unique visitors.[7]

HOW THE POLLS TOLD THE STORY OF THE CAMPAIGN

As 2019 began, the Liberals had reasonable hopes of securing another majority government in October. With the exception of the brief period following Prime Minister Justin Trudeau's controversial trip to India, the Liberals had consistently led in the polls since the 2015 election. Though Andrew Scheer's Conservatives had closed the gap in Ontario, the Liberals held solid leads of at least twenty percentage points in Atlantic Canada and Quebec and so were well positioned to win at least the 170 seats required for a majority government.[8] That changed in the wake of the SNC-Lavalin affair. By mid-February, the Liberals had dropped behind the Conservatives in national polling and did not move back into a tie with the Conservatives until the first week of September – just before the election call on 11 September.

That close race in the national polls endured for the first week of the campaign. Polls gave the Liberals between 32 and 37 percent support over that time, compared to a range of 32 to 38 percent for the Conservatives. The numbers put both parties potentially on the cusp of a majority government, particularly because of the weakness of the other parties. The New Democrats were polling in the low teens and the Greens in the high single digits. This suggested that the NDP was in danger of losing recognized party status in the House of Commons (at least twelve seats) while the Greens could put up a good number in the popular vote without necessarily taking away many seats from the other parties. In Quebec, the Bloc Québécois was stuck below 20 percent.

THE IMPACT OF THE BLACKFACE SCANDAL

There were a few indications that if any party had momentum going into the first days of the campaign, it was the Liberal Party. The Liberals had closed the gap on the Conservatives in the waning days of the summer and their numbers were looking marginally better in the first days after the election call. But any hopes that the Liberals might have had that they could carry that momentum through to election day were dashed on 18 September when it was revealed that Trudeau had worn blackface on multiple occasions before entering politics. From that point in the campaign, the Liberals were unable to make any more headway in the polls.

Still, after four years of seeing the prime minister preach the values of tolerance, surveys suggested that Canadians were largely prepared to give the prime minister the benefit of the doubt. An Abacus Data poll conducted in the immediate aftermath of the scandal found that, among Canadians who were aware of the story, 42 percent said "[it] didn't bother me really." Another 34 percent said, "[I] didn't like it, but [Trudeau] apologized properly and I can move on." Only 24 percent said they were "truly offended and [it] changed [their] view of Mr. Trudeau for the worse." Nearly two-thirds of those who were most offended intended to vote Conservative. Only 12 percent of respondents said that it would make them reconsider voting Liberal, and this was highest among young voters.[9]

Despite the unprecedented nature of the scandal, there was no significant movement in the polls. The Conservatives and Liberals remained deadlocked in the national popular vote. In the thirty-eight national surveys published between 19 and 30 September, only five put the margin between the two parties at four points or more. By the end of September, the blackface scandal had already receded in the public's mind. An Abacus Data survey conducted between 22 and 26 September found that the number of Canadians who said they were offended had decreased by four points, dropping to just 20 percent.[10] The damage to the brands of the Liberal Party and Trudeau had already been "baked in" by this point – damage caused by the SNC-Lavalin affair, significant dissatisfaction with the Liberal government in the Prairie provinces, and disillusionment with the prime minister among progressive voters. A late-campaign Ipsos poll found that 58 percent of Canadians said the SNC-Lavalin affair was very or somewhat important in their voting decision, compared to just 32 percent who said the same about the blackface scandal.[11] The blackface scandal might have made it more difficult for the Liberals to recover from the other issues weighing them down, but it did not have a significant impact on their existing support. According to Dan Arnold, the Liberal Party's director of research, while participants in focus groups reported disappointment with Trudeau, they also said they did not believe the prime minister was a racist and considered his apology to be sincere.[12] The capital that Trudeau had built up on issues of tolerance during his years in office mitigated the potential damage the blackface scandal could have had.

THE TURNING POINT IN QUEBEC

With the race still deadlocked, the three debates held between 1 and 10 October took on special importance. Polls suggest that the debate that had the most impact was the one organized by the TVA television network, pitting Trudeau and Scheer against NDP leader Jagmeet Singh and Bloc leader Yves-François Blanchet. Held entirely in French, the debate gave Blanchet his first big platform of the campaign, while it exposed Scheer's struggles with the French language and how his party's policies were out of step with mainstream Quebec opinion, particularly on issues like abortion, same-sex marriage, and pipelines. A survey by Léger found that, among those Quebecers who had watched the debate, 58 percent chose Blanchet as the winner, compared to 20 percent who chose Trudeau, 11 percent who chose Singh, and just 3 percent who chose Scheer. Unlike supporters of either the Liberals or New Democrats, Conservative voters did not choose their own leader as the winner of the debate – by a margin of nearly five to one, Conservative voters in Quebec chose Blanchet as the winner of the debate over Scheer.[13] Other polls corroborated Léger's findings that Blanchet was the winner of the debate.

This was a turning point for the campaign in Quebec, with significant repercussions for the overall dynamics of the election campaign. On 1 October, the aggregate of the Poll Tracker had the Conservatives at 21 percent support in Quebec and the Bloc at 20 percent, both parties trailing the Liberals, who were at 35 percent support. Over the next twenty days, the Bloc made a daily gain of about half a percentage point in Quebec as support for the Liberals, Conservatives, and Greens slipped. The polls indicated better results for the New Democrats from this point, though that did not materialize on election day.

The rise of the Bloc – the party captured 32.5 percent of the vote – changed the electoral calculations for the other parties. Before the TVA debate, the Liberals had reasonable hopes of making gains in Quebec, perhaps as many as ten to fifteen seats. All else being equal, the Liberals would have been returned with a majority government had they secured these gains. The Conservatives, who had their own hopes of doubling their seat count in Quebec from 2015's result of twelve, lost a couple of seats in the province instead. Before the debates, the Bloc was in the running for perhaps fifteen seats. It won thirty-two instead, blocking the path to a majority government for the Liberals, winning two seats from the Conservatives, and contributing to the virtual wipeout of the New Democrats in Quebec. Two of the NDP's strongest incumbents in the province – Ruth Ellen Brosseau in Berthier-Maskinongé and Guy Caron in Rimouski-Neigette-Témiscouata-Les Basques — were defeated by Bloc candidates.

THE IMPACT OF THE ENGLISH-LANGUAGE DEBATE

Two factors contributed to making a majority government for either the Liberals or the Conservatives increasingly unlikely as election day approached. The rise of the Bloc was the more important one. The other factor was the rise of the New Democrats following Singh's performance in the English-language debate. When it was held on 7 October, the event organized by the debate commission came when Singh's campaign was going relatively well. Unlike Trudeau, Scheer, or Green leader Elizabeth May, who had each been distracted at some point in the campaign by self-inflicted errors, Singh's campaign was going smoothly. He had been widely lauded – even by some of his opponents – for his heartfelt and personal response to Trudeau's blackface photos. But it was the English-language debate that seemed to have the most galvanizing effect on NDP support.

At the outset of the campaign, it appeared that the NDP's greatest foe was the Green Party, which was coming off a series of provincial and federal election breakthroughs in the previous year. A number of surveys, though not most, put the Greens either tied with or ahead of the NDP in the run-up to the election call. But by the beginning of October, the New Democrats had put some space between themselves and the Greens. When the writs were drawn up, the Poll Tracker put the Greens behind the NDP by just two points. On 7 October, the gap was nearly six points. Nevertheless, the trend line was relatively flat for the NDP – the widening gap was more the result of a drop in support for the Greens. Singh was improving his own personal ratings at this stage (see below), but it wasn't yet translating into significant gains in support for his party.

The English-language debate was a crowded affair, making it difficult for any leader to stand out. Scheer and Trudeau spent much of the debate bickering and talking over each other, providing Singh an opportunity for a few good one-liners that endeared him to members of the audience – both those inside the Museum of History in Gatineau, Quebec, and those watching on television. According to a post-debate poll conducted by Abacus Data, 59 percent of people who had watched or heard about the debate came away with a positive reaction towards Singh.[14] Only 11 percent had a negative reaction. That was by far the best result for any leader, with 39 percent having a positive reaction to May and 36 percent for Scheer and Trudeau (both had marginally more respondents who said they had a negative reaction to them).

Twenty-nine percent of respondents said Singh had done the most to earn their vote, edging out Trudeau and Scheer, who each scored 23 percent. But just 6 percent said Singh had done the most to lose their vote, compared to 30 percent for Trudeau and 35 percent for Scheer. In other words, Singh's performance was a net positive for his party. Trudeau's and Scheer's were a net negative. Other surveys showed similar findings, pegging Singh as the English-language debate winner – though perhaps by a lesser margin than Blanchet in the first French-language debate. Following the debate, the NDP's numbers began to rise. From 14.5 percent in the Poll Tracker on 7 October, the NDP gained four percentage points through to election day – a gain of about two points per week in the final stages of the campaign. This further narrowed the field for the Liberals and Conservatives, leaving fewer seats on the table for either party to cobble together the 170 seats needed for a majority government.

THE FINAL POLLS

By the last days of the campaign, media coverage was dominated by the question of how the leaders would make a minority Parliament work. Scheer portrayed the options as a choice between a Conservative majority government or a costly Liberal-NDP coalition. Trudeau argued the country needed a "progressive government" in Ottawa to prevent a return to the "Harper years," while Singh, May, and Blanchet asked Canadians to give them the balance of power. This discussion was definitely influenced by the polls, which showed a majority government to be unlikely. Voters motivated to vote strategically – which post-election polling suggested could have been as many as a third of voters[15] – were given mixed signals from the polls. The close race suggested that the Liberals were at risk of losing the election, though the potential for a Conservative majority government was also relatively small, potentially lowering the stakes for strategic voters. Still, the NDP did under-perform expectations in the Greater Toronto Area to the benefit of the Liberals, a possible sign of strategic voting. But this also could have helped the NDP elsewhere. The improvement of the New Democrats' standings in the polls signalled to voters on the left that it was that party, and not the Greens, that was the best vehicle for their vote. This might have contributed to the disappointing performances for the Greens on Vancouver Island, the one region of the country in which the NDP and Greens were in direct competition for seats.

The final polls still put the Liberals and Conservatives neck-and-neck in the national popular vote, as they had done throughout the campaign. The final numbers also suggested that the momentum for the New Democrats and Bloc Québécois might have stalled, indicating that there was unlikely to be a major surprise from either party on election night. Polls conducted at least partially over the last three days of campaign showed that support for both the Liberals and Conservatives had slumped since September. The Conservatives polled between 30 and 33 percent and the Liberals between 31 and 34 percent – a lower floor and ceiling from the first week of the campaign. Three polls gave the Conservatives a lead of between 0.6 and 2 points, 6 gave the Liberals a lead of between 0.6 and 4 points, and 5 had the gap at 0.5 percentage points or less. The NDP was pegged at between 16 and 21 percent, the Greens between 5.5 and 9.5 percent, the Bloc between 5 and 9 percent (or between 22 and 37 percent in Quebec) and Maxime Bernier's People's Party between 1.5 and 3.5 percent.

The final results were largely within these ranges, particularly when taking into account the margins of error of the polls. The Conservatives out-performed the polls slightly with 34.4 percent of the vote, the Liberals were also on the higher side of estimates with 33.1 percent, and the New Democrats were overestimated, finishing with 15.9 percent of the vote. The Bloc and Greens were well within the final estimates, with 7.7 percent and 6.5 percent, respectively, while the People's Party finished on the low end with just 1.6 percent of the vote.

FINAL POLL ACCURACY

While it was not a perfect call for the polls, it was very close to it. Of the twelve pollsters who released national numbers in the final week of the campaign, all but three estimated the Conservatives' final results to within 3.4 percentage points, while all but two had the Liberals within 2.1 points and the NDP within 3.1 points. There was no single polling method that out-performed the others. The final surveys by Léger for *Le Journal de Montréal* and by Abacus Data had the lowest total error and were both conducted online. The Mainstreet Research/*iPolitics* and Ipsos/Global News surveys were the next two closest to the mark, with Mainstreet surveying by IVR and Ipsos using a hybrid telephone and online mode of contact. The performance of the average online, telephone, or IVR poll was largely similar, despite the significant differences in methodology and the challenges each mode of contact has in assembling a representative sample. Nanos Research, which conducted its polls over the telephone with live interviewers, reported a 7 percent response rate in its final poll of the campaign.[16] Forum Research, using the IVR method, reported a response rate of just under 2 percent.[17] These response rates are in line with industry norms but illustrate the trade-off between the two telephone methods. Polling with live interviewers gets a better response rate and generally requires less weighting of the sample than IVR, but it is far more expensive. IVR polling gets a worse response rate but is significantly cheaper, making it easier to assemble a large sample. But respondents are less willing to stay on the phone for a long time with a machine, which limits the length of the survey and so the number of questions that can be asked. Internet surveys, with a cost somewhere in between the two but the ability to go into great depth with respondents, are still dependent on the quality of the assembled panel. Table 7.1 shows the performance of each pollster.

Every pollster underestimated support for the Conservatives by between 1.4 and 4.4 percentage points and by an average of 2.7 points overall. There are a number of factors that could explain this, including the tendency for the Conservatives to have more support among

Table 7.1
Final polls of the campaign and the total error compared to results

Pollster	Dates	Lib	Con	BQ	NDP	Grn	PPC	Oth	Error
Léger (Int.)	16–18 Oct.	33%	33%	8%	18%	6%	2%	0%	5.6
Abacus (Int.)	17–19 Oct.	34%	32%	8%	16%	8%	2%	1%	5.8
Mainstreet (IVR)	19–20 Oct.	31.6%	32.2%	7.9%	18.3%	6.1%	2.8%	1.1%	8.2
Ipsos (Tel. + Int.)	17–19 Oct.	31%	33%	7%	18%	6%	3%	1%	8.4
Nanos (Tel.)	20 Oct.	31.7%	32.5%	7.2%	20.8%	6.0%	1.5%	0.1%	10.0
Research (Int.)	18–20 Oct.	32%	31%	7%	19%	8%	2%	1%	10.4
Forum (IVR)	18 Oct.	32%	30%	9%	18%	8%	3%	1%	12.0
Dart (Int.)	16 Oct.	29%	33%	8%	21%	7%	2%	1%	12.0
Angus Reid (Int.)	12–15 Oct.	29%	33%	8%	19%	8%	3%	1%	12.0
Campaign (Int.)	16–20 Oct.	31%	31%	7%	18%	9%	3%	1%	12.4
Innovative (Int.)	15–17 Oct.	34%	30%	6%	19%	8%	2%	0%	12.8
EKOS (IVR + Tel.)	17–20 Oct.	34.2%	30.0%	5.0%	18.3%	8.1%	3.5%	0.8%	14.1

older voters, who vote in greater numbers than younger voters. The Conservatives also consistently had the most committed supporters during the campaign and those who were least likely to be considering other options. But there was also a regional aspect to the underestimation of Conservative support. On average, the final surveys published by the twelve pollsters underestimated Conservative support by only 1.6 points in Quebec, 1.1 points in Atlantic Canada, and 0.8 points in Ontario. In fact, unlike at the national level, at least one pollster overestimated Conservative support in each of these regions. In western Canada, however, the Conservatives were underestimated by virtually every pollster – and often by significant amounts. The Conservatives did 3.7 points better in British Columbia than the polls suggested they would, 7.2 points better in Saskatchewan and Manitoba, and 10 points better in Alberta. This represented about 2.1 percentage points at the national level, or roughly three-quarters of the polls' total national error for the party, a significant underestimation of the result.

The Liberals were underestimated by only 1.2 percentage points, and some individual pollsters did overestimate their support. Regionally, the Liberals were most underestimated in Ontario. On average, the polls gave the party 38.3 percent support in the province, compared to the 41.4 percent the party actually received. This error was largely responsible for the general underestimation of the Liberals' seat potential in aggregators *like 338Canada.com* and the CBC's Poll Tracker, though pollsters like Mainstreet Research and EKOS Research, both of whom published seat projections but also showed greater support for the Liberals in Ontario than other pollsters, were closer to the mark.

The New Democrats were overestimated by all pollsters by between 0.1 and 5.1 percentage points. On average, the NDP under-shot its polls by 2.7 points and in every region of the country – potentially as a result of strategic voting as some New Democrats (and Greens, who were also overestimated) flocked to the Liberals in the final days of the campaign. Post-election polling suggests this was a likely possibility.[18]

Table 7.2 shows how each party performed across the country compared to its polling.

These results partially explain some of the differences between most seat projections and the final results. Nearly across the board, seat projections gave the Liberals the plurality of seats, but, on average, seat projections underestimated the Liberals by seventeen seats and overestimated the New Democrats by eleven. The Conservatives and Bloc Québécois were also slightly overestimated.[19] The under-performance of the New Democrats and the over-performance of the Liberals in Ontario and Atlantic Canada was the main contributor to seat projectors' error. The resilience of some Liberal incumbents, as well as the impact of the loss of NDP MPs in the 2015 election who did run again in 2019, was also an important factor. Like the polls, however, seat projections were only off in some of the details and not in the overall portrait of the race.

HOW CANADIANS VIEWED THE LEADERS

Surveys about party leadership showed significant shifts over the course of the campaign, in contrast to the measures of voting intention. There was general stability in Trudeau's approval ratings, but the polls recorded a sharp decrease in voters' views of Scheer and an even greater improvement in how Canadians viewed Singh.

Forum Research and Campaign Research each consistently surveyed approval ratings during the campaign.[20] In July and August, the two polling firms found Trudeau's approval rating between 33 and 34 percent, compared to a disapproval rating of 53 to 55 percent. By the end of the campaign, those numbers were largely unchanged, with

Table 7.2
Average overestimation (+) and underestimation (−) of each party's support in the final polls of the campaign

	Canada	BC	AB	PR	ON	QC	AC
Lib	−1.2	+1.0	+2.8	+2.7	−3.1	−1.8	−2.3
Con	−2.7	−3.7	−10.0	−7.2	−0.8	−1.6	−1.1
NDP	+2.7	+1.1	+3.8	+1.8	+2.4	+1.8	+3.0
BQ	−0.4					−0.9	
Grn	+0.8	+0.5	+1.7	+1.8	+0.9	+1.8	−0.4
PPC	+0.9	+1.4	+1.4	+0.6	+0.8	+1.1	+1.4

an approval rating of between 31 and 39 percent and a disapproval rating of between 53 and 54 percent. Scheer's approval rating – 27 to 29 percent – did not increase over the course of the campaign, but his disapproval rating went up by about ten points, from 48 to 57 percent according to Forum and from 43 to 53 percent according to Campaign. That gave Scheer a worse net rating than Trudeau.

Singh saw even more significant movement. Forum found the NDP leader's approval rating shooting from 24 percent in July to 52 percent in the final days of the campaign, his disapproval rating dropping twelve points to just 27 percent. Campaign Research found similar improvements, with his approval rating jumping twenty-six points to 49 percent and his disapproval dropping eleven points to 22 percent. This means Singh went from having a net-negative approval rating before the campaign to a net-positive one by the end of it. However, this did not translate into similarly significant gains for the New Democratic Party at the ballot box – compared to final results, the NDP only did about two percentage points better on election day than it was doing in the polls over the summer.

Polling by Abacus Data found similar trend lines over the course of the campaign on the question of whether Canadians had a "positive or negative" impression of each of the leaders. Trudeau began the campaign with 35 percent of Canadians saying they held a positive impression of him, compared to 46 percent who had a negative one. Those numbers held firm throughout the campaign, with the one exception of the post-blackface survey conducted by Abacus. That poll found Trudeau's positives had gone down to an all-time low of 31 percent and his negatives were up to 49 percent. But the Liberal leader was back to 35 percent holding a positive impression of him by the first week of October, and he ended the campaign with a 38 percent to 45 percent positive-to-negative ratio. Perhaps key to the Liberals' election success was that Trudeau's positive ratings increased by seven points in Ontario between the start and end of the campaign.

Scheer was unable to make a positive impression not only during the campaign but also throughout 2019. According to Abacus Data, 29 percent of Canadians held a positive impression of Scheer in February. By the end of the campaign, only 31 percent had a positive impression. His negative score consistently went up throughout the year and increased from 38 percent the day before the election call to 47 percent two days before the election was held. His numbers had deteriorated significantly in both Ontario and Quebec, the two provinces in which the Conservatives lost support compared to the 2015 election.

In the head-to-head match-up of who Canadians preferred to be prime minister, Trudeau held a wide advantage over Scheer, despite being pegged neck-and-neck in party support. Abacus found 37 percent of Canadians preferred Trudeau to be prime minister, compared to just 31 percent for Scheer. The gap had widened between the two leaders from two to six points over the course of the campaign. Still, Trudeau faced some serious challenges concerning his own personal image. Léger found that 37 percent of Canadians said that Trudeau was "the most hypocritical" of the federal leaders, far out-pacing Scheer's 23 percent. He was also seen as "the most fake" by a margin of 36 to 23 percent and "the most elitist" by a 29 to 18 percent split. On who was considered the most honest or the most trustworthy, the two leaders were roughly tied.[21] But Scheer also had his own problems with his personal image. Innovative Research Group found that 44 percent of Canadians thought Scheer was much or somewhat more negative than positive, while just 23 percent said he was more positive than negative during the campaign. Trudeau's numbers were more evenly divided, with 36 percent saying he was more negative and 30 percent saying he was more positive. Singh was the highest-scoring leader on this question, with just 16 percent saying he was more negative and 45 percent saying he was more positive.[22]

Singh's positive impression scores sky-rocketed after the English-language debate in the Abacus polls. At the beginning of the campaign, 30 percent of Canadians had a positive impression of Singh, compared to 28 percent with a negative impression. In Abacus Data's pre-debate poll, that had hardly changed – 32 to 25 percent. But the next survey showed Singh's positives jumped to 41 percent, while his negatives fell to 22 percent. The increase was significant in Ontario and British Columbia but not in Quebec – where the New Democrats were reduced from sixteen seats in 2015 to just one seat in 2019. Elizabeth May did not have the same success over the campaign. She began it with 33 percent having a positive impression and just 19 percent a negative one. In Abacus's 19 October survey, her positive score was down to 27 percent and her negative rating had increased to 25 percent. Singh's personal image improved on a number of fronts during the campaign, according to surveys by Innovative Research Group. At the outset, just 8 percent of Canadians said Singh was the leader best described as having "strong leadership." By the end of the campaign, that had nearly doubled to 15 percent. His score on being "competent" increased from 9 percent to 16 percent, and by the campaign's end he was narrowly ahead of Trudeau and Scheer as the leader who most "represents positive change" and "cares about people like me." Green leader May, who was marginally ahead of Singh on representing positive change in the first two weeks of the campaign, dropped well behind the NDP leader by the end – a telling example of where the Greens missed an opportunity in this election. Meanwhile, both Trudeau and Scheer saw their scores on leadership, competency, representing positive change, and caring about "people like me" decrease slightly over the course of the campaign. The survey also found that, while Trudeau's numbers remained largely constant, the proportion of Canadians saying Scheer was the leader most seen as "too negative" or "dishonest" increased by seven percentage points.[23]

THE IMPORTANT ISSUES OF THE CAMPAIGN

Polls before and during the campaign consistently showed a number of issues being top of mind for voters: pocketbook issues like the economy, taxes and cost of living, and climate change. At the beginning of September, a survey by Léger for the Canadian Press found that 35 percent of Canadians listed both "income tax and tax levels" and "job creation and economic growth" as one of their top two most important issues, with 30 percent selecting "fighting climate change."[24] No other issue scored higher than 20 percent. Respondents were far more likely to list "job creation and economic growth" in Alberta, while Quebecers and younger Canadians disproportionately cited "fighting climate change" as one of their top issues.

Abacus Data's final poll of the campaign allowed respondents to choose five issues that would "have the most to do with how you decide to vote" and found 60 percent chose cost of living – the only issue selected by a majority of respondents.[25] Three other issues scored between 42 and 44 percent: access to health care, taxes, and climate change and environment. Issues such as "government spending and deficits" and "the carbon tax" only scored 27 and 26 percent, while other issues that dominated discussion during the campaign scored even lower: pipelines/oil at 19 percent, ethical and accountable politics at 15 percent, and abortion at just 6 percent.

Both inside and outside Quebec, Bill C-21 was another dominant focus of the campaign: on the one hand, whether each of the federal leaders would respect Quebec premier François Legault's demand to leave the law unchallenged and, on the other, why federal leaders were not pledging to fight the law in the courts. Polling by Léger suggested why this issue was politically complicated.[26] A mid-campaign survey for *Le Journal de Montréal* found nationwide opinion split on the elements of Bill C-21. But in Quebec, 64 percent said they were in favour of "a ban on wearing visible religious symbols for civil servants in a position of authority (i.e., police officers, judges and grade/high school teachers)" in their province, with just 27 percent opposed. Support increased to 73 percent among French-speaking Quebecers. In the rest of the country, only 38 percent of respondents said they were in favour of such a ban, with 48 percent opposed. This showed that, while a plurality of Canadians outside of Quebec were opposed to something like Bill C-21, opposition was not nearly as widespread as was support for Bill C-21 in Quebec. Complicating matters further for the federal leaders was that just over a third of Liberal and NDP voters, and just over a majority of Conservative supporters, said they favoured the bill. Support was nearly unanimous among voters backing the Bloc Québécois, and Blanchet was the only federal leader – with the exception of Bernier – who defended Bill C-21. This undoubtedly put him in an advantageous position in his own province.

Nevertheless, the decisiveness of Bill C-21 in influencing voters' behaviour should not be overstated. A mid-campaign survey by Léger found that just 10 percent of Quebecers said that "immigration and identity" was the issue that would influence their vote the most.[27]

A WELL-UNDERSTOOD CAMPAIGN

In the aftermath of an election campaign, retrospectives on the polls tend to focus on what was missed, what wasn't understood, or what explained the surprises that occurred on election day. The dynamics of the 2019 federal election, however, were generally well understood throughout the campaign. There was always some uncertainty about the likely outcome. With the benefit of hindsight, perhaps it wasn't as uncertain as it appeared since the result widely thought to be the most likely, by the media and by the voters, did come to pass. But just because the results unfolded largely as expected doesn't mean they were inevitable.

The election was historically close. There have been closer outcomes in terms of seats, but the margin between the Liberals and the Conservatives in the popular vote – at about 1.3 percentage points – was the smallest since the 1962 election. That potentially made the election a challenging one for pollsters, which makes their success all the more noteworthy. That the election was close, that the Liberals had an advantage because of their support in Ontario and Quebec, that the Conservatives were having difficulty appealing to voters in the key swing regions of the country, that the French-language debate was a turning point for the Bloc Québécois, that the English-language debate might have brought the New Democrats back from the brink of disaster – all of these elements of the campaign were laid out and explained to voters before they went to the ballot box. Thanks to public polling, the Canadian electorate in 2019 was an informed electorate.

NOTES

1 "Opinion Polling for the 2019 Canadian Federal Election," *Wikipedia*, https://en.wikipedia.org/wiki/Opinion_polling_for_the_2019_Canadian_federal_election.
2 David Coletto, "Polling and the 2015 Federal Election," in *The Canadian Federal Election of 2015*, ed. Jon H. Pammett and Christopher Dornan (Toronto: Dundurn, 2016), 307.
3 *iPolitics*, "Elections 2019," https://ipolitics.ca/premium-election-coverage/.
4 Nanos Interactive Data Portal, https://www.nanos.co/register/nanos-data-portals-4-cad-per-month/.
5 CBC News, Poll Tracker, 20 October 2019, https://newsinteractives.cbc.ca/elections/poll-tracker/canada/. Full methodology can be found here: https://www.cbc.ca/news/politics/grenier-vote-seat-methodology-1.4054947.
6 "Polls Analysis and Electoral Projections," *338 Canada*, http://338canada.com/.

7   Information provided by Philippe J. Fournier and the author.
8   Unless otherwise noted, the polling figures are from the polling averages from the CBC Poll Tracker, https://newsinteractives.cbc.ca/elections/poll-tracker/canada/.
9   Bruce Anderson and David Coletto, "A Sensational Week, Yet a Tight Race Remains," Abacus Data, 23 September 2019, https://abacusdata.ca/a-sensational-week-yet-a-tight-race-remains/.
10 Bruce Anderson and David Coletto, "Election Poll: A Better Week for Trudeau's Liberals," Abacus Data, 27 September 2019, https://abacusdata.ca/a-better-week-for-trudeau-liberals/.
11 Darrel Bricker, "One Week from E-Day, Canadians Say They're Hearing More Negativity about Candidates and Leaders than Policy Options and Campaign Promises," Ipsos, 17 October 2019, https://www.ipsos.com/en-ca/news-polls/One-Week-from-E-Day-Canadians-Hearing-More-Negativity-About-Candidates-Leaders-than-Policy.
12 Éric Grenier, "'It Definitely Woke up the Electorate': Liberal Pollster on the Events that Shook up the Campaign," CBC News, 1 November 2019, https://www.cbc.ca/news/politics/pollcast-liberal-polling-1.5342558.
13 La Presse Canadienne, "La Politique Féderalé au Québec," Leger 360, 10 October 2019, https://leger360.com/wp-content/uploads/2019/10/Politique-fe%CC%81de%CC%81rale-au-Que%CC%81bec-10-oct-2019.pdf.
14 Bruce Anderson and David Coletto, "Election Poll: Singh Impresses at Debate While Trudeau and Scheer Break Even," Abacus Data, 10 October 2019, https://abacusdata.ca/english-debate-who-won-election-2019-canada-poll/.
15 Léger, "Federal Politics – Post-Election, 29 October 2019, https://leger360.com/surveys/federal-politics-post-election/.
16 Nanos Research, "Nanos Election Call," https://secureservercdn.net/198.71.233.47/823.910.myftpupload.com/wp-content/uploads/2019/10/2019-1445-CTV-Globe-ELXN-20191020.pdf.
17 Forum Research, news release, http://poll.forumresearch.com/data/6fb7bbcf-bdb3-479c-9e2e-0ccb6e11e75aFed%20Final%20Oct%20 20%202019.pdf.
18 For example, https://leger360.com/surveys/federal-politics-post-election/.
19 Anthony Piscitelli, "Evaluating the Election Projections," *ThreeHundredThirtyEight.com*, 22 October 2019, https://threehundredthirtyeight.com/914-2.
20 CBC News, "Éric Grenier's Leader Meter," https://www.cbc.ca/news2/interactives/leadermeter/index.html.

21 "Federal Politics- Post-Election," *Leger 360*, 7 October 2019, https://leger360.com/surveys/election-polling-2019-october-7-2019/.
22 "2019 Federal Election – Perceived Negativity," Innovative Research Group, 20 October 2019, https://innovativeresearch.ca/2019-federal-election-perceived-negativity/.
23 "2019 Federal Leadership Tracking," Innovative Research Group, 20 October 2019, https://innovativeresearch.ca/2019-federal-election-leadership-tracking-2019-10-20/.
24 "Federal Politics – September 11, 2019," *Leger 360*, https://leger360.com/surveys/federal-politics-september-11-2019/.
25 Bruce Anderson and David Coletto, "Election Poll: Regional Races and Turnout Will Decide an Election with 2-Points Separating Liberals and Conservatives in Canada," Abacus Data, 20 October 2019, https://abacusdata.ca/final-abacus-2019-canada-election-poll/.
26 "Debate on Secularism," *Leger 360*, 16 September 2019, https://leger360.com/surveys/debate-on-secularism/.
27 "Federal Politics – 25 September 2019 (Full Report)," *Leger 360*, 30 September 2019, https://leger360.com/voting-intentions/federal-politics-september-25-2019-full-report/.

8

The Media: Challenges of Covering the Campaign

Paul Adams

Like the contest among the parties, the story of the national media during a campaign typically confirms some expectations and confutes others. There was considerable fear before the campaign that the mainstream national media might be overwhelmed by malicious bots and trolls.[1] It was also predicted that the effects of the waves of newsroom cuts in recent years would be profound and that the media would be preoccupied with themes of personalities and polls that suited the modern media's preoccupation with narrative and storytelling. These expectations proved only partly true. The mainstream media, and particularly television, continued to dominate the information flow to voters. There was evidence of newsroom cuts in the coverage, but these effects were most dramatic at the local level and affected national coverage less. And although personalities and polls did play an outsized role in coverage of the campaign, many outlets and individual journalists dutifully analyzed the party platforms and raised policy issues that the parties did not adequately address. And for one week at least – with the teenage climate activist Greta Thunberg in the headlines – the media devoted considerable attention to what many polls suggested was for voters among the most important issues in the campaign: climate change.[2]

What had not been widely anticipated was the degree to which displeasure with the seeming emptiness and then nastiness of the campaign was displaced onto the media itself – a critical problem for the media at a time when both its credibility and its business model are at stake. A photograph of an all-white press corps on Justin Trudeau's campaign plane drew criticism on social media, which then renewed itself with force after the photos of a blackface Trudeau surfaced. The media played an important role in sustaining the strikingly personal nature of the campaign, surfacing, then aggressively pursuing not just the blackface story but questions about Andrew Scheer's past employment and current citizenship, and even the issue of whether a photo of Elizabeth May had been photoshopped to remove a disposable cup and replace it with a reusable container and metal straw.[3] There was a contentious debate about whom the media should allow a platform and even who could properly be considered a journalist. And journalists covering Election 2019 discovered that, in the age of social media, not only would they receive continuous commentary and feedback on their work but also that they would be routinely subject to vile personal abuse, sometimes racist and misogynist.

What follows is an account of the major themes in the national English-language media coverage of the 2019 campaign.

SOCIAL MEDIA VERSUS TRADITIONAL MEDIA

Given its enormous growth in adoption and influence in the last decade, it may be tempting to imagine that the emergence of social media threatened to occlude the role of the mainstream media at election time. But the evidence suggests that traditional media remain the most important sources of election information. A survey by Abacus Data found that more than half of respondents cited the evening national TV news as a source upon which they relied in forming their views of the election, followed by news and talk radio (45 percent), both ahead of "family and friends." Just 30 percent cited social media feeds, behind both newspaper coverage and columnists. And, of course, those citing social media as a major source for forming their views are likely to have been influenced in part by media articles to which they had been channelled.[4]

Perhaps less surprisingly, there was a decided generational skew to the data. Those eighteen to twenty-nine years of age tended to be most reliant on family and friends (59 percent), followed by social media (53 percent), followed only then by news radio, national TV news, and newspapers.[5] This is not in itself news, but it does suggest that, while mainstream media remain the most important forum in which the election plays out, their grip is likely to continue to diminish over time, if not so completely as some might imagine.

Table 8.1
How much have you been relying on these media to form your views about this election?

	A lot	Quite a bit	Not much/not at all
Nighttime national TV news	15%	38%	47%
News and talk radio	10%	35%	55%
Friends and family	10%	33%	57%
Daily newspaper coverage	9%	32%	59%
Columnists/opinion writers	5%	27%	68%
Social media feeds	9%	21%	70%

Source: Abacus Data, sample: three thousand adult Canadians, 8–10 October 2019.

There was considerable commentary during the campaign suggesting that it was unusually negative in tone.[6] Whatever the media's role in creating this much-remarked atmosphere, the preliminary evidence suggested that the public believed it saw the tone reflected in the media it consumed. An Ipsos poll conducted after the leaders' debates found that 71 percent of Canadians said that what they had heard or read about the election was negative information about candidates,[7] including party leaders; in comparison, 29 percent said what they had heard or read was focused on party platforms and what they would do if elected. In a similar vein, Innovative Research Group asked respondents mid-campaign whether they had read, seen, or heard anything in recent days about each leader.[8] By a margin of two to one, those who had heard anything about Liberal leader Justin Trudeau said it led them to think less favourably of him. Almost precisely the same was true of Conservative leader Andrew Scheer.

CORE COVERAGE

Of course, the choices made by the parties were a critical element to this negativity. It is an important function of the media at election time to allow the parties and their leaders to speak directly to voters – as well as to argue among themselves in public view – and that inevitably means reflecting their tone as well as sharing their content. Budget cuts at news organizations meant that the leaders' tours were less heavily staffed than in the past. However, most national news organizations covered the tours extensively, relying on the Canadian Press wire service, pool television feeds, and locally based reporters who turned up at individual events. Policy announcements were often

Table 8.2
Reliance on these media to form your views about this election

	A lot	Quite a bit	Not much/not at all
National TV news Age 18–29	7%	36%	57%
National TV news Age 60+	22%	44%	35%
Friends/family Age 18-29	17%	42%	42%
Friends/family Age 60+	6%	25%	69%
News/talk radio Age 18–29	11%	33%	56%
News/talk radio Age 60+	10%	36%	54%
Daily paper Age 18–29	8%	32%	60%
Daily paper Age 60+	11%	32%	57%
Social feeds Age 18–29	20%	33%	47%
Social feeds Age 60+	2%	10%	88%
Columnists Age 18–29	5%	24%	71%
Columnists Age 60+	5%	29%	66%

Source: Abacus Data, sample: three thousand adult Canadians, 8–10 October 2019.

designed by the parties to produce news, including visual elements, such as Scheer's pledge to cut income taxes, which was unveiled in a family home in White Rock, British Columbia.[9] Despite their ubiquity, these routine stories may sometimes be overlooked in discussions of campaign coverage; they perform a vital function for both the parties and voters in communicating policy and tone alike.

It is also the case that the major media devoted considerable resources away from the leaders' tours to analysis, fact-checking, social-media monitoring, and enterprise stories. In fact, it may be that some news organizations that stayed off the leaders' tours due to their prohibitive costs produced more interesting journalism as a result. The claim that the media ignored substance in favour of negative news is easily refuted. At the *Toronto Star*, columnist Chantal Hébert wrote about the policy dilemma created by a Quebec court ruling on assisted dying,[10] and her colleague Heather Scoffield carefully analyzed the parties' promises of affordability.[11] The *Globe and Mail* produced a superb, intensively researched story on suburban debt linking directly to the parties' shared concern about "affordability"[12] and a deeply reported story on an under-covered issue in the campaign, the First Nations water crisis.[13] There were policy pieces on housing affordability[14] and the dependency ratio,[15] and examinations of party platforms on child care[16] and the environment,[17] just to offer a few examples.

Of course, as the polls demonstrated, television remains the most important way in which voters consume election news. Many of the campaign's most memorable moments were visual. More specifically, they were televisual, and this also meant that they lent themselves to social media. It is impossible to imagine the blackface controversy (about which, more below) having the impact it did in the absence of photographs. Justin Trudeau's two apologies were striking as television because it was possible to observe his affect as well as to hear his words. Yet more memorable was Jagmeet Singh's reaction, speaking from the perspective of a person of colour.

Singh's rise in the polls (albeit not entirely carrying through to voting day) was closely related to these televisual moments: not only his reaction to Trudeau's blackface but also his response to a reporter's question about the cost of clean water in Indigenous communities,[18] his reaction to a man who confronted him on a Montreal street saying he should remove his turban to "look like a Canadian,"[19] and his performance in the televised debates. Andrew Scheer's most successful moment of the campaign may have been at the start of the English-language debate when he ignored the initial question but launched into a highly clipable prepared attack on Trudeau's fitness for office. As Trudeau tried to recover from the blackface controversy, his managers placed him in what were, to the media, irresistibly visual settings – in a canoe and in a boxing ring.

Broadcast media is more difficult to track than print, even unsystematically. However, a sampling of national newscasts did not suggest radical departures from traditional styles of coverage. Newscasts tended to be dominated by breaking news, often from the leaders' tours, with the usual mix of campaign announcements, gaffes, controversies, and sometimes polls. With an hour-long newscast, CBC aired more in-depth segments on policy, though not usually near the tops of newscasts, but CTV and Global also produced pieces on policy.

CBC's national newscast ran a series of forty-five-minute "face-to-face" interviews with the party leaders. In each, the leaders were questioned by a series of individual voters, with follow-up questions from the journalist Rosemary Barton. In many ways these interviews were more successful than the official English-language debate between the leaders in creating meaningful discussions of issues and providing leaders with the opportunity to explain and defend their positions at length and to be observed at length by voters.

The official English-language leaders' debate was widely panned for a format that put a premium on conflict and made it difficult to sustain a policy argument,[20] with leaders' interrupting or talking over each other in abbreviated bursts to gain the floor. In fact, the format seemed designed to encourage conflict and create an entertaining TV show rather than an educative experience for voters. However, the debate was a box-office success, with a "reach" of nearly 10 million Canadians and an average viewership of nearly 4 million people per minute. In addition, nearly 900,000 people listened to the debate on radio, and there were 2.7 million digital views.[21] By any standard, this made it an important campaign event, and the audience was more than double the audience of the most-watched debate in 2015.[22]

This was the first debate organized by the Leaders' Debate Commission, established by legislation under the Trudeau government to address the situation in 2015, when there was no formal structure and several debates were organized with different participants and rules and with limited network airplay. The lesson for any future body organizing debates is that simultaneous network airplay remains key to making the debates a widely shared voter experience, but that it is unwise simply to hand the production of the debates over to television producers rather than imposing a frame in which the voters' interests to learn about the leaders and their positions are paramount. In the French debate, which occurred a few days later, the format was tweaked to allow the leaders more time and to discourage cross-talk, producing a more satisfying forum for engaged citizenship.

The cable news channels provided extensive coverage of the campaign, including live coverage of leaders' events, packaged stories, and relentless commentary. The targeted political programs such as CTV's *Power Play* and CBC's *Power and Politics* had extremely extensive commentary on the campaign, including policy, but the dominant lens on policy was its strategic significance and impact on the polls.

I do not attempt to monitor local media coverage here. However, the Ryerson University scholar April Lindgren has documented the precipitous decline of local media in Canada. On the eve of the election, she pointed out that, since 2008, 275 local news outlets have closed in Canada, while only 105 new ones have launched.[23] Significant communities, such as Brampton, population 603,000, have become "news deserts" with little or no local coverage. Smaller communities, such as Red Deer, population 104,000, have lost a newspaper and seen a dramatic reduction in the size of remaining newsrooms. The *Ottawa Citizen,* Lindgren notes, has fallen from 160 journalists in the late 1990s to just fifty today (and it has absorbed the once-separate *Ottawa Sun* newsroom).

What this means is that, in some communities, there is literally no journalism at all on local candidates, who must connect with voters through social media and face-to-face contact. Even where outlets remain, skeleton news staffs mean there is more "rip and read" – that is, the reprocessing of press releases as news, with little independent verification, balance, or analysis. In this environment, there is often no one to look at national campaign developments or policy proposals and flesh out their implications for local communities. The exceptions are those communities with a robust CBC presence. In some communities, commercial talk radio also lavishes time on local issues; however, it works with very thin news staffs and is often reactive in its coverage, relying heavily on listeners phoning in for content.

Podcasts became a significant element in the election discourse for the first time in Election 2019. Mainstream media organizations produced many with significant election content, including *Frontburner, Pollcast, Party Lines,* and *Attention Control.* Independent podcasts such as *Safe Spaces* and *Oppo* featured voices, viewpoints, and preoccupations that were often less present in the mainstream media. Podcasts were an important venue for journalists of colour who were less well represented in the mainstream media following the leaders. Some podcasts emphasized issues such as the opioid crisis and Indigenous issues that were arguably under-covered in the general media. A common feature of many podcasts is that when they addressed policy issues, they did so at greater length and in more detail than was common even in the cable TV political talk shows, where partisan politics was often the dominant lens through which policy was discussed. The breakthrough podcast of the campaign among political insiders and the political commentariat, though, was certainly

The Herle Burly, whose success, paradoxically, may have been derived in part from the fact that it did not include any journalists along with its relentless focus on party strategy and organization from three experienced partisan campaign organizers – often to the deliberate exclusion of considering policy as substance.

NEGATIVITY

Of course, neither of the two main parties ever intended to rest their appeals to the public entirely on their promises and proposals. It was a critical element of the Conservative campaign to argue that Trudeau personally had proven himself unfit to govern, including through his role in the SNC-Lavalin affair. The Liberals, for their part, recognized that Scheer was not yet a fully defined personality for many Canadians and they were determined to fill that void themselves, reminding voters of Scheer's social conservatism and identifying him closely with former prime minister Stephen Harper and current Ontario premier Doug Ford, both unpopular among some groups of voters. These strategic decisions by the parties to be negative and personal made it inevitable that, to a degree, media coverage would also be negative and personal if it was to reflect the campaign accurately. It is a valid question whether the media could have taken measures to attenuate the disagreeable tone of the campaign or, indeed, whether it would have been appropriate to do so.

As is common in modern campaigns, especially in the age of social media, the first few days of media coverage were peppered with embarrassing incidents arising from candidates' pasts. Every party had candidates who were confronted with compromising information, in a half-dozen cases leading to candidate resignations.[24] While this was not in itself a new occurrence, some features of this media cycle were. Embarrassing information may become public in a variety of ways, including through digging by reporters or members of the public simply stepping forward. But in every election, party "war rooms" play a role, conducting research in the months and years leading up to election campaigns and then strategically seeding it in the media. In the past, this was often done by quietly leaking the information to a reporter, who would then run down the facts. If it failed the test of verification, the research might disappear without a trace. If it was confirmed by a reporter, however, it could appear in the pages of the *Globe and Mail* or on the CTV National News and be conveyed to the public with all the credibility of fully researched news.

The downside of this system from the parties' perspective was that they lost control of the process. In this election, the Liberal war room seems to have recognized three novel things. In the age of social media, getting something wrong does not run the same political danger that it once did, so the requirement of media verification is not as strong. Second, unlike the tedious documents of old, which required the careful interpretation of a reporter, a viral video or Facebook post appears to proclaim its truth without need of assistance from journalists. And third, when you give your "oppo" research to a reporter, you lose control of the timing. The Liberal war room had apparently been hoarding embarrassing video on Conservative candidates that, in the first week of the campaign, it used to harass and disrupt Scheer's national tour.

For several days running, the Liberals dropped embarrassing revelations on Twitter featuring candidates that Scheer was scheduled to campaign with that day. These included Rachel Willson in York-Centre, who had called for anti-abortion legislation on video; Arpan Khanna in Brampton North, who had made homophobic posts on Facebook; and Justina McCaffrey in Kanata-Carleton, who appeared to be friends with Faith Goldy, a right-wing media commentator who has been open in her sympathies for white supremacists and was banned from Facebook earlier in 2019. In each case, this tactic left the Conservatives with an unpalatable choice: cancel the appearance and give the story extra oxygen or go ahead with the event and serve up the precise visual the Liberal war room had selected for that day with Scheer standing beside the offending candidate.

For reporters travelling on Scheer's tour, this material proved irresistible. On their way to a routine appearance by the Conservative leader, who was set to reiterate familiar policies and arguments, and thus somewhat discounted as news, reporters were handed a genuinely newsworthy piece of information along with the prospect of the leader and the offending candidate available to ask questions of. For reporters who are already multitasking and newsrooms who are short staffed, this was the gift of news. All the more so when McCaffrey fled reporters and cameras, making a piquant visual.

In effect, the Liberal's "hacked" into the media by recognizing specific news values such as novelty and conflict and how they could be played to advantage. In a small way, this replicated Donald Trump's success in the 2016 election campaign when he employed his virtuoso ability to command media attention and dominate the news cycle.

Here in Canada, the use of such tactics by political parties should trigger serious reflection by the media. The issue of the relationship of the Conservative Party to socially conservative, alt-right, and white supremacist viewpoints was legitimately newsworthy. Reporters were the recipients of genuine news from the Liberal war room, but in a way that was clearly manipulative, and this added significantly to the negative tone of the campaign.

Ultimately, Scheer tried to inoculate himself against the Liberal attack by telling a middle-of-the-night scrum on his tour plane that, in future, candidates who apologized and recanted would be allowed to remain as candidates. The inevitable result was that the very next day, as Scheer announced what was likely the most important platform promise of his campaign – a multi-billion-dollar tax cut – reporters wanted to talk not about that but about the candidate controversy. In this way, the Conservative plan to communicate a major policy proposal to the public was disrupted by a Liberal tactic that was based on an insight into how reporters and the media were likely to react.

BLACKFACE

Early in the campaign, before it had fully taken shape, my Carleton University colleague Elly Alboim argued that modern media prize storytelling as a significant value and as their preferred vehicle for organizing and communicating information. He wrote that this approach favoured news elements such as novelty over the kind of repetitive, reiterative messages parties favour at election time when communicating policies and platforms. He said this often leads to a focus on gaffes and "bozo eruptions." More significant, he suggested, is the media's reliance on broad narratives to organize or frame the campaign. "In recent Canadian elections, that media narrative has two dominant components – the state of the competition (the horserace) and as has been true since the days of Greek drama, the story arcs that characterize the personalities who are the leading actors in the overall drama."[25]

In my view, as I allude to above, this schema understates the volume and quality of journalism on matters of substance. But this may be the difference between looking at the individual products of the media and their overall effect. A conscientious national news consumer might have been well served if she or he were looking for serious, substantive, high-quality reporting, analysis, and commentary. At the same time, a more casual news consumer might have been more influenced by the stories that made the front page or the top of the newscast and started a fire on social media. Alboim's analysis is most telling at the level of the media "meta-narratives" of the campaign, which indeed focused on polling and personalities. I address polling coverage more thoroughly below. As he noted himself in the early days of the campaign, Alboim's second narrative arc, based on the leaders' personalities, was less obvious.

That changed in very dramatic fashion on the evening of 18 September, when *Time* magazine posted an article featuring a picture of a twenty-nine-year-old Justin Trudeau at a gala fundraiser for a school where he then taught, dressed in a turban and robes with face and hands painted deep black.[26] Other photos of similar incidents soon surfaced in what came to be known as the "blackface," or sometimes the "brownface," controversy. In terms of the debate that developed over the media's role, this was foreshadowed on the first day of the campaign when a photograph of the apparently all-white press corps on Trudeau's campaign plane was tweeted out by one of the reporters and instantly became the subject of comment on social media,[27] particularly among people of colour. Asmaa Malik, an associate professor of journalism at Ryerson University, retweeted the image with the comment "accurate snapshot of Canadian newsrooms."

Malik's tweet somewhat overstated the case. There were a few prominent journalists of colour, such as *HuffPost*'s Althia Raj and CBC's Salimah Shivji, covering the national campaign. Nonetheless, lack of diversity in Canadian newsrooms is a long-standing issue. The main beneficiaries of the drive to diversify the media in recent decades – and this may be especially true in the Parliamentary Press Corps – have been white women. This is not just an issue of social equity,[28] it is also a matter of journalistic capacity to address issues of race as they exist and, as in the case of the blackface controversy, as they suddenly arise. Strikingly, as the blackface issue exploded across the front pages, the mainstream media relied heavily on their own small number of racialized journalists as well as freelancers such as Vicky Mochama and Fatima Syed, and outside experts such as Ritika Goel, to explain the racial implications of Trudeau's exploits.

Here is where Alboim's schema was predictive. At the risk of overgeneralizing, most of the racialized commentators recruited by the media in those days emphasized two things: (1) that the issue of whether Trudeau was "a racist" or not was a misleading frame and

(2) that the controversy should open a broader discussion about systemic racism.[29] However, the dominant themes in the media coverage were twofold: what did these incidents tell us about Trudeau as a personality,[30] and what effect would the controversy have on the polls?[31] And when the polls seemed to suggest (perhaps somewhat misleadingly) that Trudeau's party had not sustained the devastating blow that some had anticipated, the blackface controversy quickly faded to become a secondary theme in campaign coverage.

A study published by the Public Policy Forum suggested that interest in the blackface exploded on social media the day after *Time* published the photo, with 13,400 tweets an hour. However, the social media explosion faded fast, falling to 2,614 three days later.[32] It found that (opposition) politicians and journalists continued to tweet about it for the rest of the week, but in dwindling numbers. This roughly paralleled the arc of media coverage.

JOURNO BAR THE DOOR?

The emergence of the internet and, subsequently, the emergence of social media has considerably weakened the traditional media's gate-keeping function. Because the media tend to wrap themselves in the ideology of the free press, they are sometimes slow to acknowledge explicitly the role they have played in deciding which voices are permitted to participate fully in public and political discourse and which are not. The issue of this gate-keeping function arose in a variety of ways in Election 2019 and in many forms, including who would be permitted access to major media platforms, who would be permitted to participate as journalists in debate coverage, and which spurious stories circulating on social media would be reported on or published.

The best explanation I have seen of the structure of permitted expression in the media was articulated by an American scholar, Daniel Hallin, at the time of the Vietnam War.[33] Hallin described what he called "three spheres" in journalistic discourse. The first sphere is what he called the sphere of consensus. This includes topics on which the media take the view that consensus is so broad that no opposing view needs to be offered. So journalists take for granted that slavery is bad, for example, and that democracy is preferable to dictatorship. They feel no need to offer "balance" or another point of view when touching on such topics. The second is the sphere of legitimate controversy. In the election campaign, this sphere would include the debate about the size of the deficit, for example, and whether to build a pipeline. In this sphere, reporters feel a responsibility to maintain neutrality, to "balance" their reports and to maintain a professional disinterest in the outcome of the debates upon which they are reporting. In this sphere also, columnists and editorial boards are free to weigh in with their views. The third is the sphere of deviance. These are ideas such as those espoused by ISIS or neo-Nazis, for example, which are considered outside the sphere of legitimate discourse, and they may also include ideas that are regarded as laughable, ridiculous, or simply unfounded. They may be covered as news events, but the substance of their arguments is dismissed and is not permitted in opinion pieces.

Of course, the boundaries between these spheres are continually in flux and are the subject of controversy. Both the *Toronto Star* and the *Globe and Mail* became embroiled in controversies over decisions they made during the campaign to include voices that some people, especially on the left, felt should be relegated to the "sphere of deviance." In the case of the *Toronto Star,* it was a decision to hold an editorial board meeting with Maxime Bernier, leader of the right-wing populist People's Party of Canada, which ultimately failed to win a single seat in the election.[34] *Star* columnist Bob Hepburn defended the decision in the pages of the newspaper, arguing that "it's important for voters, including those repelled by Bernier's positions, to have information to help them understand where he and those who back him are coming from and why and how he is appealing to far-right nationalists and neo-Nazis in our midst."[35] However, his fellow *Star* columnist, Shree Paradkar, wrote the same day that "many journalists of colour – there are not that many of us in the newsroom – felt let down by our employers' decision," arguing that the *Star* was helping to legitimize Bernier's views.

Meanwhile, the *Globe and Mail* opened up its op-ed page to Ezra Levant, who runs *The Rebel* website.[36] Levant is the former publisher of the *Western Standard,* a former *Sun* columnist and a former aide to Canadian Alliance leader Stockwell Day. He was, at one time, accepted as a member of the journalistic community, albeit a controversial one. However, his site has featured alt-right and Islamophobic figures who combine political agitation with more conventional reporter-like activities such as turning up at news conferences. It is fair to say as an observation that Levant has migrated in recent years from the sphere of controversy to the sphere of deviance in the sense that he is no longer routinely afforded access to major media outlets. His

Globe op-ed represented a rare recent appearance in the mainstream media and was in fact a complaint that the exclusion of his staff from some press conferences is a violation of freedom of the press. What was remarkable about Levant's op-ed was not the specific arguments he made, which could equally have come from a more conventional figure, but that the *Globe* afforded him the platform to make them.

The decisions to give Bernier and Levant mainstream media platforms were made by journalists themselves. However, this issue arose in another, surprising, context, when a court ordered the official commission organizing the leaders' debates to accredit as journalists three men from two far right outfits, Levant's Rebel Media and the True North Centre for Public Policy, and so allow them the same privileges to cover the debates as members of the established news media. The debates commission reportedly argued in court that the men should not be included because of their history of advocacy, which it argued precluded them from being accredited as journalists.[37] The case raised an unresolved tension in the age of the internet, when there are fewer barriers to entry into publication and broadcast. As the traditional media debate internally who should have access to their platforms, other institutions, and in this case the courts, are making judgments about which platforms should have access to the "guild privileges" that journalists have enjoyed, including access to political events. Not only on the right, but also on the left, some new media organizations mimic features of traditional reporting but do not necessarily respect its traditional boundaries. One of the individuals who benefited from the court ruling, *The Rebel*'s Keean Bexte, was criticized later in the campaign for accosting the teenage climate activist, Greta Thunberg, in her Alberta hotel, and aggressively questioning her. But of course, members of the traditional media are also sometimes criticized for crossing lines.

The judge in the debate case, Justice Russell Zinn of the Federal Court, released his written reasons a month after the election.[38] He rested his judgment at least in part on the vagueness and the arbitrariness of the definition of journalist applied by the debates commission to exclude the plaintiffs. This is likely to be a continuing challenge to the profession. As a practical matter, in the past, the definition often came down to who had access to a printing press or a broadcasting licence. While journalists may have formulated their own professional standards, these were seldom codified because the journalists, as they then understood themselves, preferred an expansive regime based on the general liberties of speech and press. In fact, the Parliamentary

Press Gallery, which was involved in enforcing the debates commission rules, has over the years permitted as members representatives of the official media outlets of the former Soviet Union and the current Chinese regime, so it cannot claim adherence to an idealized notion of what constitutes a journalist. This conundrum is likely to challenge the profession for years to come.

Yet another instance of the difficulties of policing media boundaries in Election 2019 is worth mentioning. In the aftermath of the blackface controversy, unfounded rumours began circulating on the internet and social media that Justin Trudeau had left West Point Grey Academy, the school at whose gala he had worn blackface, under the cloud of a sex scandal. These rumours were published by the scurrilous publication *Frank* and repeated by a number of widely read fake news sites.[39] The rumours were given further currency on social media by the political gadfly Warren Kinsella – a former Liberal "oppo researcher" who, it later turned out, had been secretly working for the Conservative Party just prior to the campaign – who suggested the *Globe and Mail* was about to break the story.[40] The Conservative Party shamefully contributed to this circuit by issuing a press release asking: "Why did Trudeau leave West Point Grey?"

Like a number of outlets, the *Globe* was apparently attempting to report on the story, and one of its reporters had asked Trudeau a question about the "unfounded rumours." It appears that reporters researching the story found nothing to confirm it as well as evidence that it was untrue, and so they did not publish. However, false rumours started circulating on social media that a secret court injunction was blocking a story from the *Globe*. This put the newspaper in the exquisite dilemma of either allowing these rumours to stand unchallenged or further fuelling them by issuing a statement correcting the record. Eventually *Canadaland*, the *National Observer*, and the *Toronto Star* each wrote stories describing the circulation of these rumours and debunking them. This is in miniature the dilemma mainstream media have with much of the spurious information circulating on the internet and on social media: At what point is it so widespread that the risk of amplifying malicious nonsense is outweighed by the need to debunk it?

A POLICY INTERLUDE:
GRETA THUNBERG WEEK

Election 2019 will not be remembered for its epic policy debates. In the early days of the campaign, all the major parties focused on similar concerns about "affordability." In many cases, their commitments were refinements on well-known positions they had previously held or versions of commitments from previous elections.[41] In several cases, such as housing or the costs of prescriptions, for example, parties expressed similar concerns but differed in the policy solutions they offered. None of these topics offered the hallmarks of dramatic news – novelty and conflict – and so while they were reported, they were generally not the stuff of bold headlines or newscast opening teasers. On one of the gravest and potentially explosive issues of the campaign, Quebec's Bill C-21, which banned government employees from wearing religious symbols such as headscarves or turbans at work, the major party leaders all steered clear of bold opposition, and the media, while continuing to quiz politicians on the topic, generally took their cue from the parties and did not attempt to make it a major campaign issue.

The most striking exception to this generalization was the issue of climate change. Polls suggested that climate change was near to or at the top of the list of issues for Canadians, along with hardy perennials such as health care and jobs.[42] Earlier in the year, some commentators had imagined that climate policy might be the principal campaign divide between the two major parties, particularly over the issue of the incumbent government's carbon tax. However, the issue was initially overshadowed in the media by the opening theme of affordability, skirmishes over candidate conduct, and then the blackface controversy.

In the forty years since climate change has emerged as a major issue, the media has struggled to cover it well. As a slow process – in news terms, if not in scientific terms – it does not have gripping defining moments of novelty. Climate conferences are complex processes, difficult to explain simply or portray in dramatic terms. The science is inherently probabilistic and difficult to convey. Even the dramatic weather events, such as hurricanes, which we have learned will become larger and more dangerous, cannot individually be attributed to climate change with certainty. In the early decades of concern, the media also reflexively employed "balance" in much of their reporting, – that is, "balancing" the findings of climate scientists with those of "climate sceptics" or "climate deniers" – in a dynamic similar to the first decades of research about the link between tobacco and cancer. In recent years, the media have responded to the criticism of "false balance" in their coverage of climate change and now normally takes it as a given that climate change is real and largely the result of human activity. However, the difficulties of covering an inherently gradual process viewed through probabilistic science has persisted.

In the 2019 election, one media outlet, the *Toronto Star*, stood out in attempting to frame the election around climate change, whatever the parties chose to talk about. The *Star* ran a series of deeply researched features on climate change in the run-up to the election, which appeared prominently on its pages and online, and continued to report more aggressively on the issue than other outlets throughout the campaign.[43] However, climate change only truly exploded into Election 2019 and its coverage towards the end of September. True to Alboim's insight that personalities drive much of modern news, international as well as Canadian media were captivated by the journey of the sixteen-year-old Swedish activist, Greta Thunberg, across the Atlantic Ocean by sailboat to attend the United Nations Climate Action Summit in New York. Thunberg's itinerary brought her from New York to Montreal. Like many other countries, Canada was the scene of enormous public protests that week demanding action on climate change that brought hundreds of thousands of people into the streets.

This presented the media with opportunities to redress their election coverage of climate change with event-driven and personality-driven stories. It also gave the media a news "hook" to publish explainers, backgrounders, and policy pieces on climate change. And naturally parties with strong climate platforms – namely, the Liberals, New Democrats, and Greens – took the opportunity to wedge against the Conservatives, with their weak and unconvincing climate change platform. For Trudeau and the Liberals, this provided a welcome opportunity to pivot from the blackface controversy to an issue on which they differed sharply from the Conservatives and could place them on the back foot, seemingly out of touch with the broad current of public opinion.

POLLING

It was already clear at the outset of the campaign that the polls – which would prove to be generally accurate[44] – would provide a significant narrative spine for coverage. The two major parties, the Liberal Party and the Conservative Party, were very closely matched in terms of percentage support, though the Liberals retained an edge in most seat projections for all but a few days of the campaign. Obviously, the point of an election is to determine who will govern, and with the race so close, every significant media event, from the blackface photos of Justin Trudeau to the leaders' debates, was thoroughly examined from the perspective of its potential effects on the polls.[45] On its website, the *Globe and Mail* posted daily results of a tracking poll conducted by Nanos Research, while the CBC, which did not conduct "horserace" polls of its own during the campaign, gave considerable prominence to its Poll Tracker feature in which its analyst, Éric Grenier, both aggregated the polls and made seat projections based on those aggregations.

Of course, polling information does not need to be explicitly present in a news story to influence its shape. The narrative of the election created by the polls becomes the meta-narrative within which much of the news operates. The perception of which party or leader is ahead or behind, rising or falling, often determines what stories are assigned, for example, as well as their tone. The favourable coverage and commentary NDP leader Jagmeet Singh enjoyed in the second half of the campaign was clearly affected by his buoyant polling numbers,[46] which turned out to be somewhat illusory.[47] Indeed, all the major parties' messaging in the last week of the campaign was significantly dependent on the perception created by the polls of their relative strength, as was media coverage.

Singh was queried on (and criticized for) his possible willingness to form a coalition with the Liberal Party, an issue clearly premised on the polls' intimation that he might hold the balance of power after the election.[48] Using this debate as its premise, Andrew Scheer's closing message in the campaign was dominated by warnings of an NDP-Liberal coalition (though, somewhat puzzlingly, he also talked of a potential Conservative majority).[49] Meanwhile, Justin Trudeau warned that only a vote for the Liberals could stop the Conservatives: "A vote for the Bloc Quebecois or the NDP or the Green Party would not stop Andrew Scheer, won't stop a Conservative government," he said.[50] Indeed one explanation for both the NDP and the Greens somewhat underperforming in their polls may be that the widely reported Liberal message, calling on so-called progressive voters to stop a Conservative government by voting tactically, actually worked to a degree, as it had done in some previous elections.[51]

MEDIA COMMENTARY AND MEDIA HARASSMENT

As has been the case for several elections now, the 2019 campaign came during a long period of enervating tension in the media. There have been many rounds of closures, consolidations, and cutbacks. With the partial exception of the CBC, most national news organizations are struggling for their very survival while also struggling to maintain traditional levels of campaign coverage with fewer resources. Although there have been promising new internet-based outlets emerge in the last decade as significant players in election coverage, including *HuffPost, Rabble.ca,* and *Canadaland,* their impact has been mostly national. There are fewer reporters covering national campaigns than there were twenty years ago, but there are *many* fewer outlets and reporters covering local campaigns.

In addition, the internet and social media put the media under much greater scrutiny than was true in the last century. *Canadaland,* for example, has media commentary at the core of its mandate and often works an adversarial vein. It was harsh in its critique of CBC's decision to sue the Conservative Party for using network video and initially including two of its journalists in the suit.[52] Meanwhile, I myself wrote a weekly column on the election media for *Policy Options.* The existence of significant media platforms that are not themselves owned by the mainstream media considerably extends the scrutiny to which the media are subject.

Social media have given this trend a steroidal injection. It is a commonplace of contemporary media practice that outlets must sustain a large social media presence. Most reporters and columnists participate in social media, especially on Twitter, and to a degree it is considered a requirement of the job to live-tweet campaign events, for example. Social media provide instant feedback to organizations and journalists from readers (not to mention feedback from a fair share of those who have not actually read the article in dispute!), some of which is serious and informed, some less so. Anecdotally, some heavy users of social media seem to be subject to a cognitive trick: they mistake the stream of news stories appearing in their self-curated Twitter feeds for being representative of the whole of media coverage. These people might profitably get off Twitter and consult Google before declaring that the media are ignoring this issue or that.

However, an astonishing quantity of the social media comments directed at journalists during the campaign mixed legitimate concerns with personal abuse, or simply outright ignorance with abuse. Frequently, this involved accusations of partisanship against reporters whose professional identity is tied to the idea of non-partisanship. Most commonly the accusation was that the media were sympathetic to the Liberals, though that reversed itself to a degree during the height of the blackface controversy. For people of colour, Jews, and other racialized groups, the attacks were sometimes racist; towards women, often misogynist; and for those who do not meet traditional TV norms of appearance or body type, repulsively personal.

In very few professions are people expected to tolerate systematic daily personal abuse in their workplace, which social media surely constitute for today's journalists. (Of course, politicians share the burden of this modern scourge.) Journalists, by disposition and training, are supposed to shrug this off. The columnist Andrew Coyne has made a sport of retweeting abusive and often contradictory tweets aimed at him. Other columnists gleefully participate in the acid tone Twitter, in particular, has acquired. But for many journalists, opening their Twitter feeds to check on breaking news or to tweet out information, we can assume that cruel and abusive comments are painful, at least for a moment before the professional carapace is erected, and cumulatively must have an effect. This is likely to be a mental health issue for the profession and the industry over time, and it is certain to discourage some capable people from entering an already precarious field and others to leave it prematurely. At most media organizations this phenomenon has received little or no systematic attention through the lens of mental health.

All that having been said, while some individual journalists may sometimes be hyper-sensitive to criticism, the media more broadly have a proud tradition of accepting criticism and engaging in self-criticism. Their business challenges and the unconscionable character of some of the attacks on their members should not inure them from this tradition. In the aftermath of the 2016 presidential election, there were significant discussions about Donald Trump's success in "hacking" the media's appetite for novelty and conflict by maintaining a stream of norm-busting comments on Twitter, in rallies, and in interviews. There was a debate about whether major news organizations had been trapped in a straitjacket of "false balance," over-reporting Hillary Clinton's issues with e-mails, for example, to balance all the negative coverage of Trump's seeming outrages. It will not be completely clear what effects these discussions had until the 2020 US election cycle is completed. But some news practices have plainly changed in the United States as a result of the soul-searching: the willingness to be more forthright in identifying outright lies, for example, and more aggressive fact-checking of mendacious claims when they are initially reported.

In the Canadian election of 2019, the issues of media practice were not so momentous. However, there were similarities. How to handle false claims circulating on the internet and social media. How to handle misleading innuendo by parties and politicians. Who is a legitimate participant in the election discourse? Who, even, is a journalist? To what extent do media practices lend themselves to negative messages and personal attacks and create incentives for parties and politicians to indulge in them? How to maintain and monitor the flow of instant feedback to the media that the internet and social media allow, and from which the media benefit, without resorting to defensive self-censoring, all the while protecting the mental health of its employees?

All of these questions can be fruitfully explored in the uncertain interim between the 2019 and the next Canadian election.

NOTES

1 This analysis is based mainly on the English-language media. However, survey data cited below referring to media consumption includes all respondents, regardless of language.
2 Mario Canseco, "'Brownface' Controversy Fails to Dent Trudeau's Approval Rating," *Business in Vancouver*, 27 September 2019.
3 "Elizabeth May Was Holding a Single-Use Cup before Photo Was Altered to a Reusable One," *National Post*, 24 September 2019, https://nationalpost.com/news/politics/election-2019/elizabeth-may-was-holding-disposable-cup-in-photoshopped-image-contrary-to-partys-claims.
4 Abacus Data, 8–10 October.
5 Ibid.
6 See, for example, Andrew Coyne, "Forget the 'Positive' Approach, Now the Campaign Is Down to a Few Days and Fear," *National Post*, 17 October 2019; and Stephanie Levitz, Mia Rabson, and Andy Blatchford, "Introducing 'Angry Andrew': What's behind the Conservative Leader's Change in Tone?," Canadian Press, 13 October 2019, https://globalnews.ca/news/6027885/andrew-scheer-conservative-tone/.
7 Ipsos hybrid online/phone poll, conducted 11–13 October, n = 2,204 Canadians aged 18+ were interviewed, n = 1,504 online, https://www.ipsos.com/en-ca/news-polls/One-Week-from-E-Day-Canadians-Hearing-More-Negativity-About-Candidates-Leaders-than-Policy.
8 Innovative Research Group, online poll, 8–9 October, n = 1726, https://innovativeresearch.ca/2019-federal-election-english-leaders-debate-2019-10-09/.

9 Cheryl Chan, "Conservative Leader Andrew Scheer Promises Tax Cut at Campaign Stop in Surrey," *Vancouver Sun*, 15 September 2019.
10 Chantal Hébert, "Trudeau Facing Tough Choices as Quebec Judge Strikes Down Federal Limits on Assisted Dying," *Toronto Star*, 13 September 2019.
11 Heather Scoffield, "Here's What Is Missing When Party Leaders Talk about Putting More Money in Your Pocket," *Toronto Star*, 12 September 2019.
12 Rachel Younglai and Chen Wang, "How Canada's Suburban Dream Became a Debt-Filled Nightmare," *Globe and Mail*, 13 September 2019.
13 Jeffery York, "In the Neskantaga First Nation, Undrinkable Water Is a Crisis of Health and Faith," *Globe and Mail*, 16 September 2019.
14 Samantha McCabe and Jack Denton, "Well-Versed: Housing Affordability Is Complicated: Your High Rent Isn't," *Globe and Mail*, 15 September 2019.
15 Heather Scoffield, "Canada Needs More Workers, and Political Supports for Children and Seniors Can Help," *Toronto Star*, 22 September 2019.
16 Wency Leung, "Federal Election 2019: Where Do the Major Parties Stand on Family and Child Care?," *Globe and Mail*, 15 October 2019.
17 Andrew Leach, "A National Reckoning on Climate Change," *CBC.ca*, 16 October 2019.
18 "'Why Is That Even a Question?': Singh Vows to End Boil Water Advisories in Indigenous Communities," *Globalnews.ca*, 5 October 2019.
19 "Federal Election 2019: Man Tells Jagmeet Singh He Should Remove His Turban to 'Look Like a Canadian,'" *Globalnews.ca*, 2 October 2019.
20 See, for example, Andrew Coyne, "How to Fix the Leaders' Debates: To Start, We Need More of Them," *Canada.com*, 10 October 2019.
21 Christian Paas-Lang, "Viewership Up, But Format Questions Remain for Leaders' Debates," The Canadian Press, 8 October 2019.
22 Aaron Hutchins, "The Numbers Are In — and Millions Watched the *Maclean's* Debate," *Maclean's*, 12 August 2015.
23 April Lindgren, "What the Death of Local Media Means for the Federal Election," *The Walrus*, 22 August 2019.
24 Andrew Steel and John Penner, "Election Candidates Take Note: Your Social Media Posts Can and Will Be Used against You," *Globe and Mail*, 18 September 2019.
25 Elly Alboim, "The Elusive Narrative in Election 2019," *Capital Current*, n.d., https://capitalcurrent.ca/the-elusive-narrative-in-election-2019/.
26 Anna Purna Kambhampaty, Madeleine Carlisle, and Melissa Chan, "Justin Trudeau Wore Brownface at 2001 'Arabian Nights' Party While He Taught at a Private School," *Time*, 18 September 2019.

27 See https://images.app.goo.gl/bMbS75VGpibRhZBr6.
28 Anita Li, "Canadian Media, Lacks Nuance, Depth on Racial Issues," *Policy Options*, 10 September 2019.
29 Ritika Goel, "Which Party Will Address Systemic Racism in Canada?," *Maclean's*, 25 September 2019.
30 I, myself, contributed to this genre in a minor way. See Paul Adams, "In Politics, a Photo Can Carry Powerful Subtext," *Policy Options*, 9 October 2019.
31 National Post Staff, "How Did Canadians React to Trudeau's Blackface Photos? With a Big Meh, Polls Find," *National Post*, 23 September 2019.
32 Taylor Owen, Peter Loewen, Derek Ruths, Aengus Bridgman, Robert Gorwa, Stephanie MacLellan, Eric Merkley, Andrew Potter, Beata Skazinetsky, Oleg Zhilin, "Research Memo #5: Fact-Checking, Blackface and the Media," Public Policy Forum, October 2019.
33 My account of Hallin's spheres here is drawn from my article "Who Is a Journalist?," *Policy Options*, 17 October 2019.
34 *Star* staff, "People's Party of Canada Leader Maxime Bernier Sat Down with the Star's Editorial Board," *Toronto Star*, 24 September 2019.
35 Bob Hepburn, "Why It's Wrong to Ignore 'Mad Max' Bernier," *Toronto Star*, 15 September 2019.
36 Ezra Levant, "Press Freedom Applies to Everyone – Even *The Rebel*," *Globe and Mail*, 16 September 2019.
37 Paola Loriggio, "Two Right-Wing Media Outlets Win Legal Battle to Attend the Leaders' Debate," *National Post*, 7 October 2019.
38 Justice Howard Zinn, *Andrew James Lawton and True North Centre for Public Policy v. Canada (Leaders' Debates Commission)*, Federal Court, 13 November 2019.
39 See Emma McIntosh, "A Fake Justin Trudeau Sex Scandal Went Viral: Canada's Election-Integrity Law Can't Stop It," *National Observer*, 10 October 2019.
40 Elizabeth Thompson, "Seek and Destroy' Contract against PPC Came with Strings, Kinsella Says," CBC.ca, 25 October 2019.
41 Canadian Press, "Promises, Promises: A Running List of What the Major Parties Say They'll Do If They Win the Election," *National Post*, 25 September 2019.
42 Abacus Data, "Election Poll: Regional Races and Turnout Will Decide an Election with Two Points Separating Liberals and Conservatives in Canada," 20 October 2019.
43 "Undeniable: Canada's Climate Change," *Toronto Star*, https://projects.thestar.com/climate-change-canada/.

44 Éric Grenier, "Canada's Pollsters Nailed the Outcome of the Federal Election – Mostly," CBC.ca, 24 October 2019.
45 National Post staff, "How Did Canadians React to Trudeau's Blackface Photos? With a Big Meh, Polls Find," National Post, 25 September 2019; Shannon Proudfoot, "Leaders Debate Poll: Jagmeet Singh Won, and Not Just among NDP Fans," Maclean's, 9 October 2019.
46 Amira Elghawaby, "Jagmeet Singh's Surging Popularity Is a Win for Diverse Communities," globalnews.ca, 18 October 2019; Chris Campbell, "This Photo of Jagmeet Singh Says a Lot," Burnaby Now, 20 October 2019.
47 The NDP finished with just under 16 percent of the vote, compared to an average of more than 18 percent in the polls.
48 Jason Kirby, "Jagmeet Singh's Coalition Waffle," Maclean's, 15 October 2019.
49 Joan Bryden, "Conservatives Stoke Fear of NDP-Liberal Coalition as Scheer Pushes for Majority," National Post, 14 October 2019.
50 Bruce Campion-Smith, "'There Could Be a Conservative Government,' Justin Trudeau Warns Whitby Residents," Toronto Star, 18 October 2019.
51 Jennifer L. Merolla, Laura B. Stephenson, "Strategic Voting in Canada: A Cross Time Analysis," Duke University, http://www.probeinternational.org/old_drupal/UrbanNewSite/strategicvoting.pdf.
52 Jesse Brown, "The CBC Has Damaged Rosemary Barton's Brand, and Its Own," Canadaland, 14 October 2019.

9

Digital Campaigning in the Era of Misinformation

Tamara A. Small

One starting place for any discussion of digital technology in the 2019 federal election must begin in the United States in 2016. Whereas Barack Obama's use of digital technology in the 2008 election was lauded, the mood had soured considerably eight years later. Headlines such as "Did Fake News on Facebook Help Elect Trump?" or "How Russian Facebook Ads Divided and Targeted US Voters before the 2016 Election" were typical of post-campaign coverage.[1] Digital technologies, especially social media, came under fire in a number of ways in this campaign, the first of which was related to Donald Trump's use of Twitter. By throwing insults at opponents in tweets and using Twitter to bypass traditional media channels, Trump was a "vast departure from the sanitized way" social media are used in campaigns.[2] Next, the world's most popular social medium, Facebook, was at the centre of several election-related scandals. In 2018, we learned that the personal data of some 87 million Facebook profiles were exposed to Cambridge Analytica, a political consulting firm that did work for the Donald Trump campaign.[3] A personality app on Facebook, created by a Russian American researcher, had collected the data. There were concerns about data privacy on Facebook and also the connection of Cambridge Analytica to Trump. There was also the problem of online "fake news" and foreign interference. Purveyors of misinformation purchased advertisements on social media, such as Facebook ads, meant to confuse and mislead voters. Pope Francis's endorsement of Donald Trump and Hillary Clinton's involvement in weapons sales to Islamic jihadists are examples of misinformation circulated online in 2016. Foreign actors, especially from Russia, are thought to be behind much of the social media misinformation in this campaign. Some credit fake stories as leading voters astray and having a possible effect on the outcome of the election.[4] The final troubling use of technology in the 2016 election was the hacking of documents and e-mails from Hillary Clinton's presidential campaign and the Democratic National Committee by the Russian government, as outlined in the Mueller Report.[5]

Since 2016, reports of nefarious and problematic uses of digital technologies, including social media, have occurred in elections in Germany, the United Kingdom, France, and Spain.[6] A report by Canada's Communications Security Establishment (CSE) notes that half of all national elections in advanced democracies experienced some sort of cyber threat in 2018 – a threefold increase since 2015.[7] Governments worldwide have responded, and the 2019 election in Canada marks the first one in which the digital space is truly subject to electoral law. This is the focus of this chapter.

More specifically, this chapter explores how the issue of online misinformation was addressed in Canada in the lead up to and during the 2019 federal election. A word about terminology: the term "fake news" has fallen out of favour of late, with terms such as "misinformation" or "disinformation" being preferable.[8] Misinformation or disinformation includes "all forms of false, inaccurate, and misleading information designed, presented, and promoted to intentionally cause public harm or for profit."[9] Misinformation is not a new phenomenon, but social media makes it very easy to generate and share it.[10] In the broadcast era, advertising was expensive to make and expensive to air. This meant there was a finite number of political ads and that advertising was seen by large segments of the population.[11] This all breaks down on social media. First, the barriers to entry are low on social media – that is, individuals and groups can inexpensively create websites or purchase advertising on online platforms. Next, the reach of social media can be extensive.[12] Some platforms have billions of users, for whom their algorithms structure and personalize a user's experience based on content that is attractive and/or useful to them.[13] Thus, social media are an easy and attractive way for both legitimate and illegitimate political actors to communicate with people and, potentially, influence voters. Purveyors of misinformation are motivated by satirical, financial, and ideological reasons.[14]

By way of context, this chapter begins by briefly highlighting the importance of digital campaigning in Canada. The bulk of the chapter focuses on the response to cyber threats, including misinformation. First, it explores how Canadian governmental actors responded broadly to what happened in the US election. This is followed by a detailed discussion of the approach to misinformation in Canadian electoral law. Owen calls this approach "platform governance"[15] – that is, the activities of online platforms are now regulated in election law, and online platforms are "expected" to play a proactive role in addressing misinformation if they allow political actors to purchase political advertising. Finally, the chapter explores how the social media giant Facebook has responded to platform governance in Canada. Facebook is relevant for several reasons: first, because of its controversial role in 2016; second, because it is a major social media platform in Canada, having more than 24 million active monthly users; and, third, because it was one of the only major online platforms to fully comply with the new regulations.

DIGITAL CAMPAIGNING IN CANADA: BRIEF OVERVIEW

In some form or another, Canadian election campaigns have been online for more than two decades. The Liberal Party is thought to be the earliest federal party to use a website for campaigning in 1993.[16] By the next election in 1997, all major political parties were using websites as part of the campaign. The impact of the internet on these early campaigns was minimal as less than half of Canadians were online. As the internet became a more regular part of the lives of Canadians, it stopped being a novelty and became a political necessity.[17] In addition to websites, parties and local candidates now campaign on all the major social media, including Twitter, Facebook, YouTube, and Instagram. Parties also purchase digital advertising on those same social media and other online platforms.

Digital advertising has also become increasingly important for third parties in Canadian elections. A third party is a person or group other than a candidate, registered political party, or an electoral district association of a registered political party that participates in elections by advertising. In 2004, not even 1 percent of third-party spending was on digital advertising; it was 23 percent in the 2015 federal election.[18] Given the trend, it does not seem inconceivable that third-party digital advertising could surpass other forms of advertising (e.g., newspapers and radio) in future elections.

The internet and related technologies have also changed the way Canadians consume political information. Brin suggests that the traditional media habits of Canadians, such as television and print use, have fallen over the last five years.[19] For instance, research by the Public Policy Forum finds that the print media are deteriorating in Canada, with reporting on civic affairs in local print media in serious decline.[20] At the same time, more and more Canadians are using digital technologies to gain access to public affairs information. The Pew Research Center shows that, out of seventeen advanced countries, Canada ranks second when it comes to using social media for news: about 27 percent of Canadians get their news information several times a day from social media.[21]

The changing nature of the digital electoral space matters. It matters because access to information is essential for citizenship in that it ensures that voters can make responsible, informed choices. It matters because it has become a principal venue for political actors and citizens to connect. As such, the cyber threats described above, including online misinformation, call into question the integrity of the electoral process. Not only do they threaten national sovereignty but they also potentially erode public confidence in the electoral process.[22] Indeed, Canadians are concerned: 60 percent of respondents to an Abacus poll believed it likely that foreign governments would attempt to influence the 2019 federal election.[23] Canadians expected the government to respond as they were not confident that social media companies like Facebook would do so.[24]

THE RESPONSE BY THE CANADIAN GOVERNMENT

The events of the 2016 American election were a wake-up call for public servants and politicians in Canada, and discussions occurred in a variety of quarters within the government. The Communications Security Establishment (CSE), for instance, released two reports outlining numerous "cyber threats" to Canada's democratic process.[25] The threats discussed in the reports go well beyond misinformation on social media and encompass a wide variety of activities, including the use of technologies to tamper with election results or steal voter information, or the coercive and manipulative targeting of political parties or politicians. Regarding social media, they note:

> Adversaries could use social media to spread lies and propaganda to a mass audience at a low cost. Adversaries could masquerade as legitimate information providers, blurring

the line between what is real and what is disinformation. They could do so by hijacking social media accounts, or they could create websites or new social media accounts that purport to be trustworthy producers or disseminators of news and information.[26]

The CSE judged it "very likely" that the 2019 federal election would face some sort of cyber threat.

Parliamentarians were also rightly concerned about digital technologies in democracy. The Standing Senate Committee on Legal and Constitutional Affairs released a report titled *Controlling Foreign Influence in Canadian Elections*.[27] Among other things, it recommended a ban on the creation and distribution of false candidate or party campaign communication materials. Following the Cambridge Analytica scandal, the House of Commons Standing Committee on Access to Information, Privacy and Ethics began an investigation into the breach as some 600,000 Canadians had their data exposed. The scandal turned out to be an entry point into the exploration of broader issues, including the "self-regulation of platform monopolies, the use of these platforms for data harvesting purposes, and their role in the spreading of disinformation and misinformation."[28] The committee heard witness testimony in 2018, including representatives from Facebook and Google. The final report features twenty-six recommendations, some directly tied to addressing misinformation and digital advertising in Canadian elections.

Perhaps in light of these reports and investigations, the government of Canada responded in a number of ways. In March 2019, the government committed $7 million towards digital, news, and civic literacy programming, noting the "strongest defence against threats to democracy is an engaged and informed public."[29] The government also established the Critical Election Incident Public Protocol, which would monitor and inform of threats during the federal election. Karina Gould, the minister responsible for democratic institutions, also released the *Canada Declaration on Electoral Integrity Online* in May 2019.[30] The declaration stresses the need for the government and online platforms to work together to ensure the "integrity, transparency and authenticity" of the digital electoral space. More substantively, Parliament made changes to the Canada Elections Act as part of a broader package of amendments called the Electoral Modernization Act, 2018. The next section details those changes.

THE RESPONSE IN LEGISLATION

Until 2018, electoral law was "remarkably silent" on the role of digital technologies in Canadian elections.[31] The term "internet" was used only a handful of times in the Canada Elections Act (CEA), and not in reference to election advertising by political entities (e.g., political parties, candidates, electoral district associations, or third parties). It is through statements made by Elections Canada and the chief electoral officer (CEO) that what constitutes digital or online advertising gets clarified. For instance, after the 2000 election, Elections Canada notes that, regardless of the channel, online or not, "an advertising message is an advertisement purchased."[32] Prior to the 2015 election, the CEO released an extremely detailed statement clarifying the extent to which the CEA applied to material on the internet. Again, it underscored the importance of expenditures – digital or online messages are only considered election advertising if there is a placement cost. What is not election advertising on the internet is also clarified, including digital messages sent for free (e.g., text messages, e-mail, social media messages) and/or online videos posted for free on a personal website or online video sites (e.g., YouTube).

Even though digital technologies had been a part of election campaigning for more than two decades, essentially the legislative approach to addressing them was to liken digital technology to all other means of communication, including television, radio, flyers, or newspaper ads. On more than one occasion, scholars have commented on the limited approach taken in regulating the digital space. As the Standing Senate Committee on Legal and Constitutional Affairs put it, "the CEA fails to address the ways in which websites, social media ... can be used as part of advertising campaigns."[33] The law did not seem to recognize that there was something unique about social media and that the digital electoral space was different from broadcasting.

This all changed as a result of the 2016 US election. In April 2018, the Justin Trudeau Liberal government introduced Bill C-76, the Electoral Modernization Act. The act was a major set of amendments to the CEA; among other things, it reversed several changes that the previous Stephen Harper government made under the controversial Fair Elections Act:[34] it introduced a formal pre-campaign period with spending limits for political actors, created a category of regulated content called "partisan advertising," and banned foreign influence in

Canadian elections. Like other jurisdictions, including Germany, the United Kingdom, France, and the European Union, the act includes provisions in order to combat misinformation on social media.[35] Provisions to regulate online platforms, such as Microsoft, Facebook, Twitter, Google, and the websites of major news organizations – platform governance – was introduced into Canadian law.

Online platforms are now required by law to publish a "Registry of Partisan and Election Advertising."[36] Each registry must include an electronic copy of any advertising message published on the platform and the name of the person who authorized its publication, in both the pre- and official writ periods. If political parties, registered associations, nomination contestants, potential candidates, or candidates or registered third parties purchase advertising on any online platform, then that platform must list them in its registry. These actors, therefore, provide the platform the requisite information for them to meet the requirements.

Current election law makes a distinction between advertising before and during an election.[37] Partisan advertising occurs in the pre-campaign period (30 June to the issuing of the writs); it is the transmission to the public by any means of an advertising message that promotes or opposes a political party, nomination contestant, candidate, or party leader other than by taking a position on an issue with which the party or person is associated. Election advertising is the transmission to the public by any means during the election period of an advertising message that promotes or opposes a registered party or candidate, *including by taking a position on an issue with which the party or person is associated.* The italicized portion of the preceding sentence is sometimes known as "issue advertising": it is regulated during the election period if a third party spends $500 or more on advertising activities (i.e., having a placement cost). As mentioned, just talking about an issue on social media or via text message is not advertising. Paid issue advertising is not regulated in the pre-campaign. The term is necessarily vague: the issues could be "social, domestic or foreign policy, economics, or national security issues."[38] In the 2019 campaign, climate change, pharmacare, electoral reform, and Quebec's Bill C-21 would likely make a list of issues. Elections Canada warns political actors to be "mindful that any political ad for or against an issue transmitted on a platform during elections may be regulated" and that political actors are responsible for figuring out what constitutes an issue in a given campaign.[39] Certainly, issue advertising is a grey area: it could be potentially difficult for political actors and online platforms to assess the full scope of a list in any given election. Indeed, the concerns about issue advertising became national news just prior to the launch of the 2019 campaign. Reports surfaced that Elections Canada officials had implied that any groups discussing climate change would be engaging in advertising because Maxime Bernier, of the People's Party, had disavowed climate change.[40] This prompted a response from the CEO, Stéphane Perrault:

> The Act does not prevent individuals or groups from talking about issues or publishing information ... The only instance in which the Act covers the promotion of an issue, without mentioning a candidate or party, is when someone spends money on issue advertising during the election period.[41]

The Commissioner of Canada Elections ultimately decides what issue advertising is; this is because it is the Commissioner who can impose fines or lay charges for lack of compliance.

An online platform is defined as "an Internet site or Internet application whose owner or operator, in the course of their commercial activities, sells, directly or indirectly, advertising space on the site or application to persons or groups." A "monthly visit threshold" is used to determine whether an internet site or internet application is a regulated online platform. This would include the major technology platforms (e.g., Facebook, Twitter, Google, Microsoft, Instagram) and other websites that sell advertising, such as the websites of news organizations. Each registry must then remain on the platform for two years following the election, and the information from the registry must be kept for an additional five years. It is an offence for online platforms to fail to publish or maintain a registry. Regarding foreign interference, Bill C-76 prohibits foreign entities or individuals from purchasing advertising during elections. As such, it is an offence for online platform operators or owners to knowingly sell election advertising to foreign actors. Thus they must confirm the address of the purchaser before selling the ad.

These regulations place considerable legal (and fiscal) responsibility on online platforms in order to meet the integrity, transparency, and authenticity goals discussed earlier. The government expects online platforms to be proactive in addressing the misinformation crisis; as Minister Gould noted in the House of Commons, online platforms are expected to "intensify efforts to combat disinformation," "help users to understand when and why they are seeing political advertising," and "to remove fake accounts and inauthentic content from their platforms."[42] The benefit of platform governance is that it provides oversight, ensuring that only "legitimate actors are advertising and doing so within spending limits."[43] The rules should weed out illegitimate actors.

The proposed platform governance rules in Bill C-76 were met with very different reactions by the major online platforms. A report by the Standing Senate Committee on Legal and Constitutional Affairs on Bill C-76 includes reactions from Google, Twitter, and Facebook. Twitter and Google expressed concerns regarding the new law.[44] For instance, Google raised concerns about the category of issue advertising in its submission.[45] For Google, the category is so fluid and evolving as to make compliance extremely challenging. Indeed, Google Canada's submission rejected platform governance altogether. Rather than the platforms maintaining a registry, it suggests that political advertisers should "submit partisan and election ad creative and campaign information directly to Elections Canada."[46] Given the campaign finance database maintained by Elections Canada, this suggestion is not far-fetched. Facebook Canada, on the other hand, was more supportive of the platform governance approach. The brief submitted by Facebook notes its commitment and technological ability to comply with the legislation.[47]

The Electoral Modernization Act received Royal Assent in 2018, thus amending the Canada Elections Act. The new rules would be in place for the 2019 federal election, starting with the new pre-campaign period on 30 June 2019. Given the differing views about platform governance, the three major platforms approached the new regulations differently as the pre-campaign approached. As I discuss, Facebook not only complied with the new regulations but went beyond them. Google Canada opted not to sell advertising on the platform in the 2019 election. It cited an inability to meet compliance with the legislation: "We've come to the decision that the best way for Google to comply with the Elections Act in the 2019 election cycle is actually to stop accepting elections [sic] ads as defined in the legislation."[48] Twitter Canada banned political ads during the pre-campaign period due to a lack of infrastructure but did allow them during the writ period.[49] Though as an aside, in November 2019 Twitter announced a global ban on political advertising. According to a tweet by Twitter

CEO Jack Dorsey, "We've made the decision to stop all political advertising on Twitter globally. We believe political message reach should be earned, not bought."[50] Should we lament the loss of Google and Twitter? Dubois and colleagues say no. Indeed, this demonstrates that the government's approach is effective: "whether a company complies with the law or pulls its services, the goal of the public policy is ultimately served."[51] That is, there is little chance of misleading advertisements on Google and Twitter if people cannot buy ads in the first place.

THE RESPONSE BY FACEBOOK[52]

While issues of misinformation can exist all over the internet, it would be fair to suggest that Facebook had become the public face of the problem. There was widespread concern that Facebook was "the principal promoter of fake news" in 2016.[53] Accordingly, Facebook faced criticism from numerous quarters – recall the news headlines mentioned earlier. Facebook's CEO Mark Zuckerberg was hauled into a US congressional hearing to provide answers on topics as wide ranging as misinformation to child pornography. Facebook Canada's Kevin Chan also appeared before a House of Commons Committee in 2018. Siva Vaidhyanathan provides a scholarly takedown of Facebook in his book the *Anti-Social Network*.[54] He argues that: "Facebook is too big and the people who use it are too diverse. And those who profit from the most powerful, efficient, and inexpensive advertising service ever invented cannot expect those who purchase ads to resist precisely targeting hateful and destructive propaganda where it can do the most harm" (10). Given the public relations crisis that Facebook has been in for several years, it is perhaps not surprising how congenial it has been to Canada's concerns about online platforms in electoral politics. And, in some ways, it may have gone further than the legislation requires. However, it is worth pointing out that Facebook had already been making changes to the platform and policies to address electoral integrity in the aftermath of the US election. Therefore, what Facebook Canada has done is to develop a uniquely Canadian approach within its broader global goals. This section explores this Facebook's Canadian approach in more detail.

In response to the first report produced by the Communications Security Establishment, Facebook established the Canadian Election Integrity Initiative in 2017.[55] The initiative includes a number of tools directed towards helping political actors and citizens navigate

Facebook as a political space. Additionally, Facebook has an artificial intelligence tool that detects and removes fake accounts. According to Facebook, it disabled 2.19 billion accounts in the first quarter of 2019 worldwide.[56] While not all these accounts produced misleading information, their removal does reduce the possibility of the spread of misinformation. As part of this initiative, and in compliance with the Canada Elections Act, Facebook established its registry for digital advertising called the Ad Library in March 2019. The Ad Library is a searchable database that includes an electronic copy of any social or political ads (active or inactive) running across all of Facebook products, including Instagram, and also includes transparency requirements about the ad sponsor. The database also allows people to download reports in a .csv file. The Canadian version of the Ad Library is a newer version of Facebook's Ad Archive, which has operated in the United States starting in 2018. Versions of the Ad Library exist for many counties.

The Canadian database attempts to include digital ads that focus on "social issues, elections or politics" that are targeted to Canadian Facebook users. Recall that, during the election period, the vaguely defined issue advertising must be included in a registry. In order to determine what might constitute an issue in the current political context, Facebook engaged with an advisory board of prominent Canadians with considerable academic and political backgrounds to develop a list of Canada-specific social issues. The advisory board includes: Megan Leslie (CEO of WWF Canada and former deputy leader of the New Democratic Party of Canada), Antonia Maioni (dean of the Faculty of Arts, McGill University), Ry Moran (executive director, Truth and Reconciliation Centre, University of Manitoba), Ray Novak (managing director, Harper and Associates, and former chief of staff to Stephen Harper), and David Zussman (adjunct professor, School of Public Administration, University of Victoria, and former head of transition for Jean Chrétien). Facebook Canada is the first one to engage a group of experts in this way.

There are a couple of ways that political ads could be shown to a Canadian Facebook user. The first and most obvious is that a recognized political actor (e.g., a political party, a registered third party, or candidate) purchases an ad on Facebook and provides the authorization information as per the law. This scenario is relatively straightforward as we would expect these actors to understand their legal requirements. These ads feature a "paid-for-by" disclaimer (see figure 9.1). The second scenario is less straightforward. Here, someone who is not a recognized political actor purchases a Facebook ad that appears to meet the definition of a social issue. If an ad features subject matter that is on the Canada-specific list of social issues, it would be flagged by Facebook's automated artificial intelligence (AI) detection process. These actors would then be contacted by Facebook asking for appropriate authorization information regarding their identity, location, and who paid for the ad. Only when such information is provided would the ad be allowed to be posted and eventually be included in the Ad Library. It is in this second scenario that Facebook might be able to address some issues of misinformation. On one hand, a creator of such an ad could be an individual or local group that is simply unclear about the legal requirements under the CEA; on the other hand, it might be a nefarious actor looking to spread misleading information. The use of the advisory board, the Canada-specific list of social issues, and the AI tool allows Facebook to try to be as proactive as possible in addressing the vague category of issue advertising, which is expected in the government's *Declaration on Electoral Integrity Online*. Facebook is aware that this automated process may fail. If, upon the reporting of an ad by a Facebook user or other internal review process, an ad is found to be related to politics, elections, and social issues, that ad would be disabled and put into the Ad Library as an ad that ran without a "paid-for-by" disclaimer. Such advertisers would then have to go through the authorization process before being able to run any more ads related to politics, election, and social issues.

According to Facebook, electronic copies of advertising in the Ad Library will be available for seven years – five years longer than is required. The extended availability is just one aspect of the Ad Library that goes beyond the requirements of the law. This is common feature of Facebook's Ad Library model. Figure 9.1 provides an example of a political advertisement found in the Ad Library. The Liberal Party ad features a video linking Conservative leader Andrew Scheer to Ontario premier Doug Ford. As is evident, there are considerable amounts of additional information provided through the Ad Library model. Below the ad (not shown here), some summary data about the ad sponsor are provided, including the total amount of money spent on advertisements and the total number of ads in the database from that sponsor. The Ad Library provides information on "Impressions" (i.e., the number of times the ad was seen on screen) and the cost of

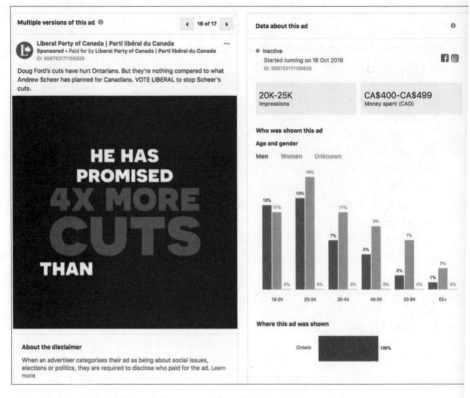

Figure 9.1 Example of political ad in the Facebook Ad Library

the ad. Demographic audience information is also provided. Estimates of the age, gender, and location of who and where the ad was shown is included. This particular version of the Doug Ford ad in figure 9.1 was shown to slightly more and younger women than men, and it was shown only in Ontario. As is evident, these numbers lack specificity.

While Facebook's Ad Library complies with the legal requirement of the CEA, the database has some issues. This in part stems from the fact that the Ad Library was not built to meet the Canadian legislation in the first instance; rather, the international Ad Library model was merely adapted by Facebook to meet the new Canadian rules.

The database is large and continues to grow. As of November 2019, there were more than ninety-eight thousand ads in the Ad Library that started in June. This number will continue to grow daily. The searching capability is not as nimble as one might hope. It is not possible to search for ads that only meet a specific category of advertiser (e.g., political party or third party). Recall that, when buying the ad, the law requires known political entities (e.g., parties, candidates, third parties) to provide the online platform with the requisite information for compliance. Thus, it is a strange omission that one cannot simply search for all party, candidate, or third-party ads as a category. Nor is it possible to search by event (e.g., pre-campaign or official writ period); searching is limited by the last day, last seven days, last thirty days, last ninety days, and all dates. Even on election day, one could not get a complete set of writ period ads because the 2019 campaign ran for forty days. For instance, trying to view just the ads produced by the NDP in the pre-campaign is near impossible. Being able to assess the impressions or demographic information for that time period is also difficult. This in some ways makes that additional information less relevant than it might be.

The registries of other online platforms, while basic, at least make it extremely clear which ads were published during the election. For instance, the Global News or the CBC/Radio-Canada registry simply provides links to the electronic copy of the ad with authorization data.[57]

The database may also include ads that do not meet the statutory definition of issue advertising. This could happen for two reasons. First, the advisory board's definition of social issues may be broader than what Elections Canada decides is issue advertising. However, Elections Canada notes that online platforms are better to be safe than sorry: "when there is doubt about whether an ad should be included in the registry, there is no penalty for including it as a cautionary measure."[58] Second, recall that the minimal placement cost for issue advertising is $500. In other words, groups that spend less than $499 are not required to register with Elections Canada. However, any ad that meets Facebook's social issues definition will be included regardless of cost. Neither of these things is necessarily a problem, it just means that data that exist in the Political Financing database on the Elections Canada website will not match up with what is in the Ad Library. The Ad Library may provide transparency in advertising overall, but transparency within the pre-campaign and/or the election period is muddled, especially the longer we are from the day of the election.

Even though the demographic, impression, and expenditure numbers are not particularly granular, this additional information does provide knowledge about digital advertising that was previously unknown. Narrowcasting or targeting refers to the practice of "sending particular political messages to particular people."[59] Elsewhere, I argue that online narrowcasting by Canadian political parties is the aspect of political advertising least researched by scholars.[60] While there was much speculation that parties and other political actors engaged in the practice of targeting political advertisements to Canadians, it was extremely difficult to assess individualized information and content on digital technologies. Thus, the Ad Library does provide a unique window into how political actors engage in online narrowcasting. It increases the transparency of the actions of political actors as everyone can see all the ads, even those that were not targeted to them and therefore would not have shown up in their feeds. The database will be a very interesting tool for the study of political advertising in the digital age.

On this point, some scholarly and media analyses of the Ad Library demonstrate some interesting trends vis-à-vis how digital advertising was used by political parties and third parties in this campaign. The Digital Democracy Project and CTV's Michael D'Alimonte note similar trends in the Facebook ads by the major political parties.[61] Facebook advertising was really the purview of two parties in 2019: the Liberal Party and the Conservative Party. More than three thousand ads (including multiple copies of the same ad) were produced by the two parties. According to D'Alimonte, by the end of the campaign the Liberals had spent roughly $490,000 on ads sent out from the Liberal Party Facebook page and $347,000 from the Justin Trudeau page.[62] The Conservatives spent just over $840,000 on ads sent out from their main Facebook page, with roughly $20,000 from the Andrew Scheer page. The NDP, Greens, BQ, and People's Party spent considerably less. The People's Party, for instance, produced fewer than seventy ads in the pre- and official campaign. In terms of third parties, the right-wing group Canada Proud (which targets the Liberals) and Canada's largest private-sector union, Unifor, were the top third-party spenders. They each spent more than $300,000 in the pre- and official campaign.

Around one in three of the 147 third parties that were registered in the 2019 election produced Facebook ads.

CONCLUSIONS

Early reports in the media suggest that the 2019 election was "largely clean" of misinformation.[63] Beyond reports of the Conservative Party's Chinese language ads on Facebook, which suggested the Liberals intended to legalize hard drugs,[64] there were few reports of misleading ads on the platform. This could be evidence that the regulation of online platforms in Canada and the Facebook Ad Library were successful. To be sure, we know that registered political actors, including parties, third parties, and candidates, produced digital ads on Facebook and other online platforms. In terms of increasing transparency of the digital electoral environment, this has certainly been effective. However, Canada's registries model has some flaws. While Canadians may have learned about Facebook's Ad Library over the course of the election through the numerous media articles published about it, knowing about and locating the other registries is extremely difficult. Only a handful of registries were located in the research for this chapter. Elections Canada would be wise to create a page on its website that links to the registries that exist. This would certainly create greater transparency of the platform governance approach overall.

As for combatting misinformation, time will tell as complaints made to the commissioner of Canada Elections are reported. Canadians may have been exposed to content on Facebook or another online platform that they concluded was misinformation and that they reported to Elections Canada. To be sure, the Electoral Modernization Act closes a gaping hole in the regulations surrounding political advertising on the internet. But what of misinformation in this campaign that was not advertising in the first place? Paying for placement is a central component of the definition of what constitutes political advertising in Canada. But one does not have to pay to use social media channels. Regular accounts on social media could produce misleading information content through organic posts, such as status updates or tweets.[65] In Facebook's 2017 congressional testimony, the company reported that organic posts spread misinformation to far more users than all the advertising combined.[66] It could be a user's friend sharing misinformation unintentionally or a "bot." Bots are automated processes run by computer programs that are designed to look like real people.

Political bots can be used for political manipulation by projecting large-scale consensus on political issues on social media.[67] Thus, other types of misinformation could have existed in the 2019 campaign.

In the early days of digital technology, the internet was seen as a tool of democracy and citizen empowerment. Its political impact would be nothing short of a revolution.[68] Social media were considered even more of a political impact than the early Web.[69] In some ways, the events of the US presidential election in 2016 were revolutionary, but these were ways that were largely unanticipated. It dramatically changed how we understand the place of digital technology in election campaigning. Modern elections are vulnerable to problems of digital campaigning, and the internet and its related technologies need to be managed. The 2020 decision by Facebook to ban and remove deepfakes is a recent instance.[70] A deepfake is a video or audio that has been altered through some form of AI machine learning.[71] Deepfakes can make it seem as if a politician (or anyone, for that matter) is saying or doing things she/he had never (and would never) say or do. For a humorous example, see Oscar-winning filmmaker Jordan Peele's video *You Won't Believe What Obama Says in This Video!*[72] Altered videos and audio are an extremely troubling new aspect of digital misinformation, especially in light of the upcoming US presidential election. Facebook's new policy does not seem to apply to videos or audio that have merely been altered. The infamous altered video of Nancy Pelosi, in which her words are slowed down so much that she appears intoxicated, is still apparently fine. It is not difficult to imagine the potential disruption that a deepfake of a political leader could cause. As Paris and Donovan put it: "If video can no longer be trusted as proof that someone has done something, what happens to evidence, to truth?"[73] This should remind us of the ever-changing nature of digital technology. Indeed, platform governance likely marks the beginning of attempts to regulate digital campaigning in this country.

NOTES

1 Danielle Kurtzleben, "Did Fake News on Facebook Help Elect Trump? Here's What We Know," *NPR.org*, 2018, https://www.npr.org/2018/04/11/601323233/6-facts-we-know-about-fake-news-in-the-2016-election; Issie Lapowsky, "How Russian Facebook Ads Divided and Targeted US Voters before the 2016 Election," *Wired*, 16 April 2018, https://www.wired.com/story/russian-facebook-ads-targeted-us-voters-before-2016-election/.

2 Dan Schill and John Allen Hendricks, "Discourse, Disruption and Digital Democracy," in *The Presidency and Social Media: Discourse, Disruption, and Digital Democracy in the 2016 Presidential Election*, ed. Dan Schill and John Allen Hendricks (New York: Routledge, 2017), 28.
3 Alvin Chang, "The Facebook and Cambridge Analytica Scandal, Explained with a Simple Diagram," *Vox*, 23 March 2018, https://www.vox.com/policy-and-politics/2018/3/23/17151916/facebook-cambridge-analytica-trump-diagram.
4 Leticia Bode, Emily K. Vraga, and Kjerstin Thorson, "Fake News," in *Electoral Integrity in America: Securing Democracy*, ed. Pippa Norris, Sarah Cameron, and Thomas Wynter (New York: Oxford University Press, 2018), 114–32.
5 *Report on the Investigation into Russian Interference in the 2016 Presidential Election* (Washington, DC: US Department of Justice, 2019).
6 Pippa Norris, Sarah Cameron, and Thomas Wynter, "Challenges in American Elections," in *Electoral Integrity in America: Securing Democracy*, ed. Pippa Norris, Sarah Cameron, and Thomas Wynter (New York: Oxford University Press, 2018), 114–32.
7 Communications Security Establishment, *Cyber Threats to Canada's Democratic Process* (Ottawa: Communications Security Establishment, 2017), https://cyber.gc.ca/en/guidance/cyber-threats-canadas-democratic-process/table.
8 House of Commons Digital, Culture, Media and Sport Committee, *Disinformation and "Fake News": Interim Report* (London: House of Commons, 4 February 2019), https://publications.parliament.uk/pa/cm201719/cmselect/cmcumeds/363/36302.htm.
9 Norris, Cameron, and Wynter, "Challenges in American Elections," 7.
10 John Brummette, Marcia DiStaso, Michail Vafeiadis and Marcus Messner, "Read All About It: The Politicization of 'Fake News' on Twitter," *Journalism and Mass Communication Quarterly* 95, 2 (1 May 2018): 497–517.
11 Siva Vaidhyanathan, *Antisocial Media: How Facebook Disconnects Us and Undermines Democracy* (New York: Oxford University Press, 2018).
12 Hunt Allcott and Matthew Gentzkow, "Social Media and Fake News in the 2016 Election," *Journal of Economic Perspectives* 31, 2 (2017): 211–36.
13 Samuel C. Woolley and Philip N. Howard, eds, *Computational Propaganda: Political Parties, Politicians, and Political Manipulation on Social Media* (New York: Oxford University Press, 2018).
14 Allcott and Gentzkow, "Social Media and Fake News in the 2016 Election."

15 "Introduction: Why Platform Governance?," Centre for International Governance Innovation, 2019, https://www.cigionline.org/articles/introduction-why-platform-governance.
16 Grant Kippen, *The Use of Information Technologies by a Political Party* (Vancouver and Burnaby: SFU-UBC Centre for the Study of Government Business, 2000).
17 Tamara A. Small, "Two Decades of Digital Party Politics in Canada: An Assessment," in *Canadian Parties in Transition: Recent Trends and New Paths for Research*, 4th ed., ed. A. Brian Tanguay and Alain-G. Gagnon (Toronto: University of Toronto Press, 2016), 92–110.
18 Tamara A. Small, "Digital Third Parties: Understanding the Technological Challenge to Canada's Third Party Advertising Regime," *Canadian Public Administration* 61, 2 (2018): 266–83.
19 Colette Brin, "Digital News Report: Canada," Reuters Institute for the Study of Journalism, 2019, http://www.digitalnewsreport.org/survey/2019/canada-2019/.
20 Public Policy Forum, "Mind the Gaps: Quantifying the Decline of News Coverage in Canada," 2018, https://ppforum.ca/publications/mind-the-gaps/.
21 Amy Mitchell, Katie Simmons, Katerina Eva Matsa, and Laura Silver, "Publics Globally Want Unbiased News Coverage, But Are Divided on Whether Their News Media Deliver," Pew Research Center, 2018, https://www.pewresearch.org/global/2018/01/11/publics-globally-want-unbiased-news-coverage-but-are-divided-on-whether-their-news-media-deliver/.
22 Lisa Young, "Election Law in the Age of Digital Globalization: A Preliminary Analysis of the Government of Canada's Approach," Annual Meeting of the Canadian Political Science Association, 2–4 June 2019, Vancouver, British Columbia.
23 Bruce Anderson and David Colleto, "Most Canadians Expect Foreign Governments May Try to Influence Canada's Election," Abacus Data, 21 February 2019, https://abacusdata.ca/most-canadians-expect-foreign-governments-may-try-to-influence-canadas-election/.
24 Ibid.
25 Communications Security Establishment, *Cyber Threats to Canada's Democratic Process* (Ottawa: Communications Security Establishment, 2019); Communications Security Establishment, *2019 Update: Cyber Threats to Canada's Democratic Process* (Ottawa: Communications Security Establishment, 2019), https://cyber.gc.ca/sites/default/files/publications/tdp-2019-report_e.pdf.
26 Ibid., 20.

27 Standing Senate Committee on Legal and Constitutional Affairs, *Controlling Foreign Influence in Canadian Elections* (Ottawa: Senate of Canada, 2017), https://www.sencanada.ca/content/sen/committee/421/LCJC/Reports/Election_Report_FINAL_e.pdf.
28 Standing Committee on Access to Information, Privacy and Ethics, *Democracy under Threat: Risks and Solutions in the Era of Disinformation and Data Monopoly Report of the Standing Committee on Access to Information, Privacy and Ethics* (Ottawa: House of Commons, 2018), vii, https://www.ourcommons.ca/DocumentViewer/en/42-1/ETHI/report-17.
29 Democratic Institutions, "The Government of Canada's Plan to Safeguard Canada's 2019 Election," Government of Canada, Democratic Institutions, 21 March 2019, https://www.canada.ca/en/democratic-institutions/news/2019/03/speech-thegovernment-of-canadas-plan-to-safeguard-canadas-2019-election.html.
30 Government of Canada, *Canada Declaration on Electoral Integrity Online*, 27 May 2019, https://www.canada.ca/en/democratic-institutions/services/protecting-democracy/declaration-electoral-integrity.html.
31 Small, "Digital Third Parties."
32 Elections Canada, *Report of the Chief Electoral Officer of Canada on the 41st General Election of May 2, 2011* (Ottawa: Elections Canada, 2011), http://www.elections.ca/res/rep/off/sta_2011/stat_report2011_e.pdf.
33 Tamara A. Small, "Regulating Canadian Elections in the Digital Age: Approaches and Concerns," *Election Law Journal* 8, 3 (2009): 189–205; Fred Fletcher and Andre Blais, "New Media, Old Media, Campaigns and Canadian Democracy," in *From New Public Management to New Political Governance: Essays in Honour of Peter C. Aucoin*, ed. Herman Bakvis and Mark D. Jarvis (Montreal and Kingston: McGill-Queen's University Press, 2012), 151–78; Holly Ann Garnett, Michael Pal, Christian Leuprecht, and Elizabeth Judge, *Defending Democracy: Confronting Cyber-Threats to Canadian Elections* (Ottawa: Canadian Defense Association Institute., 2019).
34 For an overview of the Fair Elections Act, see Louis Massicotte, "Roll Back! The Conservatives Rewritten Election Law, 2006–2015," in *The Canadian Federal Election of 2015*, ed. Jon H Pammett and Christopher Dornan (Toronto: Dundurn, 2016), 165–94.
35 Centre for International Governance Innovation and Alliance of Democracies Foundation, *Election Risk Monitor: Canada* (Waterloo, ON: Centre for International Governance Innovation, 2019), https://www.cigionline.org/publications/election-risk-monitor-canada.

36 Elections Canada, "New Registry Requirements for Political Ads on Online Platforms," 2019, https://www.elections.ca/content.aspx?section=pol&dir=regifaq&document=index&lang=e#q3.
37 These definitions are found in section 2 (Interpretation) of the Canada Election Act, 2000.
38 Elections Canada, "New Registry Requirements for Political Ads on Online Platforms."
39 Ibid.
40 Peter Zimonjic, "Environmental Groups Can Still Talk Climate Change during Election, Says Canada's Chief Electoral Officer," CBC News, 20 August 2019, https://www.cbc.ca/news/politics/climate-elections-canada-perrault-1.5253580.
41 Elections Canada, "CEO Statement Regarding Third Party Requirements on Issue Advertising," August 2019, https://www.elections.ca/content.aspx?section=med&document=aug2019&dir=spe&lang=e.
42 Katrina Gould, "The 2019 Federal Election," Pub. L. No. 420, § House of Commons, 2019.
43 Elizabeth Dubois, Fenwick McKelvey, and Taylor Owen, "What Have We Learned from Google's Political Ad Pullout?," *Policy Options*, 10 April 2019, https://policyoptions.irpp.org/fr/magazines/avril-2019/learned-googles-political-ad-pullout/.
44 "Observations to the Twenty-Ninth Report of the Standing Senate Committee on Legal and Constitutional Affairs (Bill C-76)" (Ottawa: Senate of Canada, 2018), https://sencanada.ca/content/sen/committee/421/LCJC/reports/LCJCC-762018-12-06v7_e.pdf.
45 Google Canada, C-76: *Online Platforms Issues and Recommendations (Brief)* (Ottawa: Senate of Canada, 2018), https://sencanada.ca/content/sen/committee/421/LCJC/Briefs/Google-C-76-_e.pdf.
46 Ibid., slide 18.
47 "Written Submission to the Standing Committee Legal and Constitutional Affairs," Ottawa, Senate of Canada, 2018, https://sencanada.ca/content/sen/committee/421/LCJC/Briefs/LCJCCorrectedSubmission_e.pdf.
48 Google Canada in Tom Cardoso, "Google to Ban Political Ads Ahead of Federal Election, Citing New Transparency Rules," *Globe and Mail*, 4 March 2019, https://www.theglobeandmail.com/politics/article-google-to-ban-political-ads-ahead-of-federal-election-citing-new/.
49 Michele Austin, "An Update on Canadian Political Advertising," 29 August 2019, https://blog.twitter.com/en_ca/topics/company/2019/update_canadian_political_advertising_2019.html.
50 Jack, Twitter, https://twitter.com/jack/status/1189634360472829952

51 Dubois, McKelvey, and Owen, "What Have We Learned from Google's Political Ad Pullout?"
52 My thanks to Kevin Chan, global director and head of public policy at Facebook Canada, for access to documentation about the Ad Library.
53 Nathaniel Persily, "The 2016 US Election: Can Democracy Survive the Internet?," *Journal of Democracy* 28, 2 (2017): 64.
54 Vaidhyanathan, *Antisocial Media*.
55 See http://facebookcanadianelectionintegrityinitiative.com/about.html for more information about diverse projects that make up the Canadian Election Integrity Initiative.
56 See https://transparency.facebook.com/community-standards-enforcement #fake-accounts.
57 Global New registry is located at https://globalnews.ca/pages/advertisers-election-registry, while CBC/Radio-Canada is located at https://cbc.radio-canada.ca/en/impact-and-accountability/regulatory/political-ads-registry.
58 Elections Canada, "Ne Registry Requirements for Political Ads on Online Platforms."
59 Philip N. Howard, "Deep Democracy, Thin Citizenship: The Impact of Digital Media in Political Campaign Strategy," *Annals of the American Academy of Political and Social Science* 597, 1 (2005): 158.
60 Small, "Two Decades of Digital Party Politics in Canada."
61 Digital Democracy Project, "Research Memo #6: Political Advertising on Facebook," Public Policy Forum, 2019, https://ppforum.ca/articles/ddp-research-memo-6/; Michael D'Alimonte, "The Facebook Campaign Trail: Analysis of Ads Shows Shifting Priorities for Parties in Campaign's Final Stretch," CTV News, 20 October 2019, https://election.ctvnews.ca/the-facebook-campaign-trail-analysis-of-ads-shows-shifting-priorities-for-parties-in-campaign-s-final-stretch-1.4646985.
62 My thanks to Michael D'Alimonte for sharing the data he collected from the Facebook Ad Library with me.
63 Canadian Press, "Canada's Election Has Been 'Largely Clean' of Misinformation, Research Shows," *Global News*, 10 October 2019, https://globalnews.ca/news/6017741/canada-election-misinformation-research/.
64 Sean Boynton, "Scheer Defends Conservative Chinese Facebook Ads Saying Trudeau Will Legalize Hard Drugs," Global News, 12 October 2019, https://globalnews.ca/news/6025644/conservative-facebook-ads-drugs-liberals/.
65 Ellen P. Goodman and Lyndsey Wajert, "The Honest Ads Act Won't End Social Media Disinformation, But It's a Start", 2017, https://papers.ssrn.com/abstract=3064451.

66 Ibid.
67 Woolley and Howard, *Computational Propaganda: Political Parties, Politicians, and Political Manipulation on Social Media* (New York: Oxford University Press, 2018).
68 Dick Morris, *Vote.Com: Influence, and the Internet Is Giving Power Back to the People* (Los Angeles: Renaissance Books, 1999); Joe Trippi, *The Revolution Will Not Be Televised: Democracy, the Internet, and the Overthrow of Everything* (Los Angeles: ReganBooks, 2005).
69 Yana Breindl and Pascal Francq, "Can Web 2.0 Applications Save e-Democracy? A Study of How New Internet Applications May Enhance Citizen Participation in the Political Process Online," *International Journal of Electronic Democracy* 1, 1 (2008): 14–31.
70 Monika Bickert, "Enforcing against Manipulated Media," *Facebook Blog*, 7 January 2020, https://about.fb.com/news/2020/01/enforcing-against-manipulated-media/.
71 Brit Paris and Joan Donovan, *Deepfakes and Cheap Fakes: The Manipulation of Audio and Visual Evidence* (New York: Data and Society, 2019), https://datasociety.net/wp-content/uploads/2019/09/DS_Deepfakes_Cheap_FakesFinal-1.pdf.
72 Buzzfeed, "You won't believe what Obama Says in This Video," https://www.youtube.com/watch?v=cQ54GDm1eLo.
73 Paris and Donovan, "Deepfakes and Cheap Fakes: The Manipulation of Audio and Visual Evidence."

10

From Sunny Ways to Cloudy Days: Voting in the 2019 Federal Election

Harold D. Clarke and Marianne C. Stewart

On the evening of 19 October 2015, Justin Trudeau and Canada's federal Liberal Party celebrated a major election victory. After losses in three preceding federal elections, the resurgent Liberals had swept back to power with strong support throughout most of the country. Addressing supporters on election evening, Trudeau reiterated the remarks made by an earlier Liberal prime minister, Sir Wilfrid Laurier, more than a century earlier. In his famous speech, Laurier had extolled the politics of "sunny ways." Trudeau claimed that Laurier had been right to argue that a politics of fairness and justice was not only the right thing to do but was also electorally efficacious. Almost exactly four years later, the results of the October 2019 federal election cast doubt on the latter assertion. The inability of the Liberals or their rivals to win a majority of parliamentary seats meant that Canadians would be faced with the "cloudy days" of minority government.

This chapter investigates forces that shaped the choices Canadians made in the 2019 federal election. As in many earlier such contests, voters' judgments about actual or anticipated performance on salient issues such as the economy and health care played major roles. Large majorities of people prefer an economy characterized by vigorous growth and low levels of unemployment and inflation. There is also virtually unanimous consent that a readily accessible and affordable health care system is essential, as are high-quality education and protection from threats posed by terrorists and common criminals. Since these issues engender widespread agreement on the ends of public policy, political debate focuses on "how" and, especially, "who" is able to do the job.

In 2019, concerns with environmental protection and climate change joined this list. Long a concern for many scientists and a minority of the public, the environment climbed to prominence on the issue agenda and joined health care and the economy as major topics of discussion during the election campaign. Like these issues, the environment is, by itself, very much a valence issue – all sane people want a clean, safe environment that will sustain life on the planet in the future. However, achieving that goal may involve implementing policies that have significant effects on economic activity – particularly the production and consumption of fossil fuels. As is discussed below, how voters thought about an environment-economy trade-off factored into the choices they made in 2019.

Given the importance of the issues at stake and many attendant uncertainties about what policies might actually produce, voters rely heavily on cues provided by party labels and images of the party leaders.[1] Below, we demonstrate that, as in many earlier Canadian elections, these valence politics forces heavily influenced voters' choices in 2019. The analyses are based on an internet survey of a representative national sample of 1,517 members of the Canadian electorate conducted by Abacus Data immediately after the 2019 election.[2]

THE MAIN ISSUES IN 2019

The economy is often designated as the canonical valence issue, and it typically occupies a prominent place on the issue agenda during election campaigns in Canada and other mature democracies.[3] Accordingly, analysts argue that the current state of the economy can tell us a great deal about whether an incumbent government will be returned to office. Data on trends in Canada's economy since 2015, when Justin Trudeau's Liberals swept to office, and October 2019 paint a generally positive national picture. At the time of the 2015 election, the country was technically in recession, having suffered two consecutive quarters of negative growth. Growth was not spectacular afterwards, but it was positive, running at .91 percent for the second quarter of 2019. The trend in unemployment was also encouraging – joblessness had declined from 7.0 to 5.5 percent. There was other good news as well. Many investors witnessed their assets appreciating, with the total share price index climbing from 95.97 to 116.29 since 2015. For its part, the Canadian dollar was trading at 1.32 per US dollar, virtually unchanged from four years earlier. However, inflation was becoming worrisome. Housing prices, particularly in major urban markets, were especially concerning; overall, the housing price index had moved up by fully 21 percent since 2015.[4]

Still, hardships occasioned by rising prices were not enough to offset positive trends in the economy in the minds of many voters in 2019. As figure 10.1 shows, a clear majority (57 percent) of respondents participating in the Abacus post-election survey judged the economy positively, while 43 percent had negative opinions. These figures are the mirror image of those from 2015, when 43 percent had offered positive endorsements and 57 percent negative ones (see figure 10.1). Although the 2019 numbers were less positive on balance than comparable figures for 2011 when Stephen Harper's Conservatives had won a majority government, they suggest that, outside Alberta and Saskatchewan, where the oil slump had caused major problems, voters' judgments about the state of the economy were, on balance, positive and would boost the Trudeau Liberals' efforts to be re-elected.

Although various aspects of the economy were prominent on the issue agenda in 2019, a number of other issues were also on voters' minds. When queried about the three most important issues facing the country, 45 percent of the survey respondents chose the cost of living, but substantial numbers chose other economic issues, like taxes, the deficit, inequality, or "the economy" generally (see figure 10.2). Health care, the environment, and immigration were also major concerns. When it came to health care, the focus in 2019 was on "pharmacare" – providing Canadians with affordable, high-quality drugs. In the event, health care was the second most frequently mentioned issue at 42 percent, with the environment close behind at 38 percent.

Although the need to protect and improve Canada's health care system has featured prominently in previous federal elections, parties, with the exception of the Green Party, generally have placed less emphasis on climate change or the environment. In a notable exception, former Liberal leader Stéphane Dion had made the issue the centrepiece of his party's 2008 platform with his "Green Shift" policy, but his efforts were largely derailed by the global crash in financial markets that occurred during the campaign.[5] In 2019, no such intervention occurred and, as figure 10.2 illustrates, environmental concerns emerged as a prominent topic.

Decades of research indicates that Canadians' judgments about parties' abilities to deal with salient valence issues are key factors when they cast their ballots.[6] The data displayed in figure 10.3 indicate that,

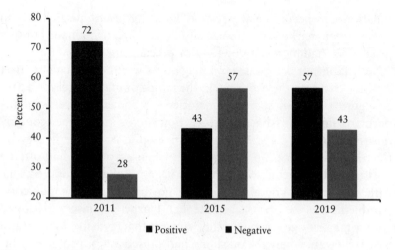

Figure 10.1 Evaluations of the Canadian economy, 2011, 2015, 2019

Source: 2011 Political Support in Canada pre-election survey, 2015 Abacus pre-election survey, 2019 Abacus post-election survey.

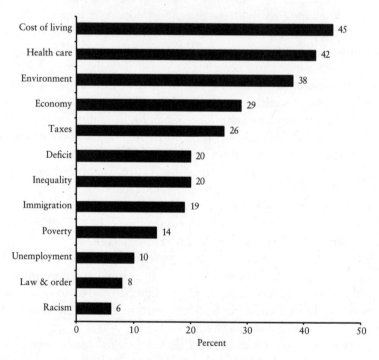

Figure 10.2 Three most important issues facing the country

Source: 2019 Abacus post-election survey.

Voting in the 2019 Federal Election 225

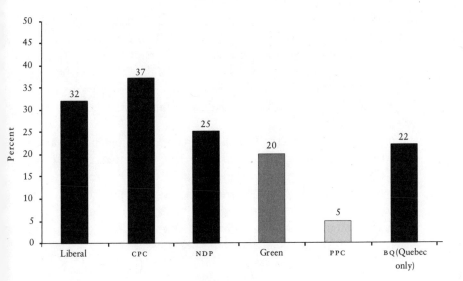

Figure 10.3 Party best on most important issue
Source: 2019 Abacus post-election survey.

despite a relatively robust national economy, in 2019 the governing Liberals trailed the Conservatives (by 32 percent versus 37 percent) when the Abacus survey respondents were asked which party could best deal with important issues. The NDP, the Greens, and the People's Party of Canada (PPC) lagged behind with 25 percent, 20 percent, and 8 percent, respectively.

These global figures conceal large differences in voters' judgments about party competence on specific issues. As illustrated in figure 10.4, the Conservatives enjoyed large leads over the Liberals on several economic issues, such as the deficit (51 percent to 19 percent), taxes (51 percent to 29 percent) and the economy generally (48 percent to 32 percent). However, the Conservative edge on the cost of living issue, a topic of concern to many Canadians, was much smaller (35 percent to 33 percent). For their part, the Liberals outranked the Conservatives in their perceived ability to deal with economic inequality (38 percent to 11 percent) and several non-economic issues, including health care (38 percent to 29 percent), racism (47 percent to 10 percent), and poverty (32 percent to 19 percent).

The inability of the Liberals to get more credit for the state of the economy is noteworthy. It may be that the generally good economic news was being discounted in the minds of many voters by news about the economic hardships in western Canada caused by the decline in the oil industry. Also, the Conservatives tried to make the economy a focal point of attention, with their campaign slogan "It's time for you to get ahead." Arguing that, if elected, they would "leave more money in your pocket," it is evident that the message crafted by party leader Andrew Scheer and his Conservative colleagues resonated with a sizable number of voters.

On the environment, the Liberals' perceived competence dwarfed all of the other parties, being ranked highest by 41 percent as compared to only 14 percent for the Conservatives, 21 percent for the NDP, and 11 percent for the Greens. Thus, although the Liberals trailed the Conservatives on the global "party best" issue measure, they were well placed on health care and, especially, the environment – two of voters' most widely cited important issues in 2019.

PARTY LEADERS

Canadians always pay a great deal of attention to party leaders when deciding how to vote. The parties inevitably make their leaders the centrepieces of their election campaigns, and the comings and goings of the leaders as they traverse the country in search of votes are a constant focal point of media coverage as the campaigns unfold. In the intervals between elections, close attention to the leaders continues on an almost daily basis. Given this preoccupation with what the leaders are saying and doing, it is not surprising that Canadians use leader images as a principal heuristic (cue) when deciding how to vote. In a sense voters are "smart enough to know they are not smart enough" to make decisions on the basis of proposed policies advocated by rival parties, and so they rely heavily their impressions of the character and competence of party leaders for guidance.[7]

In 2015, many Canadians were attracted by Justin Trudeau, who appeared as a young and progressive figure, as well as being the son of former prime minister Pierre Elliott Trudeau. Although the Conservatives deployed a series of attack ads to claim that the younger Trudeau lacked experience and intellectual heft and "was just not ready" to be prime minister, he was able to convince a large segment of the electorate otherwise. In a series of nationally televised debate appearances Trudeau demonstrated that he was able to hold his own with then Conservative prime minister Stephen Harper and NDP leader Thomas Mulcair, whose party had displaced the Liberals as the

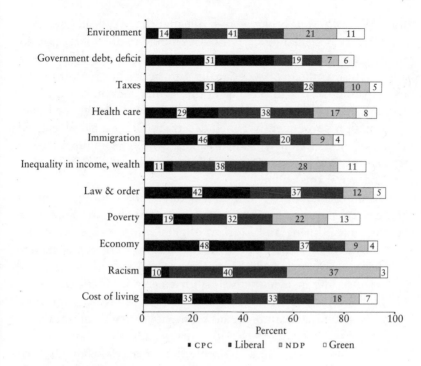

Figure 10.4 Party best on specific important issues

Source: 2019 post-election survey.

official opposition in 2011. Trudeau's convincing debate appearances and generally strong performance on the campaign trail paved the way for his party's 2015 victory.[8]

Four years later, things were different. Rather than having a "low bar" to jump as in 2015, Trudeau's claim of the many positive accomplishments that his "sunny ways" politics could accomplish had set a high standard that he ultimately found difficult to meet, despite the aforementioned improvements in the economy. Symbolizing Trudeau's problems was the policy stalemate caused by his government's inability to decide, in light of mounting concerns about climate change and protests by First Nations groups, whether to build new pipelines to carry western oil to national and international markets.

Trudeau's indecision on energy policy and the environment was not his only problem. His reputation as a "kinder, gentler" politician bound by honesty and integrity suffered as well. Two high-profile scandals captured widespread attention. In February 2019, the *Globe and Mail* broke a story alleging that Trudeau had pressured Attorney General Jody Wilson-Raybould to drop charges in an ongoing criminal case against SNC-Lavalin, a major Quebec-based construction company. SNC-Lavalin had been charged with bribing Libyan government officials in the regime of brutal ex-dictator Mummar Ghaddafi. Although he denied any wrongdoing, the Ethics Commission subsequently concluded that Trudeau had exercised improper influence on Wilson-Raybould, whom he had removed as attorney general and subsequently dismissed from the Liberal caucus (see chapter 2, this volume).

A second scandal broke in mid-September 2019 during the midst of the election campaign. Pictures taken in 2001 showing Trudeau in "brownface" during an "Arabian Nights" fundraising event at a Vancouver school where he was then teaching were published and received massive press coverage in Canada and abroad. Pictures and videos of similar incidents subsequently emerged. Amidst charges of racism and hypocrisy, Trudeau apologized for behaving inappropriately and promised to improve his sensitivity to visible minorities.

The 2019 Abacus post-election survey indicates that the SNC-Lavalin scandal resonated with sizable, but not overwhelmingly large, numbers of people. Specifically, 38 percent agreed that Trudeau should have resigned because of the affair, while 35 percent disagreed and 27 percent said they "didn't know" (see figure 10.5). The brownface pictures left voters unsure: 28 percent agreed that they showed Trudeau was a hypocrite when he claimed to be a champion of minorities and 29 percent disagreed, while a large plurality (43 percent) placed themselves in the "don't know" category. Although these figures testify that voters' reactions to the scandals were deeply divided, the affairs clearly would not help to burnish the prime minister's image.

The impact on Trudeau's image is reinforced by responses to questions asking the survey respondents their overall impressions of the party leaders. Figure 10.6 shows these data for leaders in 2015 and 2019. In 2015, a large plurality (44 percent) reported that they had a positive image of Trudeau, and only 30 percent said they had a negative image. Four years later, the balance had shifted sharply, with 36 percent stating they had a positive impression of him and 46 percent saying they had a negative one (see figure 10.6).

When evaluating this negative shift in Trudeau's image and its possible impact on voting, it is important to observe that Trudeau's main rival, Conservative leader Andrew Scheer, was negatively received by

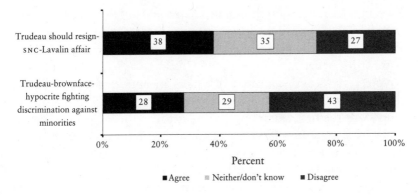

Figure 10.5 Reactions to Trudeau scandals
Source: 2019 Abacus post-election survey.

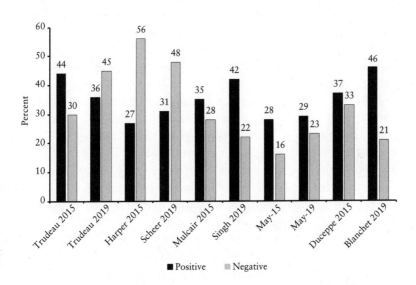

Figure 10.6 Evaluations of party leaders, 2015 and 2019
Source: 2015 Abacus pre-election survey; 2019 Abacus post-election survey.

even more voters. As figure 10.6 illustrates, nearly half (48 percent) of the Abacus survey respondents said they had a negative view of Scheer, and only 31 percent reported a positive impression. These numbers echoed the frosty reception received by Scheer's predecessor, Stephen Harper, in 2015. At that time, only 27 percent had rated Harper positively and fully 58 percent had scored him negatively. To have an image in the public mind similar to that of a predecessor who had been decisively defeated four years before and had long been viewed as a divisive figure in Canadian politics was definitely not a plus for Mr Scheer.

Voters' views of the other party leaders are noteworthy as well. Like the Conservatives, in 2019 the NDP had a new leader, Jagmeet Singh. Singh was the first federal party leader to be a member of a visible minority community (Sikh), and commentators had speculated on how he would be received by the broader electorate (see chapter 4, this volume). As it happened – bolstered by strong debate performances – Singh was seen positively by many voters. Forty-one percent rated him positively and only 22 percent said they had a negative impression. Singh's scores were better than those recorded by his predecessor Thomas Mulcair in 2015, who had positive and negative ratings of 35 percent and 28 percent, respectively. Green leader Elizabeth May also made a net positive impression, although, as in earlier elections, many people said they "didn't know" when asked about her. And, in Quebec, new Bloc Québécois leader Yves-François Blanchet paved the way for his party's resurgence. Blanchet was very well liked by many Quebecers, with his positive impressions (46 percent) far outpacing his negative ones (21 percent).

The data on party leader images, particularly the negative tilt in impressions of the leaders of the two major parties, Trudeau and Scheer, foreshadow their parties' failures to capture the support of the number of voters needed for a conclusive victory. In the next section, we see that data on voters' partisan attachments lead to the same conclusion.

FLEXIBLE PARTISANSHIP

In their seminal mid-twentieth-century studies of voting behaviour in the United States, researchers at the University of Michigan had concluded that many voters have long-term, stable psychological attachments to political parties.[9] Labelled party identifications, these attachments were typically formed as the result of socialization processes occurring in childhood and adolescence, and they constituted powerful cues that guided electoral choice in successive elections. However, when the Canadian Election Studies were first conducted in the 1960s, researchers found that many survey respondents recalled having identified with other parties in the past.[10] Subsequent surveys in which respondents were re-interviewed on multiple occasions have repeatedly confirmed that many Canadians do indeed have "flexible" partisan attachments.[11] This flexibility in loyalty to a party facilitates individual-level movements in voting for various parties from one election to the next, and it makes large-scale changes in voting behaviour and election outcomes ongoing, if not always realized, possibilities.[12]

It bears emphasizing that the flexibility of partisanship in Canada does not gainsay the importance of feelings about the parties at any given time as a cue for making voting choices in particular elections. Moreover, based on judgments about actual or anticipated party performance, the balance of partisanship can shift in consequential ways between successive elections. Figure 10.7 indicates that this is exactly what occurred between 2011 and 2015 when the percentage of federal Liberal Party identifiers increased markedly, climbing from 21 to 31 percent. In contrast, the share of Conservative identifiers fell from 31 to 26 percent, while the share of NDP identifiers declined from 17 to 13 percent. Statistical analyses indicate that erosion in the number of Conservative and NDP identifiers combined with the sharp surge in Liberal partisans helped to propel the Trudeau Liberals to power.[13]

Between 2015 and 2019, aggregate changes in party identification were more muted. Figure 10.7 shows that the Conservative and NDP partisan shares remained unchanged, at 26 and 13 percent, respectively. The Green Party enjoyed a small increase, with the number of Green identifiers moving from 3 to 4 percent, thus doubling the percentage of partisans (2 percent) they had two elections earlier, but still much lower than they had hoped (see chapter 6, this volume). Most notable is the decline in the percentage of federal Liberal identifiers, which fell by 5 percent to a level of 26 percent. This decrease in the number of Liberal partisans combined with the erosion in Prime Minister Trudeau's approval ratings and his party's less than stellar issue performance ratings were key factors driving electoral choice in 2019.

AN ECONOMY-ENVIRONMENT TRADE-OFF?

As in many earlier Canadian federal elections, voting behaviour in 2019 was guided by three powerful forces - judgments about party performance on important issues, party leader images, and partisan identifications. Above, we observed that evaluations of economic performance typically play an important role when voters make their party performance judgments. In 2019, the impact of such judgments

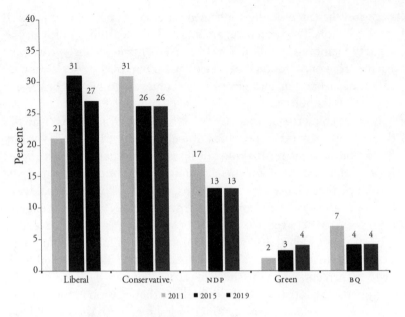

Figure 10.7 Federal party identification, 2011, 2015, 2019

Source: 2011, 2015 Canadian Election Survey, post-election wave; 2019 Abacus post-election survey.

was complicated by the enhanced salience of concerns about climate change and environmental protection. As observed, nearly two-fifths of the Abacus survey respondents rated the environment as one of their top three important issues. Moreover, when asked about whether they would give priority to protecting the environment over growing the economy or vice versa, a plurality (42 percent) opted for the environment, with 37 percent choosing the economy and 21 percent saying they "didn't know."

Although it is often observed that younger people are particularly concerned with climate change and other environmental issues, age differences in these priorities were not especially large. Specifically, 48 percent of those under thirty years of age prioritized the environment as compared to 41 percent of those aged sixty or over. For the economy, age differences were larger, with 29 percent of the under-thirties and 41 percent of the over-sixties emphasizing growth at the expense of environmental protection. This pattern suggests that the relative importance of the environment as an issue may increase in future elections as successive generations of environmentally conscious

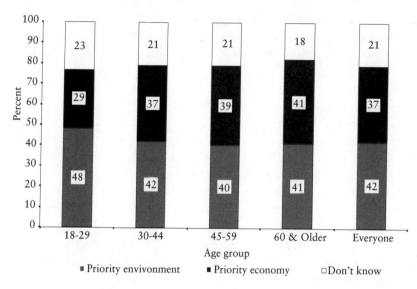

Figure 10.8 Trade-off between climate change and the economy by age group

Source: 2019 Abacus post-election survey.

young people replace older voters who prioritize a traditional mix of economic issues.

The willingness of many Canadians to sacrifice economic growth for environmental protection is a potentially significant development that may affect voters' party performance judgments and, hence, the electoral choices they make. The effect of this trade-off thinking is illustrated in an analysis of factors affecting voting in the 2019 election. In this analysis, we investigate voting for the governing Liberal Party as a function of three classic valence politics variables – judgments about the state of the economy, party leader images, and partisan attachments. In addition, we include a predictor variable that measures whether voters prioritize the environment or the economy. As observed earlier, when it came to judgments on party performance on important issues the Liberals had a huge lead as the party preferred to deal with environmental protection and climate change (see figure 10.4). Accordingly, it can be anticipated that Mr Trudeau and his party would receive heavy support from voters who prioritized the environment over the economy.

However – and ironically – this trade-off also has the potential to decrease the impact of positive economic evaluations on governing party support as environmentally conscious voters discount economic considerations in favour of worries about the earth's future. Translated into the language of statistics, this trade-off implies that both economic evaluations and according priority to the environment over the economy will have positive effects on the likelihood of voting for the governing Liberals, but there will be a negative "interaction effect" that decreases the importance of economic judgments among voters prioritizing the environment. For such people, concerns about the environment discount the importance accorded to the economy.

Table 10.1 displays the results of this analysis. As anticipated, both party leader images and party identifications have predictable effects on Liberal voting, with positive feelings about Justin Trudeau and Liberal partisanship both increasing the probability of voting Liberal and positive feelings about Andrew Scheer, Jagmeet Singh, and Yves-François Blanchet, and with Conservative and NDP partisanship reducing that probability (see table 10.1). Also as expected, both positive evaluations of the performance of the economy and according priority to the environment enhance the likelihood of Liberal voting.

The negative interaction effect between economic judgments and the economy-environment trade-off is also in evidence. Taking into account the type of statistical model used to analyze Liberal voting, figure 10.9 summarizes the results of this interaction effect. The horizontal axis of the figure shows the overall probability of voting Liberal for each of the survey respondents, while the vertical axis shows whether the interaction effect for a respondent is statistically significant. The figure illustrates that, for a large majority of voters (67 percent), the economy x environment-economy interaction effect is statistically significant ($p < .05$) and *negative*, and it is not positive and significant in even a single case.[14] This finding suggests an irony for the Trudeau Liberals and other governing parties that wish to benefit from both positive economic performance judgments and a reputation for heightened environmental awareness. Gains such parties make from good economic performance will be discounted by voters who give precedence to environmental concerns. The analysis suggests that this is what happened to the Liberals in 2019.

VALENCE VOTING 2019

As is typically the case, three major variables – evaluations of party performance on important issues, party leader images, and partisan

Table 10.1
Economic voting model of Liberal support

Predictor variable	b	s.e.
Economic evaluations	1.50***	.51
Priority to economy or environment	1.47**	.56
Interaction effect: Economic evaluations x priority to economy or environment	-.60***	.20
Party leaders:		
Trudeau	1.48***	.12
Scheer	-.47***	.10
Singh	-.30**	.12
May	-.18	.12
Bernier	-.07	.11
Blanchet	-.39***	.10
Party identification:		
Liberal	1.22***	.24
Conservative	-1.18**	.40
NDP	-1.51***	.32
Other party	-.95	.59
Constant	-5.17***	1.44

McKelvey R^2 = .76
% Correctly Classified = 88.4

*** - $p \leq .001$, ** - $p \leq .01$, * - $p \leq .05$, one-tailed test.

identifications – provide a powerful and parsimonious explanation of electoral choice in 2019. Table 10.2 documents the importance of these predictors. The analyses summarized in this table include these three predictors along with several other explanatory variables. The latter include measures of left-right ideology, reactions to Trudeau's scandals, attitudes towards immigration and minorities, and several socio-demographics (age, education, gender, income, region/ethnicity).[15] The numbers displayed in table 10.2 are changes in probability of voting for a particular party when a statistically significant predictor variable is moved across its range while controlling for the effects of other predictors.

Impressions of the party leaders had very strong effects. As shown in table 10.2, with other factors controlled, the probability of voting Liberal in 2019 increased by fully .71 points (on a 0–1 scale) as impressions of Justin Trudeau moved from very negative to very positive. The effects of attitudes towards Andrew Scheer on Conservative voting

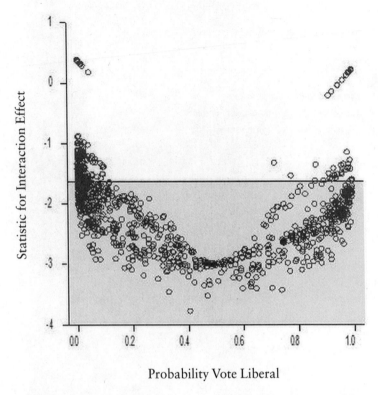

Figure 10.9 Statistically significant interactions between evaluations of the economy and climate change versus economy trade-off

Note: All cases in the shaded area have statistically significant (p< .05) negative interactions between economic evaluations and priority of environment over economy.

were even stronger, with the probability of casting a ballot for his party increasing by fully .86 points if someone held a positive as opposed to a negative image of him. Mr Scheer's problem was that many Canadians were negatively disposed towards him. If he had been more warmly greeted, this would have been very helpful to his party. However, it was not to be.

Leader image effects were smaller, but still sizable, for NDP and Green voting – a positive impression of Jagmeet Singh boosted the likelihood of supporting the NDP by .33 points and a positive impression of Elizabeth May had a positive impact of .38 points on the

Table 10.2
Change in probability of voting for various political parties produced by changes in statistically significant predictor variables

Predictor variable	Party voted for Conservative	Liberal	NDP	Green
PARTY LEADERS:				
Scheer	.86	-.28		-.09
Trudeau	-.24	.71	-.09	-.15
Singh	-.23	-.23	.33	-.03
May			-.13	.38
Bernier				
Blanchet		-.15		-.07
PARTY BEST ON MOST IMPORTANT ISSUES:				
Conservative	.23	-.10	-.09	
Liberal	-.17	.19	-.07	-.05
NDP	-.13		.14	
Green			-.05	.07
BQ	-.29	-.23	-.18	
PPC		-.21		
FEDERAL PARTY IDENTIFICATION:				
Conservative	.29	-.20	-.08	-.09
Liberal		.14	-.05	
NDP		-.24	.11	
Green		-.15		.12
Other			-.08	
Left-right ideology			-.09	.11
Scandals				-.07
Minorities		.19	-.08	
REGION/ETHNICITY:				
Atlantic				
Quebec–French	-.14	-.08		
Quebec–Non-French	-.13			
Alberta	.25		-.08	-.05
Saskatchewan–Manitoba			-.08	.09
BC				
Age			-.13	
Education				
Gender				
Income		.19		
McKelvey R^2	.88	.80	.78	.72
% Correctly predicted	93.6	89.7	92.3	97.0

Note: Binomial logit models; changes in probabilities computed by varying a statistically significant (p ≤ .05) predictor variable across its range while holding all other predictors at their means or reference categories.

probability of voting for her party. Leader images clearly mattered a lot in 2019.

As is also typical, judgments about party performance on important issues were consequential. Specifically, the numbers in table 10.2 reveal that the probability of voting Conservative increases substantially if a voter decided that the Conservatives rather than the Liberals were best on the issues they considered most important. As the table shows, if a voter preferred the Conservatives on important issues, the probability of voting Conservative increased by .40 points. However, if a voter preferred the Liberals, the decrease was .17 points. These figures imply that a move from the Liberals to the Conservatives as best on important issues, would have produced a .40 (.23 to -.17) increase in the likelihood of voting Conservative.

There is a similar, somewhat smaller, effect for Liberal versus NDP issue performance evaluations. If a voter believed the Liberals rather than the NDP was best on important issues, the probability of casting a ballot for the former party rose by .29 points (.19 to -.10). As a third example, the probability of voting NDP rather than Green climbed by .19 points (.11 to -.08) if someone identified with the former rather than the latter party.

Partisanship was very much in play as well. Other things being equal, being a Conservative identifier rather than a nonidentifier boosted the probability of voting for Mr Scheer's party by .29 points. Larger effects obtained for Conservative versus Liberal identifications, with the probability of voting for the former rather than the latter party rising by .34 points (.14 to -.20) if someone were a Conservative rather than a Liberal identifier. Similarly, moving from being a New Democrat to a Liberal identifier increased the probability of supporting Justin Trudeau's party by .38 (.14 to -.24) points.

Table 10.2 also indicates that most other predictor variables were less important. Nevertheless, some are noteworthy. For example, consistent with the Liberals' favourable ratings on the immigration issue, the probability of voting for that party increased by .19 points if someone favoured increased immigration and thought that minority cultures should be protected. Although socio-demographic factors generally had weak effects, moving from the lowest to the highest income category enhanced the likelihood of a Liberal vote by the same amount. And those with minimal educational qualifications had .13 greater probability of voting NDP. Finally, consistent with many Albertans' disaffection with the Trudeau government's energy policies, controlling for all other factors, being an Alberta resident lowered the probability of voting Liberal by fully .25 points.

Overall, the voting models in table 10.2 have impressive explanatory power. The Liberal model can correctly classify 93.6 percent of those voting for or against the Liberals, and the comparable percentages for Conservative, NDP, and Green voting are 89.7, 92.3, and 97.0, respectively.[16] And, similar to earlier elections, the vast majority of this explanatory power derives from the three valence politics variables – party performance judgments, leader images, and partisan identifications. In contrast, left-right ideology, attitudes towards minorities, and reactions to the Trudeau scandals were less important. And, as long has been the case in studies of Canadian voting behaviour, sociodemographic characteristics exhibited very weak effects. Demographics are not irrelevant for understanding electoral choice, but they operate far back in the set of causal forces responsible for the vote. Taken together, these several results combine to testify that the factors that mattered most for voting in 2019 were very similar to those operating in earlier federal elections.

FROM 2015 TO 2019: THE FLOW OF THE VOTE

In the run-up to the 2019 election, public opinion polls had shown the Liberals and Conservatives in a virtual dead-heat, with both parties running at 33 to 34 percent range (see chapter 7, this volume). The polls proved accurate – in the event the Liberals captured 33.1 percent of the vote, down significantly from the 39.5 percent they had taken in 2015 (see figure 10.10). The Conservatives improved their vote share, but the gain was not extensive, moving from 31.9 to 34.4 percent. And, despite the warm reception accorded party leader Jagmeet Singh on the campaign trail, the NDP saw its support fall by nearly four points (from 19.7 to 15.9 percent). Only the Greens and the BQ had reasons to celebrate, with both parties nearly doubling their vote totals. In the case of the Greens, their new-found support still left them with only a very small share of the national vote (6.5 percent), but the Bloc's 32.4 percent in Quebec meant that the party was once again a significant force in that province's politics.

As discussed earlier, sizable numbers of Canadians are open to shifting their party support between adjacent elections. In any given election, a party's total vote is composed of supporters from the previous election, supporters moving from other parties, supporters moving

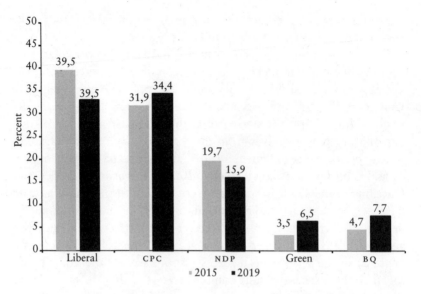

Figure 10.10 Parties' voting percentages in the 2015 and 2019 federal elections

from non-voting, minus people who decide they now prefer another party or will not cast a ballot for any party. Panel A of table 10.3 shows what voters for various parties in 2015 did four years later. The numbers indicate that the Conservatives held on to the vast majority of their 2015 vote (85.9 percent). Similarly, in Quebec, the BQ held fully 90.0 percent of its 2015 supporters. In sharp contrast, the Liberals retained only 62.5 percent of those who had supported them four years earlier. The NDP and the Greens suffered similar fates, holding the loyalty of only about half of their 2015 adherents.

The ability of parties to retain adherents from a previous election and add new ones without suffering substantial losses to other parties or non-voting is crucial for success in any particular election. Panel B of table 10.3 shows overall patterns of stability and change in support for various parties between 2015 and 2019. Considering all those who either voted or failed to do so in 2015, we see that only 52.5 percent stayed in the same place in 2019. A large majority of these people were either Conservatives (19.2 percent) or Liberals (21.8 percent), and only 5.9 percent, 2.2 percent, and 2.8 percent were NDP, Green, or BQ, respectively. We also see how patterns of vote switching either helped or hurt various parties. Perhaps most notable is the 5.7 percent who had voted Liberal in 2015 but moved to the Conservatives in

Table 10.3
The flow of the vote, 2015–19

A. Where the 2015 vote went in 2019

	\multicolumn{6}{c}{2015 vote}
2019 vote	CPC	Liberal	NDP	Green	BQ	Non-voter
CPC	85.9	16.2	10.2	14.8	2.5	31.7
Liberal	5.2	62.1	21.1	9.3	7.5	30.0
NDP	1.0	12.5	46.4	13.0	0.0	21.8
Green	1.0	4.2	8.4	53.7	0.0	8.5
BQ	3.8	4.4	11.4	5.6	90.0	5.1
PPC	3.1	0.7	2.4	3.7	0.0	2.7

B. Combinations of party support in 2015 and 2019 as percentages of everyone voting in 2019

	2015 vote					
2019 vote	CPC	Liberal	NDP	Green	BQ	Non-voter
CPC	19.2	5.7	1.3	0.6	0.1	7.2
Liberal	1.2	21.8	2.7	0.4	0.2	6.8
NDP	0.2	4.4	5.9	0.5	0.0	4.9
Green	0.2	1.5	1.1	2.2	0.0	1.9
BQ	0.8	1.5	1.3	0.2	2.8	1.2
PPC	0.7	0.2	0.3	0.2	0.0	0.6

2019. This compares to only 1.2 percent who moved from the Conservatives to the Liberals – a net gain for the latter party of 3.5 percent. The Liberals also lost 4.4 percent to the NDP while attracting only 2.7 percent of 2015 New Democrats.

Although there are many other smaller exchanges between parties across the two elections, the net Liberal losses to the Conservatives and NDP constituted a significant proportion of the erosion in support Justin Trudeau's party suffered in 2019. Equally, although the Conservatives benefited from their vote exchanges with the Liberals, these were not large enough to propel them to victory. Although many voters moved between 2015 and 2019, the volume of net transfers between the major parties was not large enough to give either of them a parliamentary majority.

FROM SUNNY WAYS TO CLOUDY DAYS

The forces driving voting in 2019 closely resembled those operating in earlier Canadian federal elections. Echoing forces at work in those contests, evaluations of party performance on important valence issues, such as the economy and health care, underpinned the choices many voters made. In 2019, another issue – the environment – joined the list. The Abacus survey data indicate that many voters favoured the Liberals on the environment. However, there is also evidence that a trade-off between according priority to the environment versus the economy worked to lessen the impact of the latter issue. In 2019, many Canadians judged the economy positively. This was good news for Mr Trudeau and his Liberal government. However, the Liberals' ability to reap political profit from these judgments was diminished by a widespread view that environmental concerns should take precedence and that, should a trade-off be required, protecting the environment should have priority over advancing the economy. The economy and the environment were both issues that helped the Liberals in 2019, but their cumulative effects would have been greater if each had operated in isolation.

Issues were not the whole story. As is typical in federal elections, voters relied heavily on cues provided by partisan attachments and party leader images when making up their minds how to cast their ballots. Views of the party leaders were especially important. In this regard, Justin Trudeau was much less well received by the electorate than had been the case in 2015. Although the Canadian economy was relatively robust in overall terms, indecision about how to bring western energy supplies to market damaged his reputation for leadership and made his government's economic record decidedly unappealing to many people in Alberta and Saskatchewan. These problems were exacerbated by widely publicized scandals that left Trudeau open to charges that, despite his talk about "sunny ways" and "positive politics," he was just another self-serving politician disguising an underlying hypocrisy in appealing, but inauthentic, rhetoric.

Trudeau was fortunate that his chief rival, Conservative leader Andrew Scheer, was even less well received. Scheer was unable to generate enthusiasm among large numbers of voters and his approval ratings were dismal across much of the electorate. Although Jagmeet Singh and Elizabeth May, the NDP and Green Party leaders, respectively, on balance were rated more positively than Scheer, many voters were not familiar with them, and this limited their appeal. The only other leader to gain substantial traction was Jean-François Blanchet, whose popularity did much to help the Bloc Québécois capture thirty-two seats and regain a position of prominence in Quebec politics.

In the end, very mixed issue performance judgments combined with mediocre leader images and the failure of any party to attract sizable groups of new partisans set the stage for a minority government outcome. Neither the Liberals nor the Conservatives could muster sufficient strength at the ballot box to win a parliamentary majority. Bolstered by very strong showings in the Atlantic provinces and Ontario, the Liberals won 157 seats, thirty-six seats more than their Conservative rivals. This enabled them to stay in power.

Lacking a majority in Parliament, the Liberals now have to govern with the support of opposition parties, principally the NDP. Historically, minority governments are commonplace in Canada, with fully ten of the twenty-four federal elections held since 1950 yielding a minority outcome. Such governments have survived only a year or two and, if the past is a guide, Canadians may soon find themselves asked to vote in yet another federal election. In the meantime, the "sunny ways" of Justin Trudeau's 2015 electoral triumph have given way to the cloudy and uncertain days of minority government. In his speech on election evening, Trudeau promised his new government would continue to pursue the progressive agenda it had initiated four years earlier. What that will mean in practice remains to be seen.

NOTES

1 Harold D. Clarke, Jane Jenson, Lawrence LeDuc, and Jon H. Pammett, *Absent Mandate – Strategies and Choices in Canadian Elections* (Toronto: University of Toronto Press, 2019); Harold D. Clarke, Allan Kornberg, and Thomas J. Scotto, *Making Political Choices: Canada and the United States* (Toronto: University of Toronto Press, 2009).
2 We thank David Coletto of Abacus Data for making these data available to us.
3 See, for example, Michael S. Lewis-Beck, *Economics and Elections: The Major Western Democracies* (Ann Arbor, MI: University of Michigan Press, 1988).

4 See the Federal Reserve Bank of St Louis (FRED) for time series data on the Canadian economy. The FRED website is https://fred.stlouisfed.org.
5 See, for example, Clarke et al., *Absent Mandate*, chap. 6.
6 Harold Clarke, Allan Kornberg, and Thomas Scotto, *Making Political Choices* (Toronto: University of Toronto Press, 2009), chap. 1.
7 Using leader images as cues to guide voting decisions is consistent with recent research in experimental economics and cognitive psychology on the importance of heuristics for making decisions in situations of high stakes and uncertainty. See, for example, Gerd Gigerenzer, *Rationality of Mortals: How People Cope with Uncertainty* (Oxford: Oxford University Press, 2008).
8 Harold D. Clarke, Jason Reifler, Thomas J. Scotto, and Marianne C. Stewart, "It's Spring Again! Voting in the 2015 Federal Election," in *The Canadian Federal Election of 2015*, ed. Jon H. Pammett and Christopher Dornan (Toronto: Dundurn, 2016), chap. 13.
9 Angus Campbell, Warren E. Miller, Donald E. Stokes, and Phillip E. Converse, *The American Voter* (New York: John Wiley and Sons, 1960).
10 John Meisel, *Working Papers on Canadian Politics*. Enlarged edition (Montreal and Kingston: McGill-Queen's University Press, 1973).
11 Partisan flexibility includes three elements: (1) instability of partisan attachments, (2) weakness of partisan attachments, (3) inconsistency in partisan attachments in federal and provincial politics. Here we focus on instability. For data on the weakness and inconsistency of partisanship, see Clarke et al., *Absent Mandate*, chap. 2.
12 Using multi-wave panel data gathered since the 1970s, Clarke and McCutcheon's statistical analyses demonstrate that large-scale instability in partisan attachments has long been a persistent characteristic of Canadian political psychology. See Harold D. Clarke and Allan McCutcheon, "The Dynamics of Party Identification Reconsidered," *Public Opinion Quarterly* 73 (2009): 704–28. See also Clarke et al., *Absent Mandate*, chap. 2.
13 Clarke et al., *Absent Mandate*, chap. 6.
14 Chunrong Ai and Edward Norton, "Interaction Terms in Logit and Probit Models," *Economic Letters* 80 (2003):123–9. Parameters in the Liberal vote model are estimated using a binomial logit analysis. See J. Scott Long and Jeremy Freeze, *Regression Models for Categorical Dependent Variables Using Stata*, 3rd ed. (College Station, TX: Stata Press, 2014).
15 Details concerning the measurement of various predictors are available from the authors upon request and are also available on their Harvard Dataverse site.

16 The percentage of voters correctly classified is computed by cross-tabulating whether a survey respondent reported voting for a party with whether she or he was predicted to vote for that party according to the analyses summarized in table 10.2. Anyone with a probability of voting for a party that is greater than .5 is predicted to vote for the party in question.

Voting Turnout in 2019:
The Long and the Short of It

Jon H. Pammett and Lawrence LeDuc

At 66 percent, turnout in the 2019 election was well above the lows recorded in the elections of 2004, 2008, or 2011 but lower than that of 2015. This occurred because there are two conflicting factors that have been at work in recent federal elections. The first is the long-term trend that has been steadily driving turnout down to new lows over the past two decades. The second is a series of shorter-term developments that have tempered that trend and acted to stabilize turnout in the mid-60 percent range. Both factors were visible in the 2019 election. In this chapter, we examine these in more detail, reaching a tentative conclusion that one more or less offset the other in this election but that the future direction of turnout is still unclear.

The longer-term trend of turnout decline has been in place since 1993. Driven primarily by demographic forces, it has seen a generation of older voters, who had reliably voted at rates of 75 percent or higher, gradually replaced by younger generations who vote at much lower rates. The underlying causes, which we discuss in more detail subsequently, have to do with attitudes towards electoral politics, feelings of civic duty, a sense of political efficacy, and the relevance of the various issues on which recent elections have been fought.

The shorter-term contrary factors, which have become visible in the past two federal elections, are a more recent reaction to the pre-existing pattern of lower turnout among the young. They represent, in part, a flattening of the longer-term trend, which has now been in place for more than twenty years; a stirring of interest in politics on the part of younger voters; and a changing issue mix. In 2015, young voters were galvanized, as was a good part of the rest of the electorate, by the desire to end the Harper government and elect a more dynamic Justin Trudeau as prime minister. In 2019, younger voters appeared determined to make their voices heard on new issues such as climate change or the costs of education. Youth participation has been facilitated by initiatives taken by Elections Canada in 2015 and in the 2019 election to make voting easier by allowing students to vote in advance polls on university campuses and through "get-out-the-vote" campaigns targeted specifically at the young. Demonstrations about the issue of climate change, which took place in several larger cities during the 2019 campaign, may also have played a role in motivating younger voters.

It is nevertheless clear that the longer-term trend of declining turnout driven by demographic forces has not gone away. Such a process, once it begins, is a very powerful driver of change and will often last for a generation or more. It is not easily reversed, but once it has run its course the pattern of change will begin to flatten. That point may now be close at hand with respect to the longer-term trend of declining turnout in Canada, but it will likely continue to be a factor in examinations of voter turnout for at least another decade. The countervailing factors, which are slowly pulling turnout back up to slightly higher levels, are more unpredictable. The speed of this development depends, in part, on the success of campaigns directed towards younger voters and on a shift of issues away from traditional areas such as health care and economic performance towards issues that resonate more directly with younger voters. However, there is increasing evidence that these issues of more concern to youth will continue to be as important in future elections as they were in 2019. In the following sections of this chapter, we explore the interplay between these two broad trends of participation as well as some of the more election-specific factors that may have played a role in motivating participation in the 2019 election.

THE TURNOUT DECLINE

Historically, Canada has been a country of relatively high voter turnout. From Confederation until the Second World War, around 70 percent of eligible voters could generally be expected to cast a ballot in a federal election. Over that long period, turnout fluctuated from one election to another only within a fairly narrow band. After 1945, turnout in federal elections rose slightly, reaching 79 percent in the 1958 election and typically registering levels of about 75 percent up

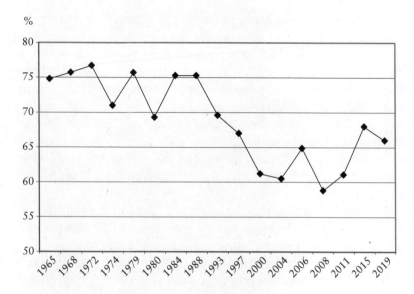

Figure 11.1 Turnout in Canadian federal elections, 1965–2019

until 1993.[1] As is seen in figure 11.1, voter turnout was above 75 percent in the federal elections of 1984 and 1988.

Turnout declined sharply in the ensuing 1993 election and then continued to decline in each of the next three federal elections, reaching a (then) historic low of 60.5 percent in 2004. A rebound to nearly 65 percent occurred in the 2006 election, which brought the Harper Conservatives to power. This upward bounce did not last as turnout in the following (2008) election hit another new historic low, falling below 60 percent for the first time and remaining at a low level (61.1 percent) in the following (2011) election. The 2015 election, however, that brought the Trudeau Liberals to power, saw a significant jump in turnout to a much more respectable 68 percent. But that substantial increase presented an important research question for political scientists. Was the turnout decline of the past two decades over? Or was 2015 an exception, brought on by an infusion of new voters motivated by animosity towards the Harper government or other short-term political considerations? This question could not be seriously addressed until another federal election had taken place, providing some initial evidence of either a resumption in some form of the turnout decline or of a stabilization or even a sustained increase that might signal its end.

A number of demographic and attitudinal factors help to explain individual decisions to vote or not vote in any given election. Length of residence in the respondent's current location is important since this provides familiarity with the local context and personalities of candidates. Household income is a more important demographic factor than education, but both have a positive relationship to voting participation. A more competitive political environment helps to boost turnout since people report being more likely to go to the polls if they feel that their vote would make a difference in the outcome of an election. Feelings of general political trust in elected representatives, as well as of political efficacy, also have a positive relationship with voting.[2]

When survey respondents are asked to give their reasons for failing to vote in any given election, these typically fall into two broad categories. Personal reasons (e.g., "too busy," "away," "forgot") are a common theme, although these of course can in some instances simply be convenient excuses. More telling, however, are the somewhat larger number of responses that indicate some degree of dissatisfaction with the political system itself.[3] The feeling that the vote is not meaningful, or that there is no one worth voting for, is not uncommon. To some degree, this is a function of the institutions within which voting in Canada takes place. Canadians cast only a single vote for a local member of Parliament. A federal election therefore is only an indirect vote on party platforms or party leadership more broadly. In some parts of the country, and in certain constituencies, the choices presented to voters are not perceived as particularly meaningful.

Although in any given election a substantial number of eligible Canadians do not vote, they are not always the same nonvoters. In earlier research, we used the term "transient voters" to describe this segment of the electorate in order to emphasize that this group was not a permanently disconnected and politically alienated segment of the population.[4] Rather, Canadians generally conformed to the idea that voting was a kind of "civic duty," and, even if they were unable to vote in a particular election, they typically expressed their intention to vote in the next one. Often, this intent was realized in that nonvoters in one election drifted into the electorate subsequently, and some citizens for a variety of reasons (often short-term personal ones) did not get to the polls. We therefore concluded that the distinctions between voters and nonvoters in any given election were in fact relatively minor and that the circulation of transient voters into and out of the electorate generally had only modest effects on election outcomes. But as turnout in elections continued to decline over the past two decades, this interpretation became somewhat more problematic.

Survey evidence also suggests that nonvoters do not necessarily see their decision *not* to vote as a fixed decision. Like voters, the decision not to vote is often made late in the campaign and can be as much a function of circumstance as a conscious determination to completely tune out the world of politics. Even citizens who are otherwise attentive to politics may sometimes decide not to vote for a variety of personal or political reasons.[5] But others for whom politics seems largely irrelevant or uninteresting may well lack the incentive to vote as election day approaches.

However, it has now been more than two decades since political scientists began to examine the sustained decline in voting turnout that has taken place in Canada since 1993 as well as in a number of other Western democracies (figure 11.2). Seen within the context of a particular election, hypotheses about the factors accounting for a decline in turnout from one election to another were sometimes seen as election-specific. But as evidence has mounted over time that the decline in turnout is much more systematic than can be accounted for by such short-term factors, explanations increasingly turned to more fundamental possible causes. With hindsight, it is clear that the 1993 decline had less to do with the specific characteristics of that election than appeared to be the case at the time. In the same period of approximately two decades, turnout in many provincial elections has been declining as well, following a similar pattern.[6]

In a study of nonvoters that we conducted for Elections Canada, several characteristics of nonvoters stood out.[7] Almost half of all nonvoters surveyed in the 2000 federal election were under thirty years of age. A majority expressed little interest in politics. Nonvoters assigned less importance to the act of voting than did voters, and the young nonvoters did not have as strong a sense of civic duty with respect to voting as did older respondents. Thus, the broader explanation of the turnout decline could be found more in the normal processes of population replacement that take place over a number of years than in patterns of turnout in any single election.

Of course, it is not unusual to find lower rates of voting participation among the young. Such patterns are well documented in the literature on nonvoting in Canada and in other countries. But lower participation rates among the young have generally been interpreted as a pattern

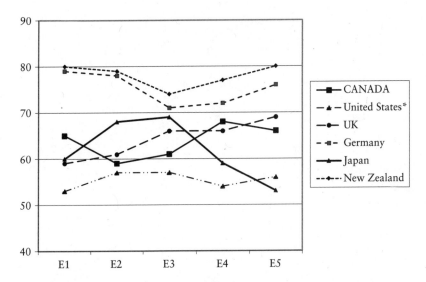

* Percentage of voting age population voting in presidential elections in United States. All others are percentage of registered voters in parliamentary elections. Elections are shown in chronological order.

Figure 11.2 Turnout in six countries (last five elections), International IDEA, www.idea.int/data-tools/data/voter-turnout.

associated with specific behavioural characteristics of the lifecycle. As people age, they become more politically aware and engaged. It is therefore to be expected that voting rates should increase over time with these normal lifecycle changes. They should also increase with rising levels of education. The evidence suggests, however, that such changes are occurring more slowly than they have in the past and that voters, when they do begin to enter the electorate, are doing so later in life and in fewer numbers.[8] Since the mid- to late 1970s, each newly eligible cohort of voters has been increasingly disinclined to believe that elections are important or meaningful – a view that stands in stark contrast to that of the generations that entered the electorate before 1974. Accompanying this growing disbelief in the efficacy of elections is a propensity to disengage, which has been observed among cohorts of younger voters for the past two decades. Nevertheless, a majority of Canadians in every age group, even the youngest ones, says that they are likely to vote in a *future* election.

The data cited above tell us a good deal about who is not participating in federal elections, but they provide only a hint of the reasons

Table 11.1
Voting turnout in recent provincial and federal elections, by province

	Most recent provincial election*	Federal elections 2015	2019
Prince Edward Island	76	77	72
New Brunswick	67	74	71
Quebec	66	67	65
Alberta	64	68	68
British Columbia	61	70	65
Saskatchewan	58	71	72
Ontario	57	68	65
Manitoba	55	68	64
Newfoundland and Labrador	55	61	58
Nova Scotia	54	71	69

* To 31 October 2019.
Source: Elections Canada, provincial sites.

younger citizens have been disengaging from electoral politics. Some further insights into these attitudes are found in small group studies in which respondents are able to discuss in more detail their feelings about politics and their attitudes towards elections and voting.[9] Combined with the more statistically reliable findings of the surveys, these data shed considerable light on some of the forces driving the larger demographic processes. Three principal themes emerged from the small group studies, which help to reveal some of the attitudinal factors that lie behind the typical reasons given for not voting in elections. The first of these is a lack of personal connection to the political world, and a feeling that electoral politics as practised in Canada may have little relevance to the lives of younger people. Wattenberg (2008) compared attempting to engage young people uninterested in politics to "getting someone who doesn't follow sports to watch a football game."[10] This lack of connection is reinforced by peer group influences and practices. Young people have radically different media habits than those of previous generations. The feeling among many young people that politics as practised in the Canadian electoral arena has little relevance for them is also reinforced by what they see around them. Politicians "know where their voters are," and the issues that tend to be emphasized in most election campaigns have typically not been those to which younger people can readily relate.

A second major theme that emerged from the small group studies – one also found repeatedly in mass surveys – is the adverse reaction of many Canadians to the negativity of politics. While older respondents are also put off by the negativity of modern electoral politics, younger people tend to be even less accepting of such practices. An illustration of this is provided by the following comment of a twenty-year-old first-time voter in one of the small group studies: "I see a lot of negative finger-pointing by all the parties. As well, most of the things each party says they will do just seem really dishonest. I mean, none of those things will ever actually get done; they're just ways to get more votes. I really don't like that." The negativity is not just a reason to dislike politics: it also provides a rationale for ignoring it altogether.

Finally, nonvoting among the younger age cohorts does not carry the same sense of social stigma that is more typically found in the older age groups. While many younger people agree that, ideally, people *should* vote in elections, they are not as likely to criticize those who come to the opposite conclusion. Older generations are more likely to emphasize the "civic duty" aspect of voting, but younger age groups approach electoral participation more pragmatically. To these people, voting is important only if it can accomplish something. Civic duty alone is not enough to persuade newly eligible voters to go to the polls if they do not feel sufficiently informed or connected.

The demographic processes that have been driving the turnout decline are relentless and slow moving, and the two-decade-old pattern of decline was therefore unlikely to be easily or quickly reversed. If the age of the electorate is rising even faster than that of the population more generally, it will not be surprising to find governments under increasing pressure to pay ever more attention to issues such as health care and pensions rather than to education or climate change. Younger voters are thus increasingly likely to feel, with some justification, that issues of greater concern to them are not addressed in election campaigns. These types of linkages tend to create a type of "vicious circle" of non-participation that is largely self-reinforcing.[11] The same may be said with respect to the increasing negativity of electoral campaigns or the declining sense of voting as a civic duty. If nonvoting is more acceptable to younger generations than it has been to older cohorts of voters, then the age gap among voters in elections is more likely to widen rather than to narrow. Therefore, the predominance of long-term social and demographic processes might well have led us to hypothesize that the 2019 election would see a resumption of the turnout decline.

ELECTION-SPECIFIC FACTORS

There are, however, exceptions to the long-term trend of turnout decline, and they are worth examining for clues about the circumstances that might mitigate the long-term trend or even bring about a reversal. We have already mentioned the 2006 and 2015 federal elections, both of which saw an increase from the previous election. In both of these elections, there was increased interest in the outcome, and in both cases there was a change in government. The Liberal government led by Paul Martin was in a minority situation leading up to 2006, and it appeared to have run its course. The Conservative government of Stephen Harper in 2015 had been in power since 2006, and by 2015 both the NDP and the Liberals looked to be in a good position to take over.[12] If political interest was high in 2019, and there was a potential close race that might unseat the Justin Trudeau government, turnout would be more likely to hold up.

In Europe, over the period since 1996, our calculations show that twenty-six of thirty-two countries have declined in voter turnout, with the average decline over that period being 10 percent. Within this general picture in Europe, short-term turnout rises of 5 percent or more occurred in Hungary (twice), Spain (twice), Czech Republic, Ireland, Poland, Germany, and the Netherlands. These instances have in common a heated political atmosphere, with features like controversial political figures (Hungary, Netherlands), corruption scandals (Czech Republic, Poland), violence (Spain), and the rise of parties on the ideological extremes (Germany, Netherlands). In all of these cases, where time has allowed us to observe a subsequent election, voting turnout has resumed its decline. A particular election mobilized a portion of the electorate that decided to vote and produced a temporary "hiccup" in the downward trend line.

Closer to home, the voting turnout picture in the Canadian provinces also shows an overall pattern of decline with occasional temporary rises due to short-term circumstances. This picture is similar to that of the European elections cited above. In the ten Canadian provinces, the voting turnout in the most recent provincial election is on average 14 percent lower than it was in the mid-1990s. Once again, however, a limited number of elections have bucked this trend temporarily. Table 11.2 displays these.

Table 11.2
Turnout rises of 4% or more since 1985 in the Canadian provinces

	Year	% Rise	Change of govt?	Subsequent decline?	Atmosphere
NL	1985	7	No	No	Brian Peckford wins third election.
	1993	5	No	Yes (-10%)	Clyde Wells opposed feds constitution plans.
PE	1986	10	Yes	Yes (-8%)	Joe Ghiz wins election.
	2015	6	No	Yes (-6%)	
QC	1994	7	Yes	Yes (-4%)	Jacques Parizeau pledges 2nd referendum.
	2012	18	Yes	Yes (-4%)	PQ minority (Pauline Marois). CAQ 1st election.
ON	2018	7	Yes		Ford PCs win election.
MB	1988	6	Yes	Yes (-5%)	PCs defeat NDP; strong Liberal showing.
SK	2007	5	Yes	Yes (-7%)	Brad Wall defeats NDP.
AB	1982	7	No	Yes (-21%)	Lougheed campaigns against federal Lib NEP.
	1993	6	No	Yes (-6%)	Ralph Klein succeeds Don Getty.
	2012	13	No	No (+3%)	Alison Redford defeats Wildrose and others.
	2019	7	Yes		Jason Kenney defeats NDP.
BC	2017	4	Yes		NDP takes power in close election.

Of the fourteen instances in table 11.2 in which provincial voting participation rose substantially, a majority is associated with changes in government. Most of the other instances occurred in two provinces, Newfoundland and Labrador, and Alberta. Two of these involved cases in which provincial leaders were campaigning against federal policies and called for strong outpourings of support: in 1982, Alberta's Peter Lougheed campaigned against the National Energy Policy established by Pierre Trudeau; and, in 1993, Newfoundland and Labrador Liberal premier Clyde Wells had been a leader in killing Brian Mulroney's constitutional reforms. In all of these cases, there were short-term controversies, close contests, or support for popular provincial leaders. In all but two of these instances, turnout went down again in a subsequent election.

The 2019 federal election, therefore, might have been expected to show a voting turnout decline from the 2015 level unless there was strong desire for a change in government, a strong desire to re-elect the Liberals, or, at the very least, a highly competitive multi-party race. Only the last of these conditions appeared credible in the run-up to the election. Polls as of August showed the Liberals and Conservatives in a virtual tie for national support, with competition in some areas from the NDP and the Greens (see chapter 7, this volume). If the competition in 2019 was strong enough, it might be enough to boost turnout. Competition itself, however, has difficulty providing the mobilization necessary for high participation if one or more of the other conditions is not present.

There is, however, another factor that might have led us to hypothesize that the revival of voting turnout that occurred in 2015 might be mirrored in the 2019 election, or at least that any decline would be small. In its post-election evaluation, Elections Canada concluded that in 2015 those between eighteen and twenty-four years of age voted at a rate of 57 percent, a substantial increase from the voting rate of the comparable age cohort in 2011.[13] If that group continued to participate at a similar rate, the turnout decline would slow.

The Importance of First Vote in Establishing Voting Habits

The recent revival of interest in political socialization reflects in part the realization that, whatever the theoretical and research difficulties the field has encountered, early learning is important. This may be especially true when it comes to political participation. Political attitudes may shift during the lifecycle according to experience and circumstances, and some of the early assumptions of the persistence of beliefs may not have held up under scrutiny. Evaluations of political leaders, parties, and issues may change or develop according to the events of the day. But when it comes to action, it has become clear that "starting early" is crucial to establishing a life-long pattern of participating, or failing to participate, in all aspects of political life.[14] Voting decisions may be heavily dependent on the political context for their direction, but the orientation towards the act of voting in the first place will likely be a product of early learning.

Increasingly, the propensity to vote, or to abstain from voting, has been conceptualized as a *habit*. The influence of the lifecycle can be seen as producing a series of factors that help to establish these habits, things like increases in attachment to community and religious or political institutions, and the ensuing development of attitudes of civic competence and political efficacy.[15] Transitions to adulthood, and the adoption of adult political roles, particularly educational experiences, marriage, leaving home, and acquiring employment, are traditionally supposed to establish these habits, though some doubt has been cast upon the validity of these assumptions, at least in places.[16] But however they are established, habits provide reinforcement of past behaviour, and the simple existence of past behaviour is associated with future behaviour, at least where voting is concerned.[17] The mechanisms underlying habit formation are psychological and can involve the acquisition of attitudes of empowerment such as political efficacy,[18] or party loyalties,[19] or lowered information costs about how voting takes place.[20]

But how likely is it that the habit of voting will be formed, and does the timing matter? In constructing a developmental theory of turnout, and emphasizing the importance of family influences in spurring early voting, Plutzer nevertheless says: "almost all habitual nonvoters gradually increase their probability of voting and eventually make the transition to being habitual voters."[21] In contrast, Franklin concludes that "those who find reason to vote in one of the first elections in which they are eligible generally continue to vote in subsequent elections [while] those who find no reason to vote in their first few elections generally continue not to vote in subsequent elections, even more important ones."[22] Consistent with this latter point of view, both public and private organizations have sponsored get-out-the-vote campaigns targeted at young newly eligible citizens in an effort to recruit them into the voter camp, on the theory that this will establish a habit of voting. Efforts to investigate voting history have concluded that consistency in either voting or not voting is much more prevalent than is a selective picking and choosing of occasional trips to the polls.[23]

Using this logic, 2015 voting among newly eligible, predominantly young, citizens may be the first step in establishing a pattern of higher voting participation. If so, we may expect that many of them returned to the polls in 2019. That might have helped to stabilize the voting turnout rate, even if the youngest, newly eligible 2015–19 cohort was not mobilized to the same extent as its immediate predecessors.

Did the Parties Emphasize Relevant Issues?

One of the most frequently heard explanations from young people to account for low political interest, and hence low voting rates, has to do with the kinds of election issues emphasized by the political parties. "They are not talking about *our* issues," some say. This point of view is most often expressed when the main election issues revolve around the health care system or other kinds of social issues. Indeed, social issues like health have been at or near the top of the issue agenda since the late 1990s, a period that coincides with the decline of the voting turnout rate.[24] And, in the kind of "vicious circle" mentioned earlier, parties have continued to tout their competence on social issues of interest to older people because older people are more likely to vote.

In 2019, however, some of the issues that might be of more interest to potential young voters were more prominent than in the past. Foremost among these is the protection of the environment and combating climate change. In general, references to "the environment" as an important election issue are an example of a classic "valence issue." These are (generally) large, problem-type issues that all parties agree are threats to national and/or personal well-being and promise to address in various ways. Other classic examples are economic growth and employment, health care and other social welfare measures, and (in the Canadian context) social cohesion and ethnic relations. With valence issues, all parties claim to be on the same side, public opinion is skewed in that direction, and the parties compete over which should be trusted to deal with the situation. Those parties that have the advantage in public trust on the issue strive to raise its salience in voter decision making, while those that do not attempt to promote other issues as being more important. In Canada, the salience of environmental issues has usually been low in the election context, partly because those parties that have established a link to that issue (like the Greens) have not been competitive on other election elements. In summary, environmental issues have had relatively minor effects on Canadian election results.[25]

Things were somewhat different in 2019. An Abacus Data poll in late March of 2019 gave an early indication that climate change was likely to be an important issue in the 2019 Canadian federal election. Results showed that 12 percent in total said it would be "my top issue." This group was composed mainly of those intending to vote Liberal (39 percent) and NDP (25 percent), with only 9 percent intending to vote Conservative. For those saying it was a low priority issue, 67 percent were likely Conservative voters.[26] To the extent that the environmental issue area was defined in terms of carbon taxation by the Conservatives, this enhanced the prominence of such approaches to dealing with climate change.

Figure 10.2 on page 224 of this volume portrays the most important issues in the minds of voters during the election period. This figure indicates that "the environment/climate change" issue was third in overall importance, being chosen as one of the top three by 38 percent of the respondents to the Abacus survey referenced in that chapter. To those respondents twenty-six years of age and younger (having come of voting age in either the 2015 or 2019 elections), however, climate change was a more important issue.[27] It came a very close second (chosen by 48 percent) to "cost of living" (49 percent) as the most important problem facing the country among the youngest potential voters. Therefore, we might expect some upward impact on youth turnout based on the issue emphasis in the 2019 election.

Figure 11.3 shows the reported percentages of respondents to the Abacus Data post-election survey (the same data source used in chapter 10) in different age groups who voted in the 2019 election. The age categories were constructed to separate out those who were newly eligible by virtue of age in the 2019 election, those newly eligible in 2015, and those newly eligible in the election of 2011. The results contain support for both of the hypotheses outlined above.

The overall turnout declined from 2015 (from 68 to 66 percent), thereby validating the influence of the long-term factors leading to a turnout decline, which have pushed it down since 1988, subject to the two exceptions mentioned earlier (see figure 11.1). The youngest age group, newly eligible in 2019, had the lowest turnout, estimated at 55 percent (see figure 11.3). The highest turnout figures, as we would predict, come from the oldest groups, reaching above average figures of 70 percent or higher. Still, these high rates of older electors did not reach the levels reported in 2015. Elections Canada research reported that the turnout of the group aged sixty-five to seventy-four in 2015 reached almost 79 percent.[28]

On the other hand, while turnout did decline, it did not reach the low levels reported in 2011 or earlier. In part, this was due to the continued voting rates displayed by the group of people who became eligible to vote for the first time in 2015. Figure 11.3 estimates that this age group, those twenty-three to twenty-six in 2019, voted at the national average rate (66 percent), eleven percentage points higher than those younger than themselves, and six points higher than the group older than they were (i.e., those who became eligible to vote in the lower turnout election of 2011). This result provides support for the "habit-of-voting" thesis outlined earlier, whereby once the first vote is cast, the person is more likely than not to continue voting.

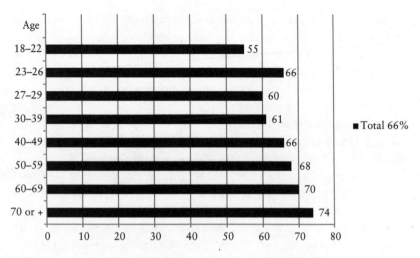

Figure 11.3 Estimated voting by age groups, 2019 federal election

Greater use of the advance polls in 2019 may also have played a role in facilitating higher turnout. Elections Canada reported a 29 percent increase in the use of advance polls in 2019 compared with the 2015 election.[29] However, the Abacus Data survey cited in figure 11.3 shows that usage of the advance polls was heavily concentrated among older voters.[30] Younger voters who chose to participate in the 2019 election were more likely to do so on election day.

CONCLUSION

The chapters in this book present a picture of the 2019 Canadian federal election campaign as relatively downbeat, characterized by a lack of substantial public enthusiasm for any of the alternatives. As such, it presented an important test case for the study of voting turnout, which had risen on the strength of enhanced public (including youth) interest in the previous election. Would turnout resume its earlier decline or would it stabilize on the strength of the solidification of voting habits by those who had participated in 2015? As it transpired, elements of both overall decline and increased indications of stabilization may be observed. The overall turnout result of 66 percent was lower than the 2015 turnout of 68 percent. On the other hand, survey evidence shows that the cohort entering the electorate in 2015 maintained its participation at levels mirroring the average voting level, contributing to a mitigation of the decline. And while voting participation of the youngest entering cohort was still substantially lower than the electorate as a whole (55 percent), it was nevertheless higher than the voting rates of many previous young voting groups. We attribute this upsurge in youth voting, at least in part, to engagement with issues of environmental protection, a situation that is likely to continue in future elections. It therefore seems reasonable to predict that Canadian federal voting turnout may be moving towards a state of stabilization, albeit in the mid-60 percent range rather than in the mid-70 percent range, as it existed three decades earlier.

NOTES

1 For a complete listing of turnout rates in all federal elections from 1867 to 2015, see Lawrence LeDuc and Jon H. Pammett, *Dynasties and Interludes*, 2nd ed. (Toronto: Dundurn, 2016), 20–1.
2 For a synthesis of some of these findings, see Lawrence LeDuc and Jon H. Pammett, "Voter Turnout," in *Election*, ed. Heather MacIvor (Toronto: Emond Montgomery, 2010), 251–68. See also André Blais, "What Affects Voter Turnout?," *Annual Review of Political Science* 9 (2006): 111–25
3 LeDuc and Pammett, "Voter Turnout," 257.
4 See Harold D. Clarke, Jane Jenson, Lawrence LeDuc, and Jon H. Pammett, *Political Choice in Canada* (Toronto: McGraw-Hill Ryerson, 1979), 359–65, for an exposition of this argument. Some evidence of movement into and out of the electorate based on panel studies in earlier elections may also be found in the third edition of a book by the same authors, *Absent Mandate* (Toronto: Gage, 1996), 56–9.
5 LeDuc and Pammett, "Voter Turnout," 258.
6 For example, in the 2008 Quebec election, turnout registered a historic low of 57 percent. In the 2007 Ontario provincial election, turnout was 53 percent – the lowest ever recorded in the province. And, in the 2008 provincial election in Alberta, turnout reached an astonishing historic low of 41 percent.
7 The sample design used in this survey called for a short screening interview with a large number of randomly selected Canadians (5,637) and a longer interview continued with 988 reported voters in the 2000 federal election and 968 reported nonvoters. Findings of that study were reported in Jon H. Pammett and Lawrence LeDuc, *Explaining the Turnout Decline in Canadian Federal Elections: A New Survey of Nonvoters* (Ottawa:

Elections Canada, 2003). See also Jon H. Pammett and Lawrence LeDuc, "Behind the Turnout Decline," in *The Canadian General Election of 2004*, ed. Jon H. Pammett and Christopher Dornan (Toronto, Dundurn, 2005), 338–60.

8 An analysis of pooled data from the Canadian Election Studies confirms this pattern. This analysis clearly shows that, across a number of elections spanning more than thirty years, each generation of newly eligible voters participated at lower rates and began to enter the electorate at a higher average age. See Jon H. Pammett, Lawrence LeDuc, Erin Theissen, and Antoine Bilodeau, *Canadian Voting Turnout in Comparative Perspective* (Ottawa: Elections Canada, 2001).

9 Lawrence LeDuc, Jon H. Pammett, and Heather Bastedo, "The Problem of Young Voters: A Qualitative and Quantitative Analysis," paper presented to the annual meeting of the American Political Science Association, Boston, Massachusetts, 2008. See also Nicole Goodman, Heather Bastedo, Lawrence LeDuc, and Jon H. Pammett, "Young Canadians in the 2008 Federal Election Campaign: Using Facebook to Probe Perceptions of Citizenship and Participation," *Canadian Journal of Political Science* 44 (2011): 859–81. See also Donald P. Green, "Civic Duty and Social Pressure as Causes of Voter Turnout," in *Duty and Choice: The Evolution of the Study of Voting and Voters*, ed. Peter John Loewen and Daniel Rubenson (Toronto: University of Toronto Press, 2019), 68–80.

10 Martin P. Wattenberg, *Is Voting for Young People?* (New York Pearson Longman, 2008).

11 Jon H. Pammett and Lawrence LeDuc, "Four Vicious Circles of Turnout: Competitiveness, Regionalism, Culture and Participation in Canada," paper presented to the Joint Sessions Workshops of the European Consortium for Political Research, Uppsala, Sweden, 2004.

12 See Jon H. Pammett and Christopher Dornan, eds, *The Canadian Federal election of 2015* (Toronto: Dundurn, 2016).

13 Elections.ca, https://www.elections.ca/content.aspx?section=res&dir=rec/part/yth&document=index&lang=e.

14 Marc Hooge, "Political Socialization and the future of Politics," *Acta Politica* 39, 4 (2004): 331–41. See also Virginia Sapiro, "Not Your Parents' Political Socialization: Introduction for a New Generation," *Annual Review of Political Science* 83, 2 (2004): 1–23.

15 John Strate, Charles J. Parrish, Charles D. Elder, and Coit Ford III, "Life Span, Civic Development and Voting Participation," *American Political Science Review* 83, 2 (1989): 443–64.

16 Theodore M. Newcomb, Katheryne Koenig, Richard Flacks, and Donald P. Warwick, *Persistence and Change: Bennington College and Its Students after Twenty-Five Years* (New York: Wiley, 1967); Benjamin Highton and Raymond E. Wolfinger, "The First Seven Years of the Political Life Cycle," *American Journal of Political Science* 45, 1 (2001): 202–10.

17 Donald P. Green and Ron Shachar, "Habit Formation and Political Behaviour: Evidence of Consuetude in Voter Turnout," *British Journal of Political Science* 30 (2000): 561–73; Alan S. Gerber, Donald P. Green, and Ron Schachar, "Voting May Be Habit-Forming: Evidence from a Randomized Field Experiment," *American Journal of Political Science* 47, 3 (2003): 540–50; Kevin Denny and Orla Doyle, "Does Voting History Matter? Analysing Persistence in Turnout," *American Journal of Political Science* 53, 1 (2009): 17–35; John H. Aldrich, Jacob M. Montgomery, and Wendy Wood, "Turnout as a Habit," *Political Behavior* 33 (2011): 535–63.

18 Mary Anderson, "Community Psychology, Political Efficacy and Trust," *Political Psychology* 31, 1 (2010): 59–84.

19 Angus Campbell, Philip Converse, Warren E. Miller, and Donald E. Stokes, *The American Voter* (New York: Wiley, 1966); Warren E. Miller, "The Cross-National Use of Party Identification as a Stimulus to Inquiry," in *Party Identification and Beyond*, ed. Ian Budge, Ivor Crewe, and David Fairlie (New York: Wiley, 1976): 21–31; Ron Shachar, "Party Loyalty as Habit Formation," *Journal of Applied Econometrics* 18, 3 (2003): 251–69.

20 James Melton, "Why Is Voting Habit-Forming?," paper presented at ECPR General Conference, Glasgow, 2014, archived at www.semanticscholar.org.

21 Eric Plutzer, "Becoming a Habitual Voter: Inertia, Resources and Growth in Young Adulthood," *American Political Science Review* 96, 1 (2002): 41–56, 42.

22 Mark N. Franklin, *Voter Turnout and the Dynamics of Electoral Competition in Established Democracies since 1945* (Cambridge: Cambridge University Press, 2004), 12.

23 Lawrence LeDuc and Jon H. Pammett, "Multilevel Patterns of Electoral Participation in Canada and Europe," paper presented at the annual conference of the American Political Science Association, Washington, DC, 2014.

24 Harold D. Clarke, Jane Jenson, Lawrence LeDuc, and Jon H. Pammett, *Absent Mandate: Strategies and Choices in Canadian Elections* (Toronto: University of Toronto Press, 2019.)

25 Ibid., chap. 4.

26 Bruce Anderson and David Coletto, "Will Climate Change Be a Ballot Box Question in 2019?," 27 March 2019, www.abacusdata.ca/.
27 This is not to imply, however, that younger age cohorts were more likely to support the Green Party as there is no evidence as yet that this was the case in 2019. The Abacus data show little pattern related to age in voting for the Greens. However, the second (22 to 24) and third (26 to 29) youngest age groups (see figure 11.3) were much less likely to support the Conservatives and tended towards the Liberals. The youngest cohort (18 to 22) was more likely to vote NDP. Abacus Data survey. Data not shown.
28 See note 13.
29 News release, 15 October 2019, www.elections.ca.
30 Data not shown. The Abacus Data survey found that voters in the two oldest age cohorts were about twice as likely as those in the four youngest to take advantage of the opportunity to vote in the advance polls.

12

The Testing Election

Jon H. Pammett

With the unexpected, yet seemingly decisive, 2015 election victory, the Liberals under Justin Trudeau seemed well on their way to becoming Canada's seventh federal political dynasty.[1] The opposition parties were disheartened. With the resignation of Stephen Harper, not just as prime minister but as party leader, the Conservatives plunged into a search for new leadership; however, many prominent figures in the party did not stand for the job because of their presumption that the party was in for a prolonged period out of power. The New Democrats, whose hopes to finally form a Canadian federal government were dashed by the election results, removed Thomas Mulcair from the leader's position in favour of an untested provincial politician who had very little hope of leading that party back to official opposition status, let alone government. The prospects seemed bright for Justin Trudeau to remain prime minister through several subsequent elections.

The chapters in this book recount the reasons that this sunny outlook for the Liberal Party clouded over. Before we summarize them again, however, we can take a look back at several previous Canadian electoral successes, some of which formed the basis of dynasties, and some of which ended up merely as interludes. The Canadian political dynasties of John A. Macdonald, Wilfrid Laurier, Mackenzie King, Pierre Trudeau, Jean Chrétien, and Stephen Harper lasted through three elections or more through a combination of leader appeal and mastery of many of the important issue areas raised in their election campaigns. But it is important to remember that, in almost all of these cases, the second elections they fought after coming to power had one thing in common. All except Laurier stumbled in their first attempt to secure re-election.

The setbacks that occurred in the federal elections of 1872, 1925, 1972, 1997, and 2008 for political leaders on their way to establishing dynasties were diverse in nature and occurred for a number of different reasons.[2] The tactics employed by John A. Macdonald in his attempts to salvage his government after Confederation were successful in keeping him in office in 1872, but the corruption involved led to his defeat in 1874. In 1925, most observers, including Governor General Lord Byng, thought Mackenzie King had lost the election and should resign, but he managed to cling to power long enough to force a new election the next year. The King dynasty was not really fully established until 1935. Pierre Trudeau's triumphant march to victory in 1968 was followed by a virtual tie in the next election of 1972, when his boast that "the land is strong" proved an unconvincing rhetorical flourish; his lack of accomplishments in his first term did not match the expectations of voters. The decimation of the Progressive Conservative Party, which led to the establishment of the Chrétien dynasty in 1993, was followed by the rise of the Reform Party and the Bloc Québécois in 1997, and a very narrow majority victory for Chrétien. Finally, Stephen Harper was unable to improve enough in 2008 to turn his minority government into a majority, and the economic crisis that struck in that year forced an ignominious retreat from many of his conservative goals.

The second election has proved to be so problematic for Canadian governments that we can consider it "a testing election," whereby virtually all prime ministers are hard pressed to sustain the popularity of their administrations over the relatively short period of time that passes after their initial victory. The cases mentioned in the previous paragraph were only those in which leaders went on to found political dynasties. Many others, though maintaining power, never recovered from setbacks that occurred when they sought re-election (Borden, Diefenbaker, Pearson, Mulroney). And some other prime ministers did not survive their second election at all (Mackenzie, Meighen, Bennett, Clark, Martin).

Justin Trudeau survived the 2019 election, but he did so narrowly, with the Liberal Party forming a minority government with a plurality of the seats achieved with fewer votes than the Conservatives. If he continues to be victorious in the next election, likely to come before four years are up, 2019 will have been a testing election for him, leading to a dynasty. If the deterioration in Liberal fortunes continues, we will have witnessed the Justin Trudeau interlude, and we will be asking the same questions about the future of the new prime minister.

Will it be the Trudeau dynasty or the Trudeau interlude? To analyze these possibilities, we must consider the factors that were important in the outcome of the 2019 election. Some of the reasons for the decline in the Liberal fortunes are undoubtedly attributable to the decline in the popular appeal of Justin Trudeau himself. As his term of office proceeded after 2015, few would have foreseen the series of missteps that contributed to the drop in his ratings as "preferred choice for prime minister" from 56 percent a year after the election to 31 percent on 2019 election eve.[3] We have seen in the chapters of this book how the ill-conducted trip to India, the seemingly duplicitous management of the SNC-Lavalin affair, and the embarrassing "brownface" scandal that was brought to light during the campaign all contributed to the dimming of Trudeau's personal image. A rebound of personal popularity is certainly possible for political leaders (Jean Chrétien managed it), but often the negative characteristics of leader image are difficult to overcome (Brian Mulroney did not).

It is in the mastery of the important issue areas that take prominence in Canadian elections that dynasties are established and maintained. In particular, the economy and social issues, led by health care, have been perennial "most important issues" in the twenty-first century. Figure 10.4 (p. 227) shows that only in the realm of social issues were the Liberals most favoured in 2019. Providing money and support for health care, alleviating poverty, and combatting racism were all topics on which the Liberals were favoured during the election campaign. Prominence on such issues, particularly health care, have played a prominent part in sustaining Liberal support since the 2000 election. To the extent they can continue this dominance, one key pillar of a dynasty will continue to stand.

To the Liberal Party's public approval on social policy can be added the area of the environment. Once again, in 2019 the Liberals had a wide lead among those primarily concerned with issues of climate change and environmental protection. From a purely political standpoint, this situation can be a mixed blessing for Trudeau and his party. It seems inevitable that environmental/climate change issues will continue to be prominent in future Canadian election campaigns, if anything increasing their importance if the climate continues to deteriorate. With this pre-eminence, however, comes the opportunity for the party to disappoint people with policy solutions that do not achieve results or that prove to detract from economic growth and job creation. A taste of this tradeoff was undoubtedly experienced during the 2019 campaign, over the issue of pipelines, especially the Trans Mountain pipeline to the West Coast. As we have seen in this book, Trudeau attempted to support the pipeline (to the extent of having the federal government purchase it) while at the same time championing the curbing of emissions from oil production. This action did not serve to obtain the support of western pipeline adherents and, at the same time, alienated a number of environmental activists. The public preference for voting Liberal on environmental issues exists in part because smaller parties with better policies are perceived to have little chance of winning. We may add to this the fear of those concerned with the environment that the Conservatives might win. Were the Conservatives to acquire more credibility in the issue area, fortunes could change quickly.

It is in the issue area of the economy where the Liberals lagged behind the Conservatives in 2019, and where the lack of public trust may have had most impact on their election results. As chapter 10 points out, and figure 10.1 shows, the public perceived the Canadian economy to be in good shape in 2019, in contrast to the situation four years earlier. Despite this, the Conservatives were the ones more likely to be favoured by voters concerned with the economy defined in general terms ("the economy"; "cost of living") or more specifically ("taxes"; "the deficit"). In some of those formulations, the preference of concerned voters for the Conservatives is understandable: that party promised a cut to taxes and criticized the Liberals for running higher deficits than it had promised. Nor is it surprising that people citing the cost of living as an important issue would not be favourable to the government. What is more disturbing for the Liberals is the lack of credit they got for the general perception of a good economy or for the negotiation of the new NAFTA treaty with the United States and Mexico.

A further issue cluster where support for the Liberals in 2019 diminished was that which dealt with national unity and diversity. This encompasses such issues as immigration and the acceptance of refugees – issues where the Liberal positions so attractive to voters in 2015 were not present in 2019. It also measures the bridging of regional differences and the skillful conduct of relations between the federal government and the provincial governments. In all of these areas, the initial promise, and promises, of the Trudeau government fell apart during its term in office. By the time of the 2019 election, the western provinces of Alberta and Saskatchewan were severely criticizing federal policies and threatening to oppose several of them. Liberal hopes to improve their position in Quebec were foiled as well, and relations with the provincial government of Quebec grew tense over the application of the provincial law prohibiting religious symbols and clothing for provincial employees. For a party that formerly prided itself as the one that kept the country together, the Liberals began to look like the party that drove its regions apart.

All the indications are that in the post-election stocktaking undertaken by the Trudeau Liberals, there is a realization that several areas need remediation if the party is going to establish a dynasty in future. In particular, an improvement in Trudeau's image would help them, as would a reclamation of the economic issue area and a thaw in intergovernmental relations. But these will be difficult to achieve, and the new Conservative leadership will themselves be attempting to put that party on the popular side of these important pillars of Canadian political dynasties. Twenty-nineteen was a testing election, but the results of the test will not be known for some time.

NOTES

1 This and subsequent references to "dynasties" utilizes the framework and criteria established in Lawrence LeDuc and Jon H. Pammett, *Dynasties and Interludes: Past and Present in Canadian Electoral Politics*, 2nd ed. (Toronto: Dundurn, 2016).
2 The circumstances of all of these elections are outlined in LeDuc and Pammett, *Dynasties and Interludes*.
3 These figures are from the reports of Nanos Research on 4 October 2016 and 20 October 2019.

APPENDIX

The Results

	Canada		NL		PEI		NS		NB		QC		ON		M		S		A		BC		Terr
	Seats	Votes	S	V	S	V	S	V	S	V	S	V	S	V	S	V	S	V	S	V	S	V	S
BQ	32	7.7								32.8	32	32.5											
CPC	121	34.4		28.0	1	27.4	1	25.7	3	32.8	10	16.0	36	33.2	7	45.4	14	64.3	33	69.2	17	34.1	
GP	3	6.5		3.1		20.8		11.0	1	17.0		4.4		6.2		5.1		2.5		2.8	2	12.4	
LIB	157	33.1	6	44.7	4	43.6	10	41.3	6	37.6	35	34.2	79	41.5	4	26.3		11.6		13.7	11	26.1	2
NDP	24	15.9	1	23.9		7.6		18.9		9.4	1	10.7	6	16.8	3	20.7		19.5	1	11.5	11	24.4	1
PP	0	1.6		0.1				1.2		2.1		1.5		1.6		1.7		1.8		2.2		1.7	
Oth	1	0.8		0.3		0.5		1.7		1.0		0.5		0.6		0.7		0.2		0.4	1	1.1	
Total	338	100%	7		4		11		10		78		121		14		14		34		42		3

Contributors

PAUL ADAMS is a writer and academic who is currently associate professor of journalism at Carleton University. He is a veteran of the CBC and the *Globe and Mail* parliamentary bureaus and is a frequent columnist and commentator on the political media. He grew up in Winnipeg and was educated at the University of Manitoba, Oxford University, and Columbia University.

HAROLD D. CLARKE, PhD, Duke University, is Ashbel Smith Professor, University of Texas at Dallas. He has served as editor of *Electoral Studies* and the *Political Research Quarterly* and as director of social and economic sciences at the National Science Foundation. His research has been supported by the National Science Foundation (US), the Economics and Social Research Council (UK), the Social Sciences and Humanities Research Council of Canada, the Canada Council, the Bill and Melinda Gates Foundation, and the Hong Kong Science Foundation. He is the author of articles in journals such as the *American Journal of Political Science*, the *American Political Science Review*, the *British Journal of Political Science*, the *Journal of Politics*, *International Studies Quarterly*, *Political Analysis*, and *Political Science Research and Methods*. He is a co-author of several books, including *Absent Mandate: Strategies and Choices in Canadian Elections* (University of Toronto Press, 2019); *Brexit: Why Britain Voted to Leave the European Union* (Cambridge University Press, 2017); *Austerity and Political Choice in Britain* (Palgrave Macmillan, 2016); and *Affluence, Austerity and Electoral Change in Britain* (Cambridge University Press, 2013).

CHRISTOPHER DORNAN is associate professor in the School of Journalism and Communication, Carleton University. This is the seventh volume in this series of election studies he has co-edited. His most recent work examines disinformation in news and social media content. See www.educatedguesses.ca.

FARON ELLIS is research chair in the Citizen Society Research Lab at Lethbridge College. His research in Canadian politics focuses on parties and elections and includes *The Limits of Participation: Members and Leaders in Canada's Reform Party* (University of Calgary Press, 2005) and various contributions to the Crosscurrents: Contemporary Political Issues series. This is his ninth contribution to the Canadian Federal Election book series.

SARAH EVERTS is the CTV chair in digital science journalism and associate professor in the School of Journalism and Communication at Carleton University. Prior to joining Carleton's faculty in 2019, she spent over a decade in Berlin, Germany, covering health, science, and the environment for a variety of media organizations, including *Scientific American*, *New Scientist*, *Smithsonian*, and *Chemical and Engineering News*.

ÉRIC GRENIER is senior writer, Polling Analysis, with the Canadian Broadcasting Corporation's parliamentary bureau. He has covered provincial and federal elections for over a decade with a focus on public opinion polling. He was the founder of ThreeHundredEight.com, and, before joining the CBC, he wrote for the *Globe and Mail*, *Huffington Post Canada*, *Hill Times*, *Le Devoir*, and *L'actualité*.

SUSAN HARADA is an associate professor, the director of the School of Journalism and Communication, and the journalism program head at Carleton University. A former national parliamentary correspondent for the CBC, she has written about the Green Party of Canada for every edition of the Canadian Federal Election series since 2004. She profiled the Greens' then leader Elizabeth May for *The Walrus* in 2012.

BROOKE JEFFREY is professor of political science at Concordia University and a long-time director of the Graduate Program in Public Administration and Public Policy. A former senior Liberal adviser, she is the author of six books on Canadian politics and public affairs, including *Divided Loyalties: The Liberal Party of Canada 1984 to 2006* and the forthcoming *Road to Redemption: The Liberal Party of Canada 2006 to 2019*, both published by University of Toronto Press.

LAWRENCE LEDUC is professor emeritus of political science at the University of Toronto. His publications include *The Politics of Direct Democracy*, *Comparing Democracies* (with Richard G. Niemi and Pippa Norris); *Dynasties and Interludes: Past and Present in Canadian Electoral Politics* (with Jon H. Pammett, Judith I. McKenzie, and André Turcotte); and *Absent Mandate* (with Harold D. Clarke, Jane Jenson, and Jon H. Pammett); as well as articles on voting, elections, and related topics in North American and European political science journals. In 2015, Professor LeDuc received the Mildred A. Schwartz Lifetime Achievement Award from the Canadian politics section of the American Political Science Association.

DAVID MCGRANE is professor of political studies at St. Thomas More College and the University of Saskatchewan. His research interests include social democracy, political marketing, elections, and political parties. He is the author of *The New NDP: Moderation, Modernization, and Political Marketing* (2019); and *Remaining Loyal: Social Democracy in Quebec and Saskatchewan* (2014). He is also a past president of the Prairie Political Science Association, chair of the Political Action Committee of the Saskatoon and District Labour Council, and past president of the Saskatchewan NDP.

ERIC MONTIGNY is professor of political science at Université Laval. He teaches Quebec and Canadian politics and is the scientific director of the Research Chair on Democracy and Parliamentary Institutions. His main research focuses on the evolution of Quebec's partisan system and Quebec nationalism. In addition to his participation in several collective works, he is the author of the book *Leadership et militantisme au Parti québécois* (2018) as well as co-author of *Le cœur des Québécois* (2016) and *Révolution Z* (2019). His most recent scientific articles deal with the generational evolution of support for Quebec independence (*French Politics*, 2019) and the use of big data during the 2018 Quebec election campaign (*Internet Policy Review*).

JON H. PAMMETT is Distinguished Research Professor (political science) at Carleton University. His research has been concentrated in the fields of voting behaviour, declines in voter participation, and electronic voting. He is co-author of *Dynasties and Interludes: Past and Present in Canadian Electoral Politics* (Dundurn, 2016) and *Absent Mandate: Strategies and Choices in Canadian Elections* (University of Toronto Press, 2019), as well as numerous journal articles on elections. He has co-edited and contributed to the Canadian Federal Election series since 1988.

TAMARA A. SMALL is associate professor in the Department of Political Science at the University of Guelph. In addition to conducting research on digital campaigning in the last six Canadian federal elections, she has published work on political memes and the regulatory framework for digital technologies in elections in Canada. She is the co-editor of *Digital Politics in Canada: Promises and Realities* (University of Toronto Press).

MARIANNE C. STEWART, PhD, Duke University, is a professor in the School of Economic, Political and Policy Sciences at the University of Texas at Dallas. Her research has been supported by the Economic and Social Research Council (UK), the National Science Foundation, the Bill and Melinda Gates Foundation, and other sources. Her recent books with colleagues include *Affluence, Austerity and Electoral Change in Britain* and *Get Brexit Done! How Britain Left the European Union* (forthcoming), both with Cambridge University Press. Her articles with colleagues have been published in the *American Journal of Political Science*, *American Political Science Review*, *Political Analysis*, and other journals. She has been editor of the *American Journal of Political Science*; associate editor of *International Studies Quarterly*; assistant editor of the *Journal of Politics*; and political science program director at the National Science Foundation.